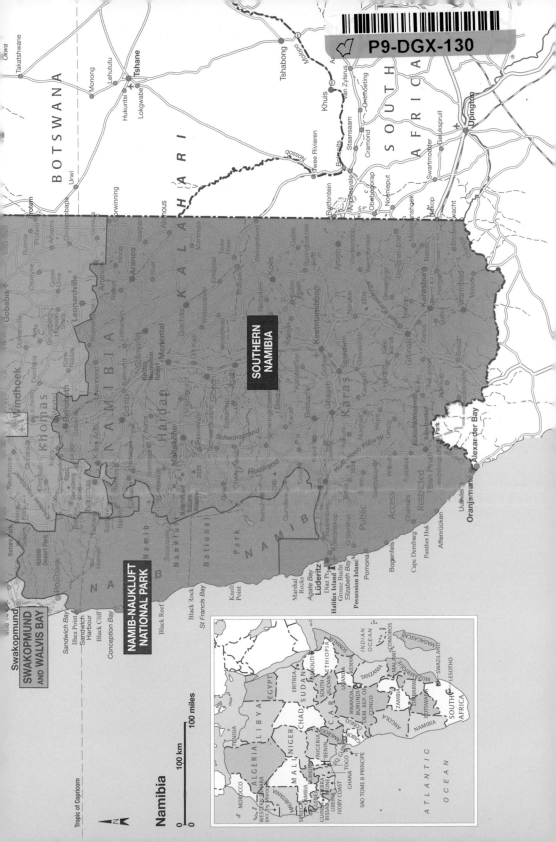

P9-DGX-130

Namibia

0   100 km

0   100 miles

Tropic of Capricorn

SWAKOPMUND AND WALVIS BAY

NAMIB-NAUKLUFT NATIONAL PARK

SOUTHERN NAMIBIA

BOTSWANA

SOUTH AFRICA

KALAHARI

NAMIBIA

INSIGHT GUIDES
NAMIBIA

Contents

THE BEST OF NAMIBIA: TOP ATTRACTIONS

From the glorious abundance of its wildlife and weird and wonderful plant species, to prehistoric rock art, the dunescapes of Sossusvlei and the sheer enormity of Fish River Canyon.

△ **Etosha National Park**. Namibia's premier safari destination, centred on the immense Etosha Pan, offers top game viewing, with lion, elephant and rhino likely to be seen alongside the endemic black-faced impala. Activity peaks in the dry southern winter, when herds of ungulates converge on the waterholes. See page 175.

▽ **Sossusvlei**. This most iconic of Namibian dunescapes, set in the vast Namib-Naukluft Park, is stunning on any occasion, and on the rare occasions when the vlei fills with water it is nothing short of breathtaking. The short walk to Dead Vlei, its cracked floor punctuated with ancient tree trunks, is a must for all photographers. See page 227.

▽ **Fish River Canyon**. One of the world's most expansive gorges, this highlight of southern Namibia is breathtaking when viewed from the rim, and even more dramatic if you walk to the floor (an option available to pre-booked hikers only). See page 238.

◁ **Waterberg Plateau Park**. Ideally suited to those who enjoy looking for wildlife on foot, this park is home to giraffe, white rhino, leopard, buffalo and antelope such as roan, sable, eland and kudu; while birds here include eagles and vultures. See page 159.

△ **Caprivi Strip**. Studded with reserves and national parks, this area offers some superb game viewing in an environment that is refreshingly moist compared to the rest of the country. See page 187.

▷ **Swakopmund**. This is the most appealing town in Namibia and the closest thing to a beach resort, with strong European roots, Art Nouveau architecture and plentiful street cafés. The town and environs hold many sightseeing possibilities and activities. See page 219.

△ **Cape Cross**. An unforgettable highlight of the Skeleton Coast north of Swakopmund, Namibia's largest colony of Cape fur seals assaults visitors on most sensory fronts – sight, sound and smell. See page 211.

▽ **Welwitschia Drive**. This self-drive trail through western Namib-Naukluft is home to the bizarre Welwitschia, a desert conifer that grows just two immense leaves and has a lifespan of more than 100 years, alongside fragile lichen communities that rely on coastal fog to fulfil their liquid requirements! See page 225.

△ **Twyfelfontein**. A fantastic collection of prehistoric rock art – mostly engravings but also paintings, some of them up to 5,000 years old – can be observed in situ in this scenic valley west of Khorixas. See page 200.

▽ **Quiver Tree Forest**. This cluster of ancient-looking tree-sized aloes, sprouting amid a field of massive volcanic boulders known as the Giants' Playground, is other-worldly.
See page 237.

THE BEST OF NAMIBIA: EDITOR'S CHOICE

National parks rich with wildlife, desolate coastal plains, colonial towns lost in time, searing landscapes of baking-hot sand dunes... Here, at a glance, are our top recommendations for a visit.

The dunes near Sesriem.

PREHISTORIC SITES

Hoba Meteorite. The world's largest recorded meteorite, a 50-tonne lump of iron and nickel, crashed down to earth more than 30,000 years ago in the vicinity of Grootfontein. See page 168.

Brandberg. This immense granite dome, visible for miles around, is home to some of southern Africa's finest prehistoric rock paintings, including the legendary but misleadingly named "White Lady of the Brandberg". See page 199.

Dinosaur footprints. Possibly more than 100 million years old, a sequence of fossilised footprints left by a two-legged, three-toed dinosaur can be seen on Otjihaenamaparero farm, located just outside Kalkfield. See page 158.

Petrified Forest. Thought to be more than 200 million years old, this immaculately preserved fossil forest of around 50 trees can easily be visited en route to Twyfelfontein. See page 200.

Dinosaur footprints at Otjihaenamaparero.

HIKING AND ADVENTURE

Orange River Canoeing. A more sedate prospect than the legendary white-water rafting at Victoria Falls, canoe trips along the mighty Orange pass through some exhilaratingly remote scenery. See page 88.

Sandboarding. The tall dune fields that separate Swakopmund from Walvis Bay form Namibia's most alluring goal for adrenalin junkies, with sandboarding, duneboarding and quad-biking all on offer. See page 90.

Dune 45. The slithering ascent of this immense dune alongside the Sesriem-Sossusvlei road can be draining – but the fabulous view from the rim justifies dragging your feet up through the thick sand. See page 228.

Fish River Canyon. Ranked among southern Africa's top hikes, the five-day trail along the canyon floor isn't for the faint-hearted (closes in summer due to the crippling heat). See page 88.

Spitzkoppe. This spectacular mountain in Damaraland offers great rock-climbing, walking trails and rock art sites. See page 200.

Khaudom National Park. Protecting a stretch of dry woodland, this little-visited park is ideal for self-sufficient 4x4 camping expeditions. See page 170.

HISTORY AND CULTURE

Lüderitz. This fantastically isolated port at the end of Namibia's emptiest road is notable for its fresh air, easy-going atmosphere and Bavarian architecture. See page 240.

Windhoek. Namibia's capital is hardly a must-see, but it's a pleasant place to while away a day or two enjoying the colonial architecture, great restaurants and refreshing climate. Altogether more down to earth than the colonially influenced city centre is the bustling residential district of Katutura, best explored on a guided bike tour. See page 141.

Diaz Point. South of Lüderitz, this windswept point – home to Cape fur seals and marine birds – is dominated by a replica of the cross erected by Bartolomeu Diaz upon his historic landing here in 1488. See page 241.

Kolmanskop. Also outside Lüderitz, this atmospheric ghost town was the thriving centre of the Namib diamond trade before being abandoned to the desert sands in 1956. Guided visits are offered. See page 240.

Bushmanland. Best visited with a sensitive local guide, this remote corner of Namibia is inhabited by the few remaining hunter-gatherer "Bushmen" whose forbears were responsible for the prehistoric rock art scattered around southern Africa. See page 169.

Lizauli Traditional Village. This open-air museum in the Caprivi Strip offers an insight into traditional farming and fishing methods. Well-made local handicrafts are for sale. See page 191.

Himba pastoralists. The charismatic Himba are staunchly traditional, many still pursuing the semi-nomadic pastoralist lifestyle. The women and children wear jewellery made of copper wand shells. See page 204.

Haus Grünewald, Bavarian architecture in Lüderitz.

BIRDWATCHING

Etosha National Park. Raptors and large ground birds tick many boxes on Namibia's checklist of 340 species. It's a good place to look for near-endemics such as white-tailed shrike and Monteiro's hornbill. See page 183.

Mahango National Park. A highlight of the Caprivi Strip, this remote and well-watered reserve is home to more bird species than any other Namibian sanctuary. Avian highlights include Cape parrot and African skimmer. See page 190.

Walvis Bay Lagoon & Sandwich Harbour. The pedestrian-friendly lagoon on the southern outskirts of Walvis Bay often hosts large flocks of marine birds. Further south, the less accessible Sandwich Harbour is southern Africa's finest site for marine birds, and is renowned for its flocks of flamingos. See page 222.

Namib-Naukluft Park. This arid park forms the core range of such dry-country endemics as the dune lark and various raptors. See page 225.

OFF THE BEATEN TRACK

Kunene River. This perennial river on the remote Angolan border is fringed by tall white dunes of the Kakaoveld, a mesmerising landscape inhabited by oryx, Hartmann's mountain zebra and several localised bird species. See page 205.

Mudumu & Nkasa Rupara National Parks. A combination of woodland and wetland habitats makes them ideal for adventurous safari-goers and birdwatchers. Once notoriously inaccessible, **Nkasa Rupara** is now the site of a luxury tented camp. See page 191.

Damaraland. This sparsely vegetated and hilly region is home to a range of dry-country dwellers including southern Africa's only desert-adapted populations of elephant and black rhinoceros. See page 197.

Skeleton Coast. Thrillingly desolate and renowned for its pristine ecology and the shipwrecks that litter its rocky bays. Coastal highlights include the seal colonies at Cape Fria and Cape Cross, as well as the dazzling agate formations in the Hoarusib Canyon. See page 209.

Pelicans abound on the Namibian coast.

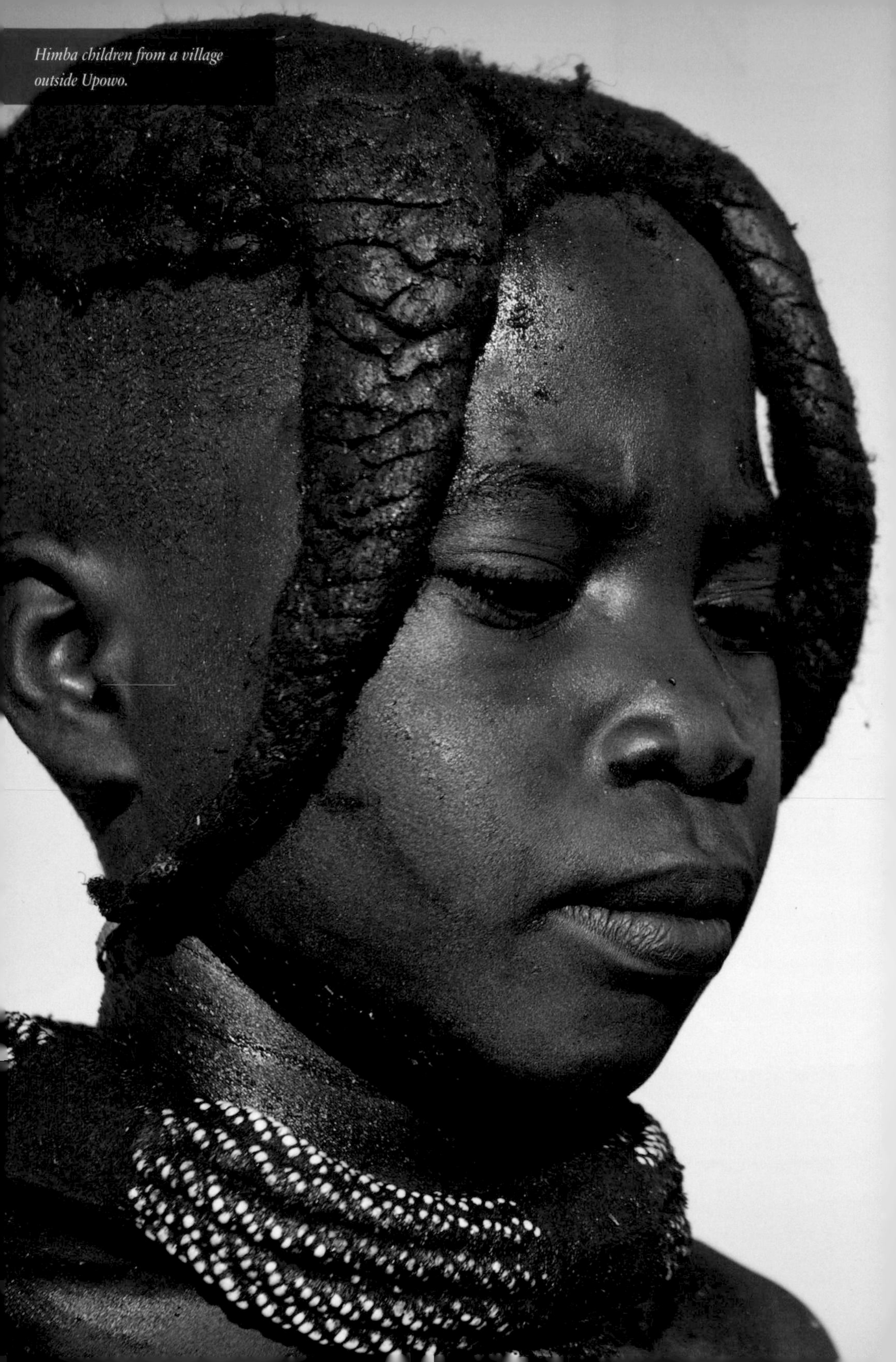

Himba children from a village outside Upowo.

San women in Tsumkwe.

Local Namibians in Swakopmund.

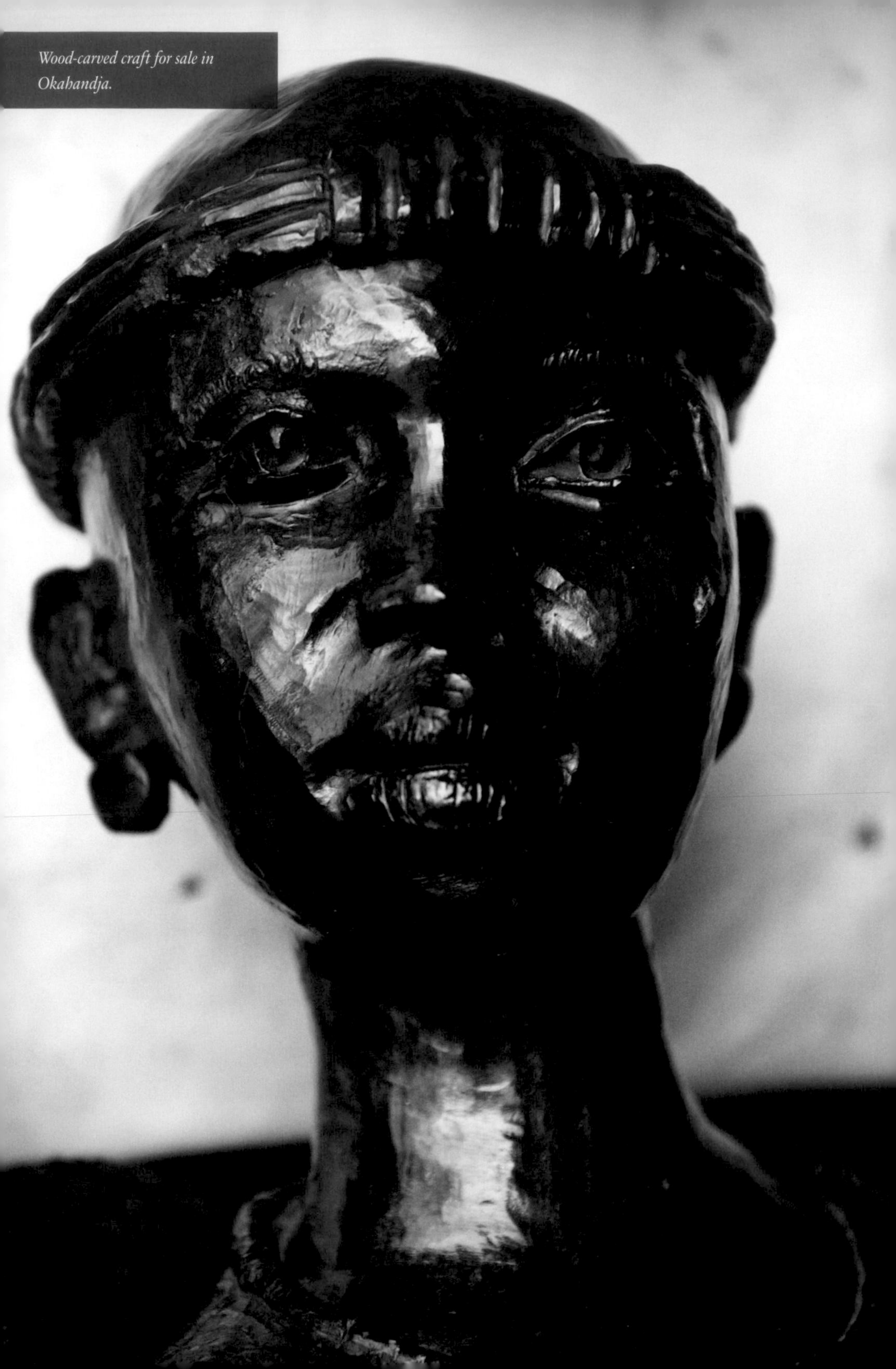

Wood-carved craft for sale in Okahandja.

UNITED COLOURS

Namibia survived the transition to
independence with comparative ease.
Why did it succeed where others failed?

Himba village.

What can explain the harmony that prevails in Namibia today, given that the population consists of at least 11 major ethnic groupings and an even greater variety of languages? The reason may be that – despite a century of ruthless colonialism, decades of apartheid and a bitter struggle for independence – the majority of ordinary people always stood together, working and suffering as one, mingling on farms and in small towns, sharing the bitter and the sweet.

The Europeans conquered Africa with their languages, religions, education, technology and agricultural know-how, but a barrier of deep mistrust remained between the indigenous inhabitants and their conquerors. As one might expect, 23 years of occupation by apartheid South Africa singularly failed to resolve the situation – yet the independence struggles of the 1970s and 1980s somehow managed to bring white and black Namibians together. It was as if they realised that by staying apart, they risked becoming enemies. White Namibians – originally Europeans, but long since people of Africa – overcame their fears of the "black peril", and black people their mistrust of the "white peril". The area in between was no longer uncharted territory.

Crafts made by the Herero women.

In 1989, the powerful political organisation known as SWAPO took the decision to get involved in independence negotiations with the South African government. Now, at last, Namibia could get on with the complex process of drafting a new democratic constitution, and finally declaring itself independent in 1994.

This comprehensive process of reconciliation – or, rather mutual safeguarding – is ongoing. Today the country possesses a political system based on sound democratic principles, with great regard for the origins, language, culture, religion and political convictions of all its peoples. And the bonhomie that has taken root among the people of Namibia is readily communicated to visitors, too.

THE PEOPLE

Namibia is a rich tapestry of cultures, with at least 11 major ethnic groups speaking dozens of different languages.

Namibia's population is as varied as its landscape: colourful and rich in different languages and lifestyles. The peoples of this thinly populated expanse of land – which ranges from the river landscapes of the Caprivi Strip, through dry forests and savannahs, to the deserts along the Atlantic – have been compared to a colourful carpet, with fringes that reach deep into the countries around it. This young country combines a palette of peoples and tribes in a geographical area whose borders were drawn through tribal lands between 1884 and 1890 to suit the interests of colonial powers. As a result, many peoples were thrown together in what was to develop into the modern state of Namibia.

The people's socio-political orientation is as many-sided as their culture. At one point, they'll seem conservative; at another, enlightened and progressive. Social isolationism is not uncommon, but neither is upward mobility. Thus, segregation – often the legacy of the apartheid laws abolished in the late 1970s – alternates with giant steps forward in national reconciliation, after decades of open and dormant conflicts.

The mobile Namibians

Long ago, the nomadic herdsmen of the Herero and Nama moved with the seasons to find good pasture; today, the inhabitants of Kaokoveld still follow this practice. In adjoining territories, competing cowherders quarrelled over pastures, water rights, and ownership of the cows themselves. Meanwhile, the oldest inhabitants of southern Africa, hunter-gatherers known to outsiders as the San (Bushmen), wandered through huge desert territories which had seemed inhospitable both to the roving herdsmen and to the

A student at a German private school in Windhoek.

CITY-SEEKERS

Although Namibia has the second-lowest population density of any sovereign state, a growing proportion of its people are concentrated in a dozen main urban areas. This is most obvious in Windhoek, where the population grew from less than 100,000 in 1981 to 233,529 in 2001, and is estimated at around 330,000 today. The populations of the twin ports of Swakopmund and Walvis Bay have more than doubled since 2000, and respectively stand at around 45,000 and 85,000 today. Aside from Rehoboth and Keetmanshoop, the rest of Namibia's 12 largest urban centres lie in the north, with Rundu the most populous at around 80,000.

settled agricultural, herding and fishing clans in Ovamboland, Okavango and the Caprivi Strip.

The first mixed-race and white settlers moved onto the land with wagons and herds of cattle. Settlement and territorial conflicts at the beginning of the century forced native peoples, the Herero and Nama in particular, from their homelands into outlying areas of the country. But despite colonial dominion by German and South African settlers, the native population was able to maintain its cultural identity.

The occupation and development of the central and southern region, and the expan-

In 1977, the pass laws were repealed. The contract-labour system was no longer practical. Since then, migrant labour has followed its own course: thousands seek employment in industry, trade or administration to escape, if only temporarily, the country's "vicious circle of subsistence economy". Many return periodically to visit their families; others are sucked more quickly into the maelstrom of big-city life.

This syndrome of urban migration has affected every part of the population, whether in the overpopulated areas of the north or the thinly populated deserts to the south and west.

A child living in Tsumkwe.

sion of the mining industry, brought about a great demand for labour. Workers were drawn from the more thickly populated north, in Ovamboland, where 'migrant workers' were common. Migrant work, which was strictly regulated according to a contract system until the 1970s, brought together people from every region of the country. The mandate government, however, attempted to prevent migrant workers from settling permanently in the south by means of pass laws. For this reason, the central and southern regions of Namibia were virtually a foreign country for northern natives. To obtain a temporary residence permit, they had to have a steady job, and these were hard to come by.

Independence has accelerated the process to a remarkable degree. The country's few cities and population centres – Ondangwa and Oshakati, Windhoek and Swakopmund – are faced with the tremendous task of quickly creating reasonable housing for all of these people, to prevent the development of urban slums.

Deportation and emigration

After World War I, in the period between the Armistice (11 November 1918) and the signing of the Treaty of Versailles (28 June 1919), the South African military government deported 4,900 Germans from occupied South West Africa, most of them soldiers, officials and "undesirables". This was a considerable number in a population of only about 15,000, of whom 12,300 were native German speakers. It hit the country's economy as well, since the skilled labourers needed could not simply be brought in from South Africa. After the deportation ordinance was lifted, some 1,000 of those who had been turned out returned to Namibia.

During the period in which apartheid laws were in effect – over 25 years – many thousands of black Namibians left the country illegally, emigrating to Botswana, Zambia, and later Angola. They were following the patriotic call to take part in the fight for Namibian inde-

of the South African military presence which accompanied independence in 1989 meant that several thousand white family members, who had for years lived in various military facilities within Namibia, now left the country.

The newcomers

Originally, South West Africa was regarded as a "settlement area" among the former German colonies, rather than merely as a source of raw materials, such as Togo or Cameroon. European settlers – mainly Germans before 1914, after the two world wars primarily homeless South

Owela Museum display in Windhoek, Namibia.

pendence, or hoping to receive higher education in foreign schools and universities. Before the great repatriation in 1989, many Namibians had spent up to 30 years in exile.

With the country's first attempt at independence in 1978, political uncertainty and economic recession induced the white population to emigrate in droves. This group shrank in number from its record height of 110,000 to about 74,000. Emigration occurred primarily among that class which had either been transferred or came looking for work from South Africa only a few years before. But the final, successful, independence process in 1989–90 did not lead to any significant emigration of white Namibians – although the withdrawal

RETURN OF THE TREKKERS

One distinct group of 20th-century immigrants were Boers from Angola, who were resettled in the regions of Outjo and Gobabis in 1928, on the initiative of the South African government. The newcomers were mainly survivors and descendants of the legendary "Dorsland trekkers", who had left Transvaal in 1878 in search of land free from British colonial rule. Doggedly refusing to yield to thirst or tropical diseases, these indefatigable trekkers had driven their cattle and ox-drawn wagons through the Kalahari and South West Africa, finally settling in South Angola, where they had remained for about half a century.

African Boers – had a major effect on the ownership of land and inevitably on its use. However, the influx of immigrants to South West Africa never reached anything like the scale of the prodigious migration of people from Europe to the Americas and Australia. Immigrants to Namibia never numbered more than a few thousand.

The most recent large-scale influx was the repatriation of exiles in 1989, the year when the international community realised plans to solve the Namibian question. The Refugee Commissioner of the United Nations set up an "air bridge" to Windhoek and Grootfontein for all Namibians

in the country. The authors of the constitution deliberately chose not to use the language of the country's erstwhile colonial rulers, German (a customary practice among newly-independent African states).

> *Afrikaans is the leading language in Namibia. Around ten percent of Namibians – coloureds, blacks and most whites – speak Afrikaans as their first language, far more than the total of English and German speakers.*

At least 97 percent of Namibia's population does not speak English at home. Although it is the country's official language, less than 2 percent of Namibians are raised as English speakers – a number approximately equal to that of those raised speaking German.

The Ovambo dialect, including both written versions of it, represents the largest linguistic family in the country, with some 680,000 native speakers. Thus, limiting the official language to English is equally unfair to members of every other linguistic family – that is, virtually the entire population. It accommodates neither the majority nor any dominant minority. Linguistic experts calculate that it will take some two generations for the change to be fully implemented; in urban surroundings, the process will be somewhat easier.

However, the mastery of English carries with it hopes of greater social and economic mobility. By means of this international language, the country has been able to hook up with international information exchanges. English has helped to forge links with neighbouring countries, and will also serve, perhaps, as the vehicle for the creation of a new national unity.

Afrikaans, by contrast, is stigmatised as a "language of oppression" because of its connection with apartheid. On the other hand, it is the native language of various extremely vital cultural groups, so there appears to be little danger of its dying out in the future.

The survival of Namibia's other languages will depend on the vigour of the cultures of the individual groups that speak them. The Ovambo dialects, which are rooted in solid, living cultures, are less endangered than the countless smaller border languages, such as those of the Bushmen (San) or some of the Nama.

Standing for a family portrait.

living in exile in Angola, Zambia and elsewhere. Every repatriate of voting age could take part in the preparations and then in the historic vote for independence in November 1989. In this way, 42,000 refugees returned to their homeland. Many of them were children and adolescents who had never seen the country of their fathers.

Official language, many tongues

The authors of Namibia's constitution selected one of the two languages which had historically been official in Namibia: English. Thus the common vernacular language of Afrikaans, after serving as an official language for some 60 years, was retired to a secondary position as first among 20 or so other tongues recognised

In sport, languages vary from one discipline to another. English is spoken on the football field and the bowling green. Afrikaans dominates at rugby matches; riding, nine-pins and hang-gliding tend to be carried out in German; and at the spectacular athletic jumping game of *omupembe*, Oshivambo is the language you will hear.

From the very beginning, residents of Namibia have had to be multilingual. As a rule, those who live here can make themselves understood in two or three local languages without any trouble; mastery of four or five is not unusual. Anyone who remained monolingual in

for example, are unique to Namibia. Such a synthesis of European and African folk cultures is typical of this country.

Each sector of the population is a tile in the mosaic of Namibia's culture. The ceramics, basket-weaving and decorative woodcarvings of the peoples in the rainy north are as much a part of Namibian culture as the prize songs of the Nama or the Bushmen's dancing rituals. Choral singing is popular and common. Songs accompanied by the rhythm of drums, or classical instruments, on the Okavango river or the Caprivi Strip, or the church choir, or the 1902

An arts and crafts store in Otjiwarongo.

a country with as many different languages as Namibia would risk social isolation. And, if anyone complains that this is an unreasonable situation, somebody is sure to point to the matter-of-fact multilingualism of the Swiss.

The quest for culture

Apart from the flag, the national anthem and the civil rights' ordinances that apply to all citizens and every part of the country, there's not much, culturally speaking, that all Namibians can immediately identify with to the same degree. However, the forms of cultural expression of certain sectors of the population are distinctive and characteristic. The traditional Victorian folk costumes of the Herero women,

SPRECHEN SIE DEUTSCH?

German, historically Namibia's first "official" language, has been able to retain its force as a means of communication and vehicle of culture. This is perhaps because of the multilingual abilities of those who speak it, rather than their numbers, which are still relatively small. Mainstays of the German language in Namibia are several schools and churches, a whole range of athletic and cultural organisations, two German newspapers, a radio station and a part of the business world, as well as the tourist and service trades – although, in the latter, people are happy to switch back and forth to English and Afrikaans.

Men's Singing Association in Swakopmund – each has its own sound, each its own appeal.

Is this Namibian culture? No, but this country's culture has many faces. And Namibia is in a position to attract creative individuals from other places – those who wish to explore the cultural legacies of fast-vanishing minorities. In the annual music contest, or the visual arts competition, Namibian artists seek out new forms, tones and colours. Faces, environment, social problems: all provide ample subject-matter.

After a hard day's work, the people are masters in the art of unwinding. Inviting barbecue

A man from Ovamboland.

fires blaze throughout the country for festivals and holidays. At sundown, they signal the locations of safari camps or garden parties. Meat dishes of every variety are a part of the diet. In this country with so many remote farms and rural communities, such hospitality plays an important role.

The last of the hunter-gatherers

The San people – also known as "Bushmen" – live mainly in the easternmost reaches of northern Namibia, a region which the South Africans called Bushmanland. These slight, lean, apricot-skinned people still live in traditional villages, although most of them now wear Western clothing and trade painstakingly

> *Although the "Bushmen" are a distinct ethnic group, they have no collective name for themselves. They are members of the Kung clan, or Ju/'hoans, or any one of a dozen other clans.*

made jewellery for money to buy basic foodstuffs. Some retain their remarkable tracking skills (they can recognise an individual by their footprints), and obtain most of their food from hunting and gathering.

Spending time with these self-deprecating people is a moving experience, for they have a strong sense of fun, a profound understanding of the environment and an unrushed quality about their lives. It is possible for small parties to visit some of the San people in Bushmanland, to see their dances and possibly go out with them on hunting and gathering expeditions.

Contact the Omatako Valley Rest Community Campsite via Spitzkoppe Reservations (tel: 081 211 6291; www.spitzkoppereservations. com). Another option is Nhoma Safari Camp 80km (50 miles) from Tsumkwe, which is open all year but best known for the five-day Bushcraft and Tracking Course offered on set dates between March and July.

Bringing the people together

Namibia's new constitution calls upon the government to distribute goods and social services in equal measure throughout the country. Discrepancies between the central regions and the under-developed border territories, in terms of modern comfort, education and structural economic development, are also to be resolved. This development will speed the process of adaptation, particularly for smaller ethnic groups. While the existing cultural diversity and regional customs will protect the country from becoming uniform and flat, they will not prevent Namibians from coming together, and growing into a new, identifiable nation. Namibians have already demonstrated this multiplicity in many different situations. A chorus in five languages sums it up:

Namibia, Namibia, ti oms, ti saub,
  geskenk van God;
Namibia, oshilongo shetu, country –
  Heimat Namibia.

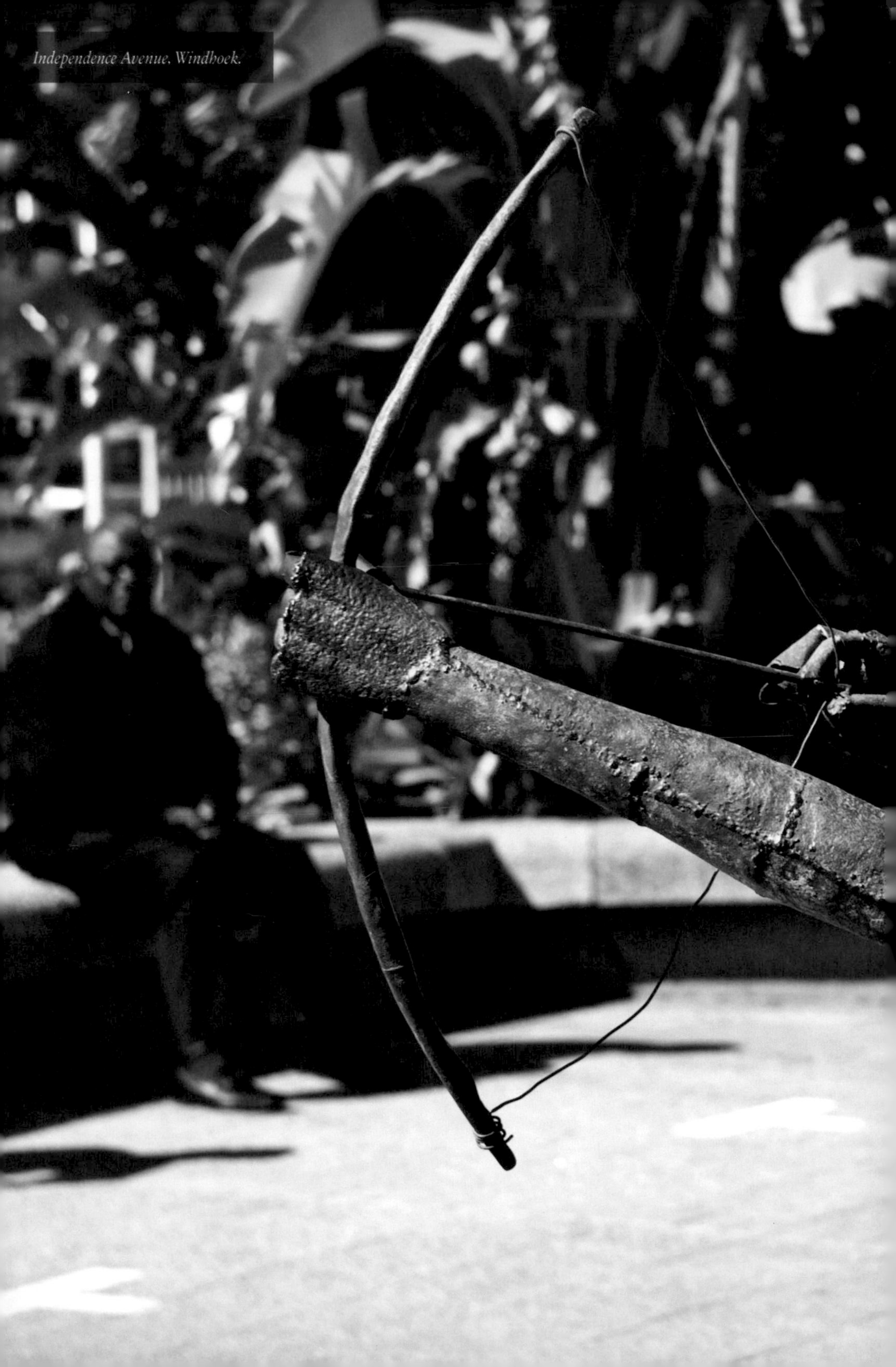

Independence Avenue, Windhoek.

DECISIVE DATES

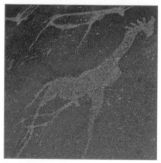

Twyfelfontein rock art.

12 million BC
The hominoid (ape-like creature) *Otavipithecus namibiensis* occupies Namibia.

25,000 BC
Namibia is inhabited by San hunter-gatherers whose art still adorns rocks at Twyfelfontein.

500 BC–AD 500
Nama migrants from Botswana bring metal-working skills.

c.900
Khoi-San pastoralists, the Damara, settle in Namibia.

Discovery and Exploration

1486
The Portuguese explorer Diego Cão lands at Cape Cross.

1488
Bartholomeu Diaz lands at Lüderitz.

1500s
Herero migrants from East Africa settle the Kaokoveld.

1820s
Khoi-San groups such as the Oorlam Nama migrate from the Cape into Namibia.

1862–70
The Nama-Herero wars.

The Colonial Era

1878
Britain annexes Walvis Bay to Cape Colony.

1884
Germany claims German South West Africa (Namibia) as a colony. Walvis Bay remains British.

1889-1890s
German troops clear indigenous Namibians from their land for settlers to farm.

1904–6
An estimated 80,000 Herero and Nama are killed or die in concentration camps following uprisings against German rule.

1915
During World War I, Namibia is placed under South African military rule.

1920
Under League of Nations mandate, Namibia is to be administered by South Africa.

1922
South Africa sets up "reserves" for black Namibians and distributes more land to settlers. Uprisings are violently crushed.

Lindequist.

1939-45
Many black Namibians serve with the South African forces fighting Nazism.

1946
South Africa refuses to hand back its mandate to the UN.

Towards Independence

1960
The South West Africa People's Organisation (SWAPO) is founded by Sam Nujoma.

A painting showing the Germans exploring South West Africa.

1961
Legal action begins at the International Court of Justice (ICJ) to end South African mandate.

1964
South Africa consolidates apartheid policies in Namibia.

1966
SWAPO undertakes its first military action. The UN ends South Africa's mandate, but South Africa refuses to withdraw.

1967
South Africa refuses the UN Council for Namibia access.

1976
The UN Security Council Resolution 385 calls for United Nations to organise elections.

1977
South Africa refuses implementation of Resolution 385.

1978
The South African Defence Force (SADF) kills 800 Namibian refugees in a raid on Kassinga in Angola. South Africa rejects election proposals accepted by SWAPO and adopted by the UN as Resolution 435.

1979–80
South Africa sets up an "internal government" in Namibia.

Modern Namibia

1981
US makes the implementation of Resolution 435 conditional upon Cubans leaving Angola.

1983
Namibia's "internal government" collapses.

Namibian youths celebrate their country's first hours of independence.

South Africa resumes direct rule.

1984
South Africa and SWAPO meet. South Africa's insistence on "Cuban Linkage" undermines any progress.

1985
MPC's internal government, the "Transitional Government of National Unity", is installed in Windhoek. The SADF increases military involvement in Angola.

1989
A formal cessation of hostilities is declared on 1 April. In November, elections to the Constituent Assembly are held. SWAPO win 57 percent of the vote.

1990
On 21 March Namibian independence is finally won.

2000
Nujoma allows Angola to attack rebels from Namibian soil, bringing reprisals by Angolan guerrillas.

2002
Ceasefire in Angola encourages economic development in Northern Namibia.

2005
Hifikepunye Pohamba (SWAPO) wins presidential elections and begins a land-reform programme.

2009
Hifikepunye Pohamba wins elections with more than 75 percent of the vote.

2011
More than 10 billion barrels of oil reserves are discovered offshore.

2013
Namibia's government ranked 3rd among mainland African countries on the Ibrahim Index, which measures success in delivering essential political goods to citizens.

Namibian President Hifikepunye Pohamba.

BEGINNINGS

Palaeontologists looking for evidence of the origins of modern man have found much to interest them in Namibia's ancient sites.

Scientists now agree with some confidence that Africa was the cradle of mankind. All the available palaeontological evidence indicates that the first humans evolved on the African continent, that, before migrating northwards into Europe and Asia. Taxonomists place these early humans in the subfamily Hominini, which all members of the human clade (including modern *Homo sapiens*) subsequent to the evolutionary split from chimpanzees.

Hominine taxonomy is a matter of considerable controversy, with experts frequently disagreeing on the status and significance of any given fossil, and theories are regularly revised as new discoveries come to light. Broadly speaking, however, the oldest genus of hominid is Ardipithecus, which first showed up on the fossil record some 5.6 million years ago and is thus far known only from the Ethiopian Rift Valley. Ardipithecus was possibly ancestral to Australopithecus (literally "Southern Ape"), several species of which are recognised, and which roamed

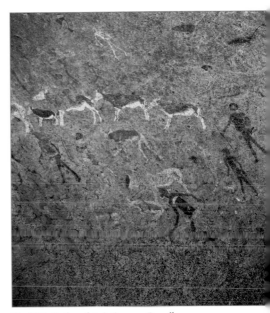

The White Lady rock painting near Brandberg.

The hunter-gatherer peoples that populated Southern Africa were once designated with blanket terms such as Bushmen or San. Since 1996, however, the relevant groups in Namibia have agreed to be described collectively as San.

widely throughout sub-Saharan Africa between 4 and 1.7 million years ago.

Opinion differs as to whether Australopithecines were ancestral to the genus Homo, which emerged some 2.5 million years ago. However, the cranially enlarged *Australopithecus garhi*, first discovered in Ethiopia in 1996, is regarded

by advocates of this theory as the missing link between the two genera. Fossil evidence suggests that the two genera co-existed in Namibia and elsewhere in southern Africa for at least half a million years before Australopithecus became extinct.

Relics of early man

Remnants of our own direct ancestor, *Homo sapiens*, have been found widely distributed throughout southern Africa. African variants of *Homo sapiens* display genetic markers that are called Negroid – as opposed to the Mongoloid and Caucasoid variants found elsewhere. Crudely stated, this implies that black people have been living in southern Africa for about 100,000 years.

Within the Negroid genetic constellation, however, different groups developed in relative isolation from each other. One sub-group which we particularly need to notice must have lived in relative isolation in the southwestern corner of the continent for about 40,000 years. These were the so-called Khoisan peoples, who once inhabited substantial parts of what is now Namibia, South Africa and Botswana.

Hand axes, cleavers, pebble choppers and other tools dating from the Early and Middle Stone Age (between 27,000 and 25,000 years ago) have been found at sites throughout the territory – even in the heart of the Namib Desert, which indicate that major climatic changes must have occurred there in the not-too-distant past. Most of the relics have been found along seasonal riverbeds and coastline, and around natural springs. One interesting find was in present-day Windhoek, which tells us that these Early and Middle Stone Age people were hunting elephant and other big game in what is now the heart of the capital.

It's estimated that small bands of these hunter-gatherers wandered from one hunting ground to another, following the seasonal

Daily life in a Himba village

OTJISEVA MAN

In 1991, a US-French team of palaeontologists led by Glenn Conroy and Martin Pickford made a thrilling discovery at Berg Aukas in the Otavi Mountains to the north of Windhoek. The scientists found the fossilised jawbone of an anthropoid from the Middle Miocene period, dating back 13 million years. This was the first discovery of its kind south of Kenya, and it was named *Otavipithecus namibiensis* or Otjiseva Man. Now preserved in the National Earth Science Museum in Windhoek, it predated the earliest known Australopithecus fossils by 8 million years, and is placed in the "super-family" that includes gibbons, apes and humans.

migrations of game. Painted and engraved stone slabs depicting their domestic life and religious rites have been found in abundance all over Namibia – most significantly in Damaraland, and in the Huns mountains to the south of the country.

The Khoisan were shorter and had lighter-coloured skin than most other Africans, their language contained clicking sounds and other unusual consonants, and they knew nothing of agriculture or iron-working.

Then, about 2,600 years ago, one group of Khoisan living in northern Botswana were initiated into cattle-keeping by other Africans. Being herders rather than hunters, they multiplied and dispersed very rapidly. They called themselves Khoikhoi – "men of men" – or Nama people, and they called the remaining hunter-gatherers San.

Migrations from the north

By the beginning of the 9th century, groups of Bantu-speaking people from central Africa started migrating into Namibia. Taller, darker-skinned and more technologically sophisticated than the Khoisan-speaking peoples, they spoke languages that indicate their cultural links with the rest of sub-Saharan Africa. Internationally, these are known as 'Bantu' lan-

20th century. Apartheid theorists were fond of describing the southwestern corner of the African continent as an empty land, peopled solely by immigrants. Apartheid maps showed fat black arrows depicting waves of Africans migrating into the region from the far north, while much thinner white arrows discreetly indicated the European incursions from the south. The intention, of course, was to give the impression that Namibians both white and black, equally, were intruders of alien origin, and that the white minority had the same moral right to the land as the black majority.

Dunes near Sesriem.

guages, a term so abused by the South African administration in Namibia during apartheid times that it is no longer socially acceptable there, in any context. Settling in the northeast (present-day Caprivi and Kavango regions), the north-central (Ovamboland) and the northwest (Kaokoland), these Africans brought with them pastoral practices as well as pottery and metal-working skills – but as they moved in, the indigenous San groupings were pushed steadily southwards.

The apartheid picture

Yet a very different picture of the origins of Namibia's peoples was painted during South Africa's long occupation of Namibia in the

For similar reasons, apartheid theorists went to great lengths to emphasise what they saw as the cultural differences between different kinds of Africans. Black Africans were alleged to belong to "tribes" that were culturally monolithic and mutually incompatible. These could not be trusted to live in peace, and had to be sharply segregated from each other. Apartheid theory also sought to disaggregate this African majority into much smaller components so that the white minority no longer seemed like a white minority, but more like one tribe among many other tribes.

Such theories are rarely met within Namibia today, but unfortunately the underlying stereotypes still persist to a surprising degree.

Detail of a pillar erected by the Portuguese explorer Diego Cão in southern Angola.

EARLY EXPLORERS

Although the Portuguese first set foot on Namibian soil as far back as 1486, nearly four centuries were to pass before European expansionism really took root.

The first European to step onto Namibian soil was the Portuguese explorer Diego Cão, who reached the Skeleton Coast in 1486 and put up a stone cross at Cape Cross to prove it. He was followed in 1488 by another explorer, his fellow-countryman Bartholomeu Diaz, who erected his own cross at Angra Pequena (which is now known as Lüderitz).

Prior to this, the coast of Namibia – like the rest of sub-Saharan Africa – was terra incognita to European navigators. Furthermore, unlike the Indian Ocean coastline of eastern Africa, which had entered into regular maritime trade with Arabia by the start of the second millennium AD and was visited by Indian and Chinese ships in mediaeval times, the west coast of sub-equatorial Africa probably existed in almost total isolation from the rest of the world at this time.

Only in the 15th century, as trade with the East took off, did European ships – more specifically, the Portuguese – start to search for a new sea route to India via the Cape of Good Hope, a route that took them along the coast of Namibia. But for centuries after Cão and Diaz first landed in what is now Namibia, the forbidding climate and inhospitable terrain shielded the land from European expansionism. For both explorers and traders, the very notion of settling on a coastline that offered neither food nor water for sustenance – nor slaves and ivory for trade – was a complete waste of time. As the captain of a passing Dutch vessel, the *Bode*, noted: "Here for nothing in the world is there even the smallest gain for our masters… there is only sand, rock, and storm."

Towards the end of the 18th century, however, the ports of Lüderitz and Walvis Bay

Drawing of Walvis Bay in the 19th century.

began to be visited more frequently by whalers and seal-catchers from France, Britain and America, and passing Indian trade. The areas around these harbours, meanwhile, began to be harvested for guano.

The Oorlam invasions

With war on the horizon in Europe, in 1793 the Dutch government claimed Walvis Bay (the only decent deepwater port along the coast) and Angra Pequena, as well as Halifax Island off the coast. When the British annexed the Cape Colony two years later they, too, hoisted their flag along the Namibian shore – although it was not until 1878 that they annexed Walvis Bay and its environs (approximately 1,165 sq km/450 sq miles) for themselves as well.

Even at this stage, however, scarcely anything was known about the Namibian interior, although the discovery of the Orange River in 1760 did open up the territory somewhat to traders and hunters as well as to missionaries.

At the turn of the 18th century, southern Namibia was thrown into a turmoil with the arrival of large numbers of Oorlam people, roving bands of dispossessed Khoisan fleeing Dutch persecution in the Cape. Although the

The mighty Herero chief, Maherero.

Oorlams were of the same origins as the Nama pastoralists already settled in southern Namibia (and spoke a similar language), many had guns and horses, giving them both mobility and a technological edge. Some were outlaws, while others had broken away from scattered Nama settlements en route to take their chances with the Oorlams as they traded, thieved and hunted their way north.

Thanks to their commando-style military structures, which they'd copied from the Boer frontiersmen, the South Africans quickly subdued the indigenous Namibians and their bows and arrows. Soon the Oorlams – led by a paramount chief named Jonker Afrikaner – had subjugated the Nama and Damara in the south

> Namibia's northernmost peoples – the Ovambo and the Kavango – remained relatively isolated from the troubles down south during the Oorlam invasions.

and reduced the Herero clans in the east and centre-north to mere vassal status.

Nevertheless, the locals fought back. Ongoing skirmishes amounting almost to low-level warfare raged throughout the region for the next 70 years, as Oorlam commandos continued to raid the cattle of local clans and pillage settlements. The inexhaustible demand for commodities to trade for arms also led to the wholesale slaughter of game stocks, especially elephant and ostriches.

Traders and missionaries

Temporary calm was brought to this unhappy situation in 1840, when Jonker Afrikaner struck a peace deal with Paramount Chief Oaseb of the Nama. Southern Namibia was effectively split between the Nama and a range of Oorlam groups, while the Oorlams obtained the rights to the land between the Swakop and the Kuiseb rivers in the centre of the country. Jonker Afrikaner was also given rights over the people living north of the Kuiseb. In practice, this meant that the Oorlams formed a buffer zone between the Nama in the south, and the Herero further north in Kaokoland – although the latter had been steadily moving south themselves ever since the middle of the 18th century.

Nonetheless, the disruption of indigenous community life continued, thanks to the reduction of cattle stock through warfare and drought and the destruction of water reserves. The resulting discontent deepened opposition to Jonker Afrikaner's rule, and forged a broad alliance between Herero, rival Nama clans, traders and missionaries. Yet Afrikaner's central Namibian "empire" continued even after his death in 1861, when his eldest son and heir, Christian, inherited the reins of power.

By this time, traders and hunters on the lookout for valuable commodities such as ostrich feathers and ivory had begun venturing deep into the Namibian interior. One of the most important figures was a certain Charles John Andersson, who – with the help of a band of hunters acting as a sort of armed guard in this lawless territory – established a trading post at Otjimbingwe and started to explore new trade routes further north and east. It was his men who in 1863 shot and killed Christian Afrikaner, who had rashly mounted a raid on Otjimbingwe.

In the traders' wake came various missionaries – in particular the London Mission Society, Wesleyan Methodists, and Rhenish and Finnish Lutherans – who established small stations throughout the south and central regions. They were able to extend their influence reasonably easily during the 1870s, a relatively calm decade thanks to a treaty signed in 1870 by the Herero chief, Kamherero and Christian's successor, Jan Jonker Afrikaner. But by the 1880s fighting had once again broken out between the various Nama groups, the Herero and the Basters – new arrivals from the Cape who had settled in the Reheboth area. All these groups had by now also started to trade extensively with the Europeans.

It was into this cauldron – pre-colonised by European technology and awesome firepower, as well as the spread of Christianity – that Germany now stepped.

Drawing by Albert Bettanier.

PORTUGUESE EXPLORATION OF AFRICA

It started in 1415, when the Portuguese navy, inspired by Henry the Navigator, captured the Moroccan port of Ceuta. Though the battle lasted less than a day, the capture of Ceuta arguably unleashed a wave of European expansionism that shaped the world as we know it. It also provided impetus to an era of Portuguese naval exploration driven by two main motives: to find a route through to the Indian Ocean and establish control over the spice and gold trade that linked East Africa, Arabia and Asia, and to locate and forge links with the legendary lost Christian Kingdom of Prester John (Ethiopia).

Portugal underestimated how far southwards Africa stretched. The Senegal River was reached in 1444, the Gambia in 1446, Sierra Leone in 1460, and São Tomé in 1474. Only in 1486, however, did Diego Cão make it as far as present-day Namibia, erecting a cross at Cape Cross shortly before he died.

Where Cão left off, Bartholomeu Diaz followed, landing at present-day Lüderitz in 1488, before he unwittingly rounded the Cape of Good Hope into the Indian Ocean. Finally, in 1499, Vasco da Gama made it all the way to India. Within another ten years, Portugal had established a permanent presence in Goa and East Africa, and while its influence over Namibia was never great, both neighbouring Angola and nearby Mozambique remained Portuguese colonies until 1975.

Major Theodor von Leutwein.

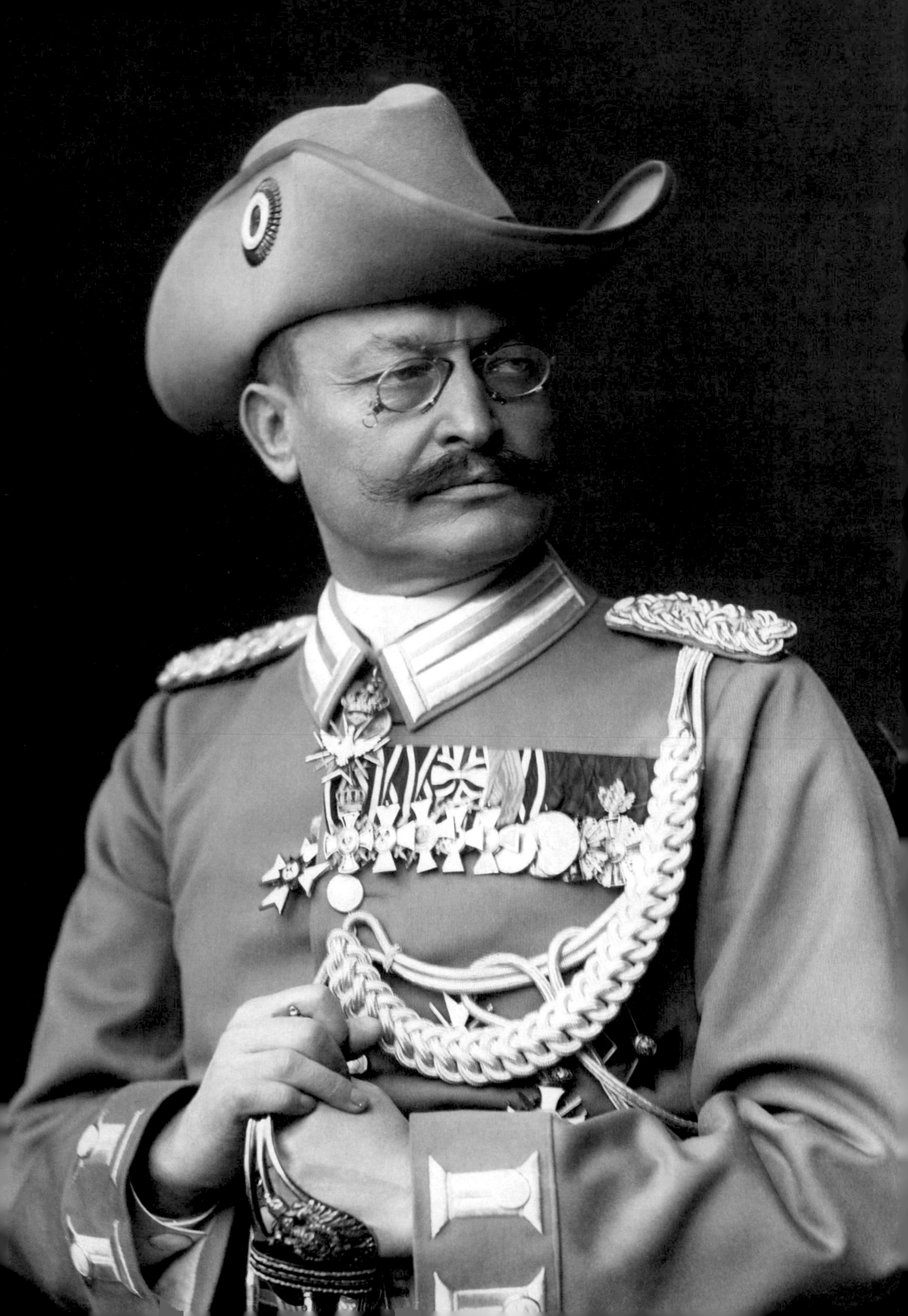

ENTER THE GERMANS

Having acquired Namibia relatively late in the "Scramble for Africa", Germany set about subduing the Namibians with a series of ruthless military campaigns.

The Germans were relative latecomers to the great "Scramble for Africa" which in the late 19th century found the British, the French, the Portuguese and the Belgians racing to carve up the continent. Although during the 1870s the German missionaries stationed in Namibia sent repeated requests to their government for military backup to help establish law and order in the war-torn southern and central regions, their appeals met with little response; a colonial policy was at this stage simply not part of Germany's overall plan.

It was only in 1884, after much wrangling, that the German government under Chancellor Otto von Bismarck decided to abandon its anti-colonial policy and enter the fray. As far as Namibia was concerned, colonisation was greatly aided by an enterprising trader from Bremen called Adolf Lüderitz, who had the previous year bought several coastal territories (including the port of Angra Pequena) from a local Nama chieftain. At the time of the sale, he had asked for German protection, and in 1884 he got it. In April of that year, two German gunboats arrived in Angra Pequena – now known as Lüderitz – and the German flag was officially raised over Namibian soil.

A protectorate proclaimed

Although Bismarck proclaimed the Lüderitz area a protectorate of the German Reich on 24 April 1884, the purchase was not without its negative aspects. This was a desert region, after all, and its economic outlook was bleak.

It was a gamble that paid off, however, for the dunes of the Namib Desert concealed a fortune. Diamonds were discovered in the region some 24 years later, although Lüderitz himself was destined never to reap any rewards from this windfall; his life ended tragically early in

Adolf Lüderitz, trader and pioneer.

Of all the international boundaries created during the Scramble for Africa, few are as perverse as the Caprivi Strip: a long, emaciated corridor of land ceded by Britain to Germany in 1890 so that the latter would have access to the Zambezi.

a mysterious accident at sea. In October 1886 he embarked on an expedition overland from Angra Pequena south to the Orange River, and back up the coast again by boat. On 22 October, he and his crew set off from South Africa's Alexander Bay for Angra Pequena – but the vessel never arrived, and the entire crew perished.

Before the discovery of the Namib diamond fields, however, Bismarck planned to turn over this new overseas territory to investors. As a result, only three officials were sent out to administer the brand-new colony of South West Africa. With the flourishing little trading post of Otjimbingwe for a base, the colonial staff's efficiency was proportional to its size; although the Imperial Commissioner Dr Heinrich Göring managed to get the powerful Herero chief Maharero to sign a "protection treaty" with Germany, he failed to build a relationship with the equally powerful Witbooi Namas, who occupied a large tranche of

At the turn of the 19th century, German settlers to Namibia were rewarded with the most fertile land.

land south of Windhoek. He also failed in his attempts to impose a prohibition on the locals' importation of weapons. As a result, unrest between the indigenous clans continued to rage; from time to time, the Commissioner was even compelled to seek shelter from them in the British enclave of Walvis Bay.

A time of consolidation

By 1889, Berlin was forced to recognise that an absentee policy in Namibia was doomed to failure. In an attempt to develop the colony's infrastructure, the first 21 German soldiers (*Schutztruppe*) were sent out to Namibia that year and ordered to erect a fortress at Windhoek; two years later, a makeshift landing stage was set up in Swakopmund. In the wake of the soldiers came the first trickle of settlers to Windhoek.

Then, on 1 January 1894, a man who was to shape Namibia's destiny stepped ashore at Swakopmund. Not only did Major Theodor von Leutwein succeed in forming a 10-year alliance with the rebellious Nama chief Hendrik Witbooi, along with numerous smaller Baster and Nama groupings – he also conducted intensive negotiations with the Herero's paramount chief, Samuel Maharero. As a result of von Leutwein's diplomacy, a truce was, for a time, effected between the Herero and their old enemies, the Nama.

In the southern and central regions, the turn of the 19th century saw a steady dwindling of power on the part of the indigenous peoples in favour of the colonial government. Newly arrived settlers, for example, bought up land from both the Herero and the Nama, who for their part bought large amounts of Western goods on credit and became heavily indebted.

This was not an auspicious situation for a lengthy peace, however diplomatically and strategically von Leutwein tried to proceed, and tensions mounted; on 12 January 1904, Maherero ordered a Herero uprising against the German settlers which took the colonial forces by surprise. No fewer than 123 settlers were killed on their farms with *kirries* (wooden clubs); their homes were burned and cattle driven away. Only women and children were spared. As a result, reinforcements were urgently summoned from Berlin.

A SERIOUS LACK OF RESOURCES

Major von Leutwein's efforts to establish order over the fledgling colony were hampered by a lack of resources. A mere four companies and one artillery battalion were not enough to make the German presence felt in this huge territory – particularly in the northern regions of Kaokoland, Ovamboland and the Okavango. Kurt Schwabe, a *Schutztruppe* member who later published his memoirs, described the situation thus: "The German government had for years no relation to the Ovambo, who were, on the map, German vassals, but who were neither themselves aware of this fact, nor would have acknowledged it if they had known it."

The Herero defeated

With German opinion at home demanding that the government "bring the rebels to their senses", Berlin's response was to replace von Leutwein with a certain General Lothar von Trotha, who had already served in East Africa and garnered a reputation for ruthlessness. With him came an entire division of reinforcement troops, including heavy artillery.

It didn't take long to break the Herero's resistance, although they fought hard. By August 1904, their warriors had been pushed back and confined to a stronghold at Waterberg. By 11

from strongholds in the Kalahari. In 1907, however, the powerful Nama leader Hendrik Witbooi was killed, and the remaining leaders sued for peace. Namibia was finally under colonial control.

An economic flurry

The six years of German rule before World War I saw the colony thrive. Not only was there an influx of settlers but the railway system was expanded and the towns grew. In 1908, a railway inspector named August Stauch discovered one of the world's richest diamond deposits

Early settlers arrive.

August, the tide had turned in the Germans' favour, although not decisively; they lacked the strength to force the enemy's complete capitulation. As a result, after this victory, von Trotha issued his notorious "extermination order", which forced thousands of surviving Hereros to flee. Most headed east into the Omaheke sandveld and from there to Botswana, burning the bush behind them as they went.

Von Trotha's implacable "all-or-nothing" campaign against the Herero had succeeded – although it was criticised by the British, in particular, who called it genocide. It also spurred the Nama people into outright revolt; for the next three years, many local clans joined forces to wage a guerrilla war against the *Schutztruppe*

in the Namib, which formed the basis for an economic boom in the south. Meanwhile, the development of the Tsumeb mines – yielding copper, zinc and lead – brought about prosperity in the north.

Black Namibians, on the other hand, were restricted to "native areas" – usually infertile land that was difficult to farm – and exploited as cheap labour. By this time, the country's borders had been more clearly defined in a series of territorial deals struck by the colonial powers.

All this changed with the outbreak of war in 1914. South Africa entered the war on the side of the Allies, attacking German troops with overwhelming force; the Germans surrendered at Khorab near Otavi on 9 July 1915.

The road to independence was long and hard.

THE PATH TO INDEPENDENCE

It would take more than 70 years of bitter struggle
to transform Namibia from colonial protectorate
to mandate and, finally, to independent state.

Imperial Germany's role as a colonial power on the international stage was short-lived. German South West Africa came to an end when the government surrendered to the South Africans at Khorab in 1915. The territory was placed under military rule for the duration of World War I. Louis Botha, the South African premier and commander-in-chief of the Union troops, could make no answer to the capitulating Imperial governor, Dr Theodor Seitz, when the latter said that South West Africa's fate would not be determined there, but by the course of the war in Europe. History vindicated Seitz's prophecy. Under the Treaty of Versailles, signed on 26 June 1919, Germany had to renounce all its colonial holdings abroad.

"The German colonies in the Pacific and Africa are inhabited by barbarians," wrote South Africa's prime minister Jan Christiaan Smuts in 1918. "They are incapable of ruling themselves, and it would furthermore be impractical to attempt to implement the idea of self-government in the European sense." Smuts's suggestion was that South West Africa should be incorporated into South Africa – although in the end the victorious Allies agreed to restrict themselves to an administrative and supervisory role as far as Germany's former colonies were concerned.

As a result, South Africa was awarded responsibility for the country, but only as a League of Nations "trust territory". Nevertheless, this meant that, for the following 75 years, Pretoria's influence would extend all the way north as far as the southern border of Angola.

A new administration

In a show of strength by South Africa, a number of German "undesirables" (officials, defence

A demonstrator picketing outside South Africa House in London to demand that South West Africa be put under United National Trusteeship, 1948.

force personnel and police) were turfed out of South West Africa immediately after the Armistice on 11 November 1918. Some 1,400 nationals returned to Germany voluntarily, while 6,374 were deported – nearly half of the territory's German population. The German diamond concession was given to Consolidated Diamond Mines, which later became the world-famous De Beers.

The agreement formulated by the Allies, according to which South West Africa was made an "integral part" of South Africa, was formally ratified by the League of Nations on 17 December 1920. The ambiguities implied by this phrase "integral part" were to prove a major stumbling block in the administration of the territory over the next few decades; a vital definition was left too open to interpretation. South Africa's responsibilities were outlined in this sentence: "The mandatory shall promote to the utmost the material and moral well-being and the social progress of the inhabitants of the territory subject to the present mandate." In the years that followed, the formulation became more specific: the territory should, under the protection of South Africa, be guided towards independence.

A last stand

The indigenous population's hopes that colonial land division and allotment would be revised after the defeat of the Germans were, therefore, soundly dashed. Nonetheless, various groups were determined to fight for their land. Chief Mandume, for example, took a stand against British-South African territorial demands in Ovamboland.

The frustrated hopes concerning the transfer of power in Windhoek, combined with South Africa's interference in the line of succession of chiefs among one of the most powerful Nama

A group of Boers working for a German transport service.

Beyond merely administering the country, the South African government concerned itself with continuing the white-settlement policy which had been initiated by the previous German administration. In a clear bid to increase the Boer population, it gradually parcelled out more and more of the land to "poor white" settler families from South Africa, rather than to Germans. Between 1915 and 1920, 6 million hectares (15 million acres) of land were given to South Africans. In the years 1928–9, another large chunk of the territory was distributed during the repopulation of Boers who had been living in Angola, while the third, and last, phase of white settlement occurred between 1950 and 1954.

SPLITS IN THE BOER CAMP

When South Africa was urged by Britain to challenge Germany over South West Africa during World War I it needed little encouragement. One of the main motivations behind the invasion was that a successful military campaign would lead to a reconciliation with the hostile Boers who had settled in the colony following the bitter Boer War of 1899–1902. This conflict had split the Boers into two camps: anti-British opponents of the war, and its pro-British supporters (such as the prime minister, Jan Smuts). The rifts ran deep, however, and South Africa did not achieve all that it had been hoping for in terms of reconciliation.

groupings, the Bondelswarts, gave rise to a major Nama uprising against the South African administration in 1922.

Unfortunately, whether resistance came from Chief Jacobus Christiaan, who lost 64 warriors, or the Rehoboth Basters, who had hoped for more autonomy after the South African takeover, the Nama had no chance against an enemy that was militarily far superior. Even the battle-hardened Bondels, for example, who had long held their own in guerrilla fighting against the German colonial forces prior to World War I, now found themselves fighting an adversary

chiefs – with varying degrees of success. Its main tactic was to bring the black population under control by installing lackey chiefs, ready to do its bidding. In this way South Africa's area of influence was gradually extended into Ovamboland and the northern territories lying beyond the so-called Red Line – an area which the Germans had tended to avoid. The extreme northern and Kalahari border regions to the east were, however, largely unaffected.

Yet despite their efforts to grab control of as much land in the territory as possible, the South Africans invested very little in Namib-

A karakul farmer shows off his painting skills, 1939.

which, having been through similar experiences in the Boer War, was well-versed in those very same tactics. The South African government responded by sending in wave upon wave of fresh troops. Retribution for the unrest was heavy; the Basters lost even the right to appoint their own "kaptein", or leader. Instead, they now had to submit to the authority of a white magistrate, a situation which continued until 1976.

Divide and Rule

Continuing the policies of the German administration that preceded it, the South African mandatory government consistently interfered in the succession and appointment of local

ia's infrastructure. An exception was the construction of several railway lines – from Swakopmund to Walvis Bay, from Otjiwango to Outjo and from Karasburg to Upington in South Africa, as well as from Windhoek to Gobabis. The continent's very first automatic telephone exchange was installed in Windhoek in 1929.

The isolated, time-warped flavour of Namibia at this time is well expressed by the missionary Dr Heinrich Vedder in the foreword to his book Old South West Africa (1934): "This book should only be read by people who love South West Africa; for it contains many things which are of lesser importance in comparison to the major world events of this period, things which could only be of value to someone who has already become attuned to our sunny country."

But in the end, it was these "major world events" that were to determine Namibia's fate – affecting as they did the political consciousness of the white settlers. Essentially, the settlers were divided into two camps, differentiated by language: Afrikaans-speakers loyal to the South African Union advocated a complete union with South Africa; the majority of German-speakers were, by contrast, largely faithful to the Geneva Mandate. It was their

Driving along the beach to reach the diamond mine.

hope that, once Germany had recovered its former strength, it would bring a swift end to South Africa's administration of Namibia and usher in a new age of independence for the territory.

The war years

In the 1930s, National Socialist propaganda and agitation served to exacerbate these divisions. The South African government empowered the territorial administration to forbid foreigners (such as German immigrants) the right to join political organisations – but there was a large loophole: many German-speakers had become naturalised citizens, or carried two passports. The Deutscher Bund (German Union) and

Die Verenigde Nasional Suidwes Party (United National South West Party, VNSWP) were the major political forces of the time, one in favour of the mandate, the other for annexation to South Africa.

The outbreak of World War II put an end to these disputes. In most cases, speaking fluent German was sufficient grounds for the South African officials to detain men of army age in internment camps, regardless of whether they were naturalised British-South African subjects, had dual German-South African citizenship, or were recent immigrants.

During the war years, the women tended the farms. As had been the case in World War I, German property and possessions were placed under the jurisdiction of a "Custodian for Enemy Property". The fate of Germans and their families interned in the South African prison camps of Andalusia and Baviaanspoort remained uncertain until long after the outbreak of peace.

Dr Malan and his National Party's (NP) narrow victory in South Africa in May 1948 put a final stop to all actions directed against South West Germans, even to the threat of deportation, and the last detainees were allowed to go back home to their farms. Until the mid-1970s, South West Germans thanked the NP by adhering to it with unswerving loyalty, although Pretoria's racial policies did not always meet with their approval.

Defying the United Nations

In 1947, South Africa formally announced to the United Nations its intention to incorporate Namibia as a fifth province, arguing that local chiefs had supported the annexation in a communal vote. However, they played down the dissenting voices of many Herero and Nama chiefs, as well as those of the African National Congress (ANC) and South Africa's Communist Party, both of which had always demanded that the UN provide for an honest administration for South West Africa, as specified by the UN General Assembly.

The UN rejected the plan, however, and from that moment on, South Africa's guardianship of the territory was increasingly called into question. Over the next 21 years, the General Assembly and Security Council convened the International Court of Justice in The Hague at least six times in reference to South West Africa.

In the invalid general election of 1978, the Democratic Turnhalle Alliance took 41 seats and the Nationalist Party six. Three smaller parties received one seat each.

However, a binding, clear statement of the territory's international status, as well as a definition of the limits of South Africa's responsibility, remained lacking.

South Africa chose to ignore the UN's legal pressure; from 1948, for example, the country

According to South Africa's policy of apartheid, the black population within the territory of the mandate was nominally permitted to regulate its own affairs. However, all the crucial issues – such as international relations – were left up to the government in Pretoria and the Cape Town Parliament.

An uphill struggle

Between 1949 and 1977, the white population of the mandated area was represented by six delegates in Parliament and four members in the South African Senate. During all this time,

The diamond industry is still a mainstay of Namibia's economy.

simply ceased to file the annual reports it was supposed to present on its "trust territory".

The great wave of African independence at the end of the 1950s and beginning of the 1960s swept over the continent without touching Namibia, although it left clear traces behind in the minds of the country's black population. Yet where black Namibians managed to organise themselves to protest against their lack of political and civil rights, they were met with heavy-handed repression, as in the events of December 1959 when 13 black demonstrators in Windhoek were felled by club-wielding police. The victims had been protesting against their forced resettlement to the new blacks-only township of Katutura.

A SAD RECORD

There can be no other country in the world – especially one with such a small population – that matches Namibia's sad record as far as clarifying its international status is concerned. In its decades of transformation from colonial protectorate to mandate to bone of international contention to – finally – universally acknowledged independent state, Namibia has amassed a collection of verdicts, papers, requests and related literature that is unequalled. Despite this, it was not until 1968 that the South Africans' presence was ruled illegal and The Hague demanded that South Africa terminate its South West African administration.

only a handful of black Namibian nationalists – such as Mburumba Kerina and Fanuel Kozonguizi – managed to get their voices heard by the United Nations Committee on South West Africa.

However, this era did see the founding of the Ovamboland People's Organisation (OPO), which led to the founding of the South West Africa People's Organisation (SWAPO) in 1960. Although SWAPO initially concerned itself only with labour-related issues, it was increasingly identified as an independence and liberation movement – all the more so after 1966,

process only affected marginal areas and was by and large limited to police zones.

The fifth province

Pretoria's determination to annex Namibia came to a head when, in 1968 and 1969, two constitutional ordinances formally declared the territory to be the fifth province of South Africa. Over the next few years, thousands of young Namibians left the country, either to struggle for independence from abroad or to attend an educational facility not under South African control.

Delegates at the historic Turnhalle Conference, whose aim was to create a constitution for an independent Namibia.

when the organisation took a decision to fight for freedom with arms.

Bolstered by their administration's complete disregard for the UN's resolutions, whites, on the other hand, must have felt sure that nothing was likely to change.

Political developments were one thing, the establishment of an infrastructure in Namibia entirely another. In the 1960s, for the first time since German rule, the country underwent a period of rapid development: roads, water and energy resources, telecommunications, agriculture, tourism and other areas reached a level which placed Namibia a cut above the average African state in terms of living conditions. In the heavily-populated rural north, however, this

FATHER OF THE NATION

The dominant figure in modern Namibian politics, Samuel Nujoma was born in Ongandjera in 1929. By 1957 he was dedicated to the liberation cause. Two years later, as leader of the Ovamboland People's Organisation (OPO), he tabled a first petition to the UN asking that his country be released from South African rule. In 1960, Nujoma helped found SWAPO, and was elected as its first president. After years of fruitless petitioning, he authorised a policy of armed resistance in 1966, initiating a war of independence that lasted 24 years. Following independence, Nujoma was inaugurated as President of Namibia in March 1990, then re-elected in 1994 and 1999.

Faced with increasing international pressure, South Africa did make a few fainthearted gestures towards granting civil rights to the black population. In 1973, Prime Minister Vorster created a "native council" for South West Africa – just as SWAPO attained observer status at the UN. In September 1975, a constitutional conference was summoned; since it met in the old German Turnhalle (gymnasium) in Windhoek, this assembly was to go into the annals as the Turnhalle Conference. Its task was to create a constitution for an independent Namibia, and delegates were strictly which had already been demanded by the United Nations in countless resolutions.

Though the Turnhalle Conference did not produce any tangible results, it did succeed in loosening the knots of apartheid. For the first time, black, white and coloured people sat round the table, striving to reach a consensus in lengthy negotiations.

South Africa only partially yielded to the suggestions of the five Western powers. In 1977, General Administrator Marthinus Steyn was appointed to govern the territory until its independence, serving as a counterpart to the

Herero men and women marching in traditional and military attire.

divided into 11 groups; political parties were still excluded.

Resolution for change

Some 18 months later, in March 1977, a first draft of the constitution was presented; much influenced by South Africa, it presented a model for an ethnically segregated country. Meanwhile, the five Western members of the Security Council – the United States, West Germany, Great Britain, France, and Canada – closed ranks. This group urged South Africa to guarantee that the Turnhalle Conference would be nullified, and that general and free elections would be held in order to exercise every Namibian's right to self-government – something UN Special Commissioner for Namibia, Martti Ahtisaari. In keeping with the spirit of the Western demands, which were officially formulated in the international arena as UN Resolution 435 a year later, Steyn removed several mainstays of the hated apartheid laws before the year was out. Segregation also began to be lifted in urban residential areas, a process that lasted until 1980.

Defying the dictates of Resolution 435, South Africa initiated general elections in Namibia in 1978 under its own auspices, without the supervision of the UN. For the first time in the country's history, elections were held on a one-person, one-vote basis. Despite SWAPO's call to boycott elections, 81 percent of the 421,600 registered voters took part. The five Western powers declared the election to be invalid.

On the advice of South Africa, the representatives formed a national congress. However, this legislative body was limited in its powers and constantly subject to South African intervention – as happened when it attempted to implement a law against racial discrimination, and when it wanted to drop South African holidays.

In January, 1983, the DTA, unable to govern under these conditions, stepped down. In the years that followed, Pretoria laboriously attempted to re-establish some measure of

San (Bushmen) trackers were recruited by the South African army during the mandate years.

Namibian self-government – for example, the general administrator, a South African official, was effectively left to stand alone as the territory's sole administrator.

In 1985, what was to become the very last "temporary government of national unity" was formed. It, too, lacked credibility, however, for in constitutional questions South Africa again demanded the consensus of all parties.

Armed conflict

At the beginning of the 1960s, SWAPO took a joint decision with the Organisation for African Unity: they would resort to arms in the struggle for independence if diplomacy should prove

fruitless. The historic first skirmish with the South African police took place not far from Ongulumbashe, in northwest Ovamboland, in August 1966 (today, 26 August is Namibia's Remembrance Day holiday). This marked the start of years of guerrilla and border warfare which were to end only in April 1989.

After Angola's independence in 1975, the armed conflict in Namibia became more and more bound up with the geopolitical interests of the superpowers and their representatives in southern Africa. The Soviet Union and Cuba supported Angola's Marxist MPLA government in Luanda; on the other side, the United States contributed aid to the pro-Western resistance movement UNITA. As long as Namibia's political parties adhered to one or the other of these alliances, all attempts at Namibian unity were doomed to failure.

After a general strike in 1971 involving Ovambo workers in particular, followed by uprisings in Ovamboland in 1972, martial law was imposed in the north for the first time, and controlled by the South African army. This remained in place right up until shortly before the 1989 elections.

After 1975, Namibia's volatile northern regions became a deployment area for South African military intervention and action in Angola. SWAPO's Angolan headquarters also came under repeated fire, most infamously on 4 May 1978, when an air attack destroyed their camp at Cassinga. Several hundred uniformed men, as well as women and children, were killed.

Superpower involvement

Despite the propitiatory announcement of a plan for the solution of the Namibia question, it would be another 11 years before Security Council Resolution 435, which had met with a broad consensus in 1978, was realised. Time and again, the parties accused one another of setting unrealistic conditions which interfered with the plan's execution. Positions became completely entrenched when the US and South Africa made the enactment of Resolution 435 contingent on Cuba's withdrawal from Angola (the so-called Cuban linkage).

In the light of the threat from UNITA, the withdrawal of its defending power's troops was totally unacceptable to the MPLA government in Angola. Nor could the United Nations make

The independence process was aided by the United Nations Transition Assistance Group (UNTAG), consisting of some 7,000 people from 110 countries.

progress on the Cuba demand, as Resolution 435 was aimed specifically at a solution in Namibia, rather than addressing the security and balance of powers in neighbouring countries.

Finally, in 1988, under the direct supervision of the USSR and the USA, the three countries of South Africa, Angola and Cuba met a number of times in Cairo, Brazzaville and New York, until Resolution 435 was inextricably linked with the total withdrawal of Cuban troops from Angola.

Agreement at last

Once agreement between the three countries was reached on 22 December 1998, things moved rapidly. Administrators and observers from more than 100 different countries started to pour into Windhoek.

Yet the Namibia question was threatened anew when on 1 April 1989 – the very day set aside for the resolution's implementation – heavily-armed SWAPO units moved in along a broad front from Namibia's northern border with Angola. Although Martti Ahtisaari, the authorised UN representative, was prompted to mobilise army units under South African command, conflict was luckily averted. After a quick conference between South Africa, Angola and Cuba, the independence process finally got underway in early May.

Not only did South Africa now lift all its remaining discriminatory laws, but SWAPO fighters were given the option of returning to Namibia as civilians. The withdrawal of all Namibian and South African soldiers still under South African command and their subsequent demobilisation went without a hitch. In June, those SWAPO leaders who had been living in exile abroad were at last able to come home – in triumph.

The repatriation of some 40,000 Namibian exiles and refugees from Angola and Zambia was carried out between May and August, aided by the UN. The next step was to register the Namibians, so that they could take advantage of their unconditional voting rights. More than

700,000 voters were registered, often under exceptionally difficult conditions.

Free elections

In November 1989, Namibia went to the polls to elect a constituent assembly, whose brief it was to create a new constitution for the country. Three parties – the National Patriotic Front of Namibia (NPF), the Federal Convention of Namibia (FCN) and the Namibia National Front (NNF) – each returned a single delegate to the Assembly. Aksie Christelik Nasionaal (ACN) had three delegates; the United Demo-

SWAPO's last rally before its victory at the 1989 elections.

cratic Front (UDF) four. The absolute majority, however, was held by SWAPO, which, with votes from 57 percent of the electorate, was represented by 41 seats in the Assembly; the strongest opposition was the Democratic Turnhalle Alliance, with 28 percent of the electorate and 21 seats. In 22 of the 23 total electoral districts, the two major parties were locked in a head-to-head race. Only in Ovamboland, the most heavily-populated region and SWAPO's home base, was the party able to use its home advantage and win the day. None of the other nine parties won a single seat here.

The UN confirmed that the election had been free and fair – the proud culmination of 70 years of bitter struggle in Namibia.

Old German architecture amidst
the modern buildings of Windhoek.

THE MODERN REPUBLIC

While independent Namibia has remained relatively stable and prosperous, regional security issues look set to prove the country's biggest headache.

Namibia's new constitution was unanimously adopted on 9 February 1990 and the country became independent just after midnight on 21 March 1990. Few people present on that historic night will ever forget the feeling of elation that swept through the country when the South African flag was lowered and the red, blue, green and yellow Namibian flag took its place – a moment witnessed by a jubilant crowd gathered at Windhoek's Independence Stadium.

As Dr Sam Nujoma, SWAPO leader and first President of the Republic of Namibia, pointed out in his inaugural address, the struggle for independence had been shaped by the nature of Namibia's colonial experience. As he put it in his speech, "it pleases me to state that we are gathered here today not to pass yet another resolution, but to celebrate the dawn of a new era in this land and to proclaim to the world that a new star has risen on the African continent. Africa's last colony is, from this hour, liberated... we have been sustained in our difficult struggle by the powerful force of conviction in the righteousness and justness of our cause. Today history has absolved us; our vision of a democratic state of Namibia has been translated into a reality... we express our most sincere gratitude to the international community for its steadfast support."

The 1989 elections finally saw a victory for SWAPO, which was granted a mandate to form a government. Prior to independence, a Constituent Assembly representing each of the country's political parties had been given the task of drafting a constitution enshrining the principles of multi-party democracy. And so it does; it's an impressive document, paving the way for a new system of Namibian

Namibians celebrate at the swearing in ceremony of President Hifikepunye Pohamba in 2010.

government consisting of three branches: an executive branch, a parliamentary branch and the judiciary. It also incorporates specific checks designed to guard against the possible abuse of power, allows for substantive judicial review by the courts and assigns broad investigative powers to an independent ombudsman.

Members of the legislature are elected through a system of proportional representation, thus giving minority parties a chance to have their voices heard. There is a strong system of regional and local government, while a Council of Traditional Leaders advises the president on issues pertaining to traditional laws.

Namibia's early years as an independent state were marked by a mood of unbounded optimism. Brian Atwood, president of the Washington-based National Democratic Institute, compared the state of the nation before and after independence in a paper delivered to the institute. The old Namibia, he said, had been "a static society, full of fear for the future". In November 1989, however, he had returned to monitor the elections and found "a highly ... emotional campaign" where "attitudes ... had changed tremendously". People were now "working together to build a multi-party system and make it work".

Namibia since independence

Initially, all went smoothly for the new state. South Africa handed back the disputed territory of Walvis Bay in February 1994, and relations between the two countries remain amicable.

December 1994 saw SWAPO returned to power in the general elections, winning 53 out of 72 seats. Nujoma was re-elected president for a further five years.

The general elections of December 1999, meanwhile, saw a landslide victory for the president, who captured a convincing 77 percent of the vote. His party, SWAPO, also won 55 par-

Namibia becomes independent under its first president, Dr Sam Nujoma.

SYMBOLS OF LIBERATION

As the era of independence dawned in Namibia, a series of national symbols was chosen to promote the concepts of nation-building and unity. The flag consists of three diagonal bands: the blue top left-hand corner symbolises the sky and water, and contains a golden sun; the green bottom right-hand corner represents Namibia's agricultural potential; and the broad red band in the middle depicts the people's heroism. The flag is the centrepiece of the coat of arms, supported on either side by one of Namibia's best-known antelopes, the oryx, and reflecting the constitution's key principles with the motto "Unity, Liberty, Justice".

liamentary seats, which gave it the two-thirds majority necessary to amend the constitution.

Although the election was deemed free and fair, there were some controversial results, because the previous SWAPO parliament had used its predominance to alter the constitution anyway, to allow a third term for Nujoma (previously, the constitution had stated that no president should be allowed to serve more than two terms in office).

Still tainted by its links with the former South African administration, the Democratic Turnhalle Alliance (the traditional opposition) won just seven seats, as did a new party – the Congress of Democrats, led by a disaffected SWAPO activist called Ben Ulenga.

Namibia's independence celebrations were presided over by then Secretary-General of the UN, Javier Pérez de Cuéllar. The outgoing colonial administration was represented by F.W. de Klerk, then the State President of South Africa.

Regional tensions

Nujoma made the economy the focus of his electoral campaign, going so far as to promise his fellow Namibians that they would have government car pool – mainly consisting of people carriers – has higher fuel consumption per vehicle than a fleet of HGVs. The implication is that members of the administration are taking fuel from government cars for their own private usage.

Dr Sam Nujoma decided not to stand for the presidential elections of November 2004, but he remained the leader of SWAPO and his chosen successor, Hifikepunye Pohamba, won a landslide victory as the representative of the same party. Although this result was fiercely disputed by the opposition parties, the majority

The parliament building, Windhoek.

living standards on a par with the developed world in just 30 years. It is true that since 1990, most Namibians have better living conditions and access to basic social services, but the average per capita income remains low. What's more, productivity is still narrow, with little industrialisation outside the mining sector.

SWAPO's opponents continue to attack the government over the country's unemployment rate of 35 percent and over allegations of official corruption. Articles are constantly appearing in the newspapers denouncing another outrageous fiddle or incidence of everyday racketeering that has become taken for granted. For example, it is alleged that the

of impartial observers noted there was minimal evidence of voting irregularities. A former exile and founder member of SWAPO, Pohamba was inaugurated as President in March 2005, and has since followed up on proposed land reforms and started to tackle corruption. In 2007, Pohamba succeeded Sam Nujoma to become the second ever leader of SWAPO. He was re-elected as President of Namibia in 2009, garnering more than 75 percent of the vote. Now 80, Pohamba will be forced to resign shortly after the 2014 elections, due to the constitutional limit of two presidential terms. His likely successor will be Hage Geingob, who served as Prime Minister from 1990 to 2002, and again from 2012 onwards.

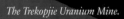
The Trekopjie Uranium Mine.

THE ECONOMIC BALANCING ACT

**Most Namibians enjoy a better standard of living since
independence, although the productive structure
remains narrow, with little industrialisation.**

For almost a quarter of a century – from the first resolution of the General Assembly ending South Africa's League of Nations mandate in 1966 to Independence Day on 21 March 1990 – Namibia's political future made international headline news. A succession of General Assembly and Security Council resolutions, plus decisions of the International Court of Justice, charted the country's passage through the political reefs.

By the end of this period, Namibia's (mostly white and conservative) business community had come round to the idea of independence for three reasons: nothing else seemed to have worked; the white regime in South Africa, afflicted by even worse troubles, was in no position to help; and the few members of the newly-elected government they had met seemed to be reasonable men prepared to abandon the rhetoric of the past and deal pragmatically with the economy.

Once the country had actually won its independence, however, a rather different picture emerged. Wealthy members of the interna-

Oyster farmers at Shear Water Oysters, in Lüderitz.

Although it is a very large country – more than a third larger than the uk and Germany combined – Namibia is sparsely populated, supporting around 2 million people in 2010.

tional community who had previously seemed enthused by the Namibian cause (and who, indeed, had jointly spent US$800 million on the year-long transition supervised by the United Nations) now lost interest. Faced with more interesting prospects in Eastern Europe, they were not disposed to be particularly generous to the newest – but by no means the poorest

– member of the community of nations.

In short, the new Namibian government had to work very hard to attract grants and investment. Proximity to South Africa proved (and continues to prove) a double-edged sword: it is an advantage for export trade, but then South Africa tends to attract much of the aid and inward investment to the region. Aid donors meeting in New York in 1990 pledged funds totalling US$696 million to Namibia. Between two-thirds and three-quarters of this was promised in the form of grants, the balance in concessional loans. Namibia's proposal to the World Bank that it be regarded as one of the "Least Developed Countries" was, however, turned down, as its per-capita GDP exceeded US$1,000, the maximum for this category. Acceptance as an LDC would have given Namibia access to a wider range of concessionary bank funding.

Communications

Namibia received US$600 million worth of aid as part of its 1996–2000 development plan from 30 donors under the United Nations Development Plan (UNDP). The UNDP describes the country as having "a stable political and economic climate and low tax rates. Namibia is well placed to serve as gateway to South Africa, boasting good communication networks and

> Namibia produces up to 1.65 million carats per year – around 1.5 percent of world diamond production – which earns it around US$500 million of foreign exchange.

charter operations and private pilots.

Two harbours – Lüderitz, a fishing port to the south, and Walvis Bay, a deep water harbour in the centre of the coast – provide access from the sea. Constitutional title to the Walvis Bay enclave was the subject of a long dispute with

Construction workers building the new viewpoint at the curve of the Fish River Canyon.

port facilities able to handle up to 800 vessels per day." The EU is the largest contributor of aid to the region, while the biggest bilateral donors are Sweden and Germany.

Namibia is well served with major infrastructure: the main towns and cities are linked by some 5,450km (3,400 miles) of asphalt roads, while another 37,000km (23,000 miles) of gravel and unsurfaced roads traverse the rural areas of the country. Some 2,400km (1,500 miles) of railway lines, carrying both freight and passengers, are integrated with the South African rail network and thence with the rest of the subcontinent. More than 350 airstrips and airports, including an international terminal outside Windhoek, serve the national carrier, Air Namibia, smaller

South Africa, which was settled amicably by negotiation in 1994.

Mining, ranching and fishing

In African terms, Namibia is potentially rich – given its small population – with valuable mineral resources, exceptionally rich fishing waters and a strong livestock farming industry. Diamond, uranium and base metal mining, and beef cattle and Karakul sheep ranching have accounted for 90 percent of Namibia's exports in the past, as well as about 40 percent of its GDP.

Namibia's fishing grounds, in the nutrient-rich waters of the southeast Atlantic ocean, are some of the richest and least exploited in the world. Pelagic (pilchards, anchovies) and demersal (hake, white fish) species abound, and support a small, but thriving, rock lobster (crayfish) industry at Lüderitz. As Namibia's 200-mile (320km) exclusive economic zone was not recognised before its independence and there was much pirate fishing, these waters have not yet provided the economic returns of which they are capable – with prudent management. The government believes that royalty payments by foreign fleets together with the value of local catches processed in Namibia could greatly increase revenue from this sector.

Livestock ranching on the southern and central plateau constitutes almost 90 percent of the

Changing trends

The pelts of Karakul lambs – once known as Namibia's "black diamonds" – were traditionally auctioned in London, but since 1995 the twice-yearly sales have been held in Copenhagen, where the pelts are sold under the Swakara brand. Karakul farmers have been vulnerable to shifting fashions in the fur industry. At the peak of demand, there were 4 million Karakul sheep in the country and no fewer than 3 million Namibian pelts were sold in London alone, in a single year. Prices recovered only slightly after the collapse of the market in the early 1980s,

Almost 70 percent of Namibians depend on farming and ranching for their survival.

value of Namibia's agricultural output for commercial purposes. The agricultural sector itself contributes only about five percent of GDP, but almost 40 percent of the population is dependent on ranching and farming for their survival.

Poor rainfall in most of the country and cyclical droughts make crop cultivation impossible in the absence of irrigation. Even cattle ranching (which in Namibia means hardy beef species like the Brahman and the Afrikaner) can be precarious – the total cattle population has ranged from 1.3 to 2.5 million in recent decades, depending on climatic conditions. Most cattle sold commercially are transported by rail or truck to South Africa for slaughter, but the government maintains an annual export quota from the EU.

A MEASURE OF WEALTH

Based on the 2012 figure of US$12.46 billion, Namibia only ranks 25th in the list of African countries with the highest GDP. However, the country's low population means that it fares far better in terms of per capita gross GDP, ranking 11th in Africa. Indeed, with a per capita GDP of around US$7,000, Namibia is officially regarded to be a low middle income country, a ranking undermined somewhat by its Gini coefficient (a figure based on comparative income of the wealthiest and poorest 10 percent of the population), which currently stands at 60, one of the world's highest.

only to crash again in 2001. Today, Karakul pelts create annual export earnings of around 5 million euros and the industry creates direct or indirect employment for about 20,000 people. Nevertheless, many farmers have shifted to joint wool/mutton production to protect themselves against the vagaries of the market.

As for minerals, the value of Namibia's mining output ranks fourth in Africa, behind South Africa, the DRC and Botswana, and comprises on average over 75 percent of the country's export earnings. The mining industry pays the bulk of corporate taxes and is the largest

a high percentage of larger gems, although the average size is falling, and mining conditions are increasingly difficult. The lifetime of deposits depends on the results of new prospecting and the assumptions made about the depths at which it is possible and profitable to mine.

Rössing Uranium, 68.6 percent owned by the British company Rio Tinto, together with a number of South African mining interests and Minatome of France, operate the world's largest open-cast uranium mine 65km (40 miles) from Swakopmund (www.rossing.com). Careful financial structuring – including a lengthy tax

Trekopjie Mine near Swakopmund.

private sector employer – indeed, taxes and royalties from mining account for 25 percent of the national revenue. Little processing or beneficiation is undertaken in Namibia, however, and most of the products are exported; the industry is thus at the mercy of shifting market prices, reflected in volatile value added output. Employment levels in the industry have fallen in recent years and Tsumeb mine closed in 1998.

Diamonds are mined from coastal deposits 30km (19 miles) off the coast of Lüderitz and on the Orange River – Namibia's southern boundary – by NAMDEB. The corporation is owned in equal shares by the government of Namibia and De Beers, although the latter retains all exploitation rights. The production includes

holiday – and long-term supply contracts at high prices, concluded in the nuclear-friendly 1970s, enabled the mine to post excellent profits throughout the early 1980s despite the low-grade ore. A combination of circumstances has, however, since made the mine vulnerable. Uranium spot prices fell sharply as plans for nuclear reactors were shelved in the aftermath of the Three Mile Island (1979) and Chernobyl (1986) accidents and new, higher grade, deposits were developed in Australia and Canada. Political and legal pressures were also brought to bear on purchasers by the UN Council for Namibia.

As its long-term contracts drew to a close, Rössing had difficulties signing new agreements after independence in 1990. Uranium sales in the US were also inhibited in the few years before independence by the passage, at the end of 1986, of the Anti-Apartheid Act, which treated Namibia as part of South Africa. Although one new long-term contract was signed with the French EDF in 1990, a 25 percent production cut-back was announced by the Rössing board in 1991. Since then, Rössing has undergone a change in fortunes, and it now produces some 5 percent of the world's uranium, making Namibia the fourth-largest producer globally. The Namibian government controls 51 percent

Local manufacturing

Because South Africa administered Namibia pretty much as a fifth province until the end of the 1970s, there was very little scope or incentive for the development of local manufacturing industry.

At the time of independence, manufacturing contributed a mere 5 percent to GDP, but today that figure is more than 20 percent.

Many people now work in the food and beverage processing area. The government actively encourages domestic and foreign investment in this sector as a means to add value and create

Wildlife Manager at Puros Village, Damaraland.

of the voting rights and 3 percent of the equity in Rössing Uranium.

Most base (copper, lead, zinc, cadmium, pyrite, arsenic trioxide and sodium antimonate) and precious (gold and silver) mineral production used to be derived from four mines run by the Tsumeb Corporation (TCL), which closed in May 1998.

Namibia's most important gold mine is Navachab, opened in 1989 near Karibib, and is operated by the multinational AngloGold Ashanti. It produces around 85,000 ounces of gold annually.

Zinc has been discovered in the south near Rosh Pinah and is bringing an influx of investment to the area around Lüderitz. Another key recent development was the discovery of vast offshore oil reserves in 2011.

MEDIA AND COMMUNICATIONS

The Namibia Broadcasting Corporation (NBC) offers radio programmes in nine languages, including English and German. Much of the country also receives a variety of TV programmes through the NBC, which will offer 21 digital channels to subscribers once the changeover to digital is complete in 2015. Electronic media lags behind the rest of the world, with around 30 percent of the population enjoying internet access in 2012. By contrast, the recent boom in mobile phone access has revolutionised communications in Namibia, with some the vast majority of adults now subscribing to fixed or mobile services.

jobs. Unilever, Guinness and Lonrho are among the major companies to have entered the market.

Water and power

Although Windhoek has experienced a total population growth of almost 200 percent since the start of the millennium, most Namibians still lead a rural existence. Development of the physical and social infrastructure in the rural areas, particularly the more populated north, is thus a priority. The improvement of schooling and health care facilities and the provision of jobs, either on the land, or in small-scale,

A construction worker in Walvis Baai (Walvis Bay).

labour-intensive, informal manufacturing enterprises, requires electrification of the rural areas. Improved crop production and better use of grazing lands by livestock are dependent on the availability of water at points far removed from its sources.

Although most of Namibia is arid, the country has huge water resources within its borders, particularly in the north, where the Okavango system alone has more water than all the rivers of South Africa together. However, plans for the final phase of the Eastern Water Carrier, which would have brought water from the Okavango River to the centre of the country, were shelved in the 1980s due to lack of funds. Likewise, Namibia has the capacity to become the largest net gas exporter in the region through its gas deposits in the Kudu field in the Orange Basin.

Tourism has been and remains an important growth area, which now contributes more to the economy than the manufacturing sector. Direct flights to Europe, improved tourist facilities and increased travel to South Africa are all encouraging this trend.

South Africa is the country's biggest trading partner. At one point, up to 90 percent of Namibia's foreign trade was with South Africa, but while this is still the case for imports, around 70 percent of which are from South Africa, less than 20 percent of exported goods are now sold to the neighbouring republic. South Africa holds more than 50 percent of investments in the key sectors of banking, mining and insurance.

Challenge for the future

The country's greatest strengths are the tolerance bred into the political culture since the mid-1970s, reinforced by its exemplary constitution; the free and active press; the basic health of the economy, despite its deficiencies; and the government's pragmatic approach. Its weaknesses are high levels of unemployment; inequalities of income and opportunity between rural and urban areas and between black and white; over-dependence on the mining sector; insufficient industrial capacity due to an underdeveloped manufacturing sector; and a shortage of critical skills in key sectors of the economy and administration.

Deprived of the ideological shibboleths and divisive loyalties of the past, Namibians since independence have had the chance to unite in support of new social and economic programmes and give substance to the idea of nationhood. The challenges are enormous: combating unemployment, promoting rapid skills development and effecting economic restructuring to maintain growth, holding down inflation and reducing present inequalities of opportunity.

The end of the civil war gently boosted development in Namibia, the two countries co-operating to their mutual benefit. Angola is rich in minerals and energy sources and shares close cultural and ethnic ties with Namibia. Moreover, fruitful avenues are opening up toward regional co-operation – with South Africa as the economic motor of the region. In this way, the necessary progress can take place to enable Namibia to face the economic demands of the 21st century.

The uranium mine near Swakopmund.

GEMSTONES

Thanks to its astonishing wealth of semi-precious stones, Namibia is a happy hunting ground for mineralogists and souvenir-hunters alike.

Not only is Namibia home to one of the richest alluvial diamond fields in the world, it's also endowed with large quantities of high-grade semi-precious stones. The first **topaz** was discovered at the end of the 19th century near Spitzkoppe in northwestern Namibia, an area rich in the translucent, brilliant crystals known as silver topaz; there have been record finds here of crystals up to 15cm (6ins) long and 12cm (5ins) wide. The mineral **beryl** also occurs in abundance, from the blue variety (aquamarine) to the pink beryl (morganite) and the yellow, known as heliodor. Most valuable of all, though, is the tourmaline, mined in numerous small quarries around Karibib, Usakos and the Spitzkoppe. This crystal often has a red core with a green "skin"; cut into slices and then polished, it is easy to see how it came by its nickname of "watermelon tourmaline.

Unique Materials

Yet it is the country's exceptional ore deposits that are of most interest to mineralogists. The Ysterpütz farm in the southerly Karasburg district, for example, is home to substantial deposits of the rare **"blue lace" agate. Pollucite**, an extremely rare caesium mineral, is mined south of Karibib. Most remarkable, however, is Tsumeb Mine in the north-central region, where one pipe has produced 217 different minerals and gemstones – 40 of which are unique to Namibia.

Diamonds are found in loose sand both on land and at sea. Virtually every grain of sand on the shoreline has been vacuumed up in the search for diamonds.

A jumble of polished stones for sale in Windhoek.

Street vendors will often sell unpolished stones, which can be of dubious quality.

Beautifully cut pieces like this aquamarine can be found on the jewellery markets.

NAMIBIA'S DIAMOND RUSH

In 1908 a mixed-race worker called Zacharias Lewala – hired to clear sand off the newly built railway line near Grasplatz – found a small, unusual stone stuck to his oiled shovel. Lewala turned the crystal over to his boss, German railway inspector August Stauch, who, fortunately for him if not for Lewala, had already applied for a prospector's claim for "minerals of all kinds" – just in case. The stone turned out to be a diamond (above), precipitating a major case of diamond fever in German South West Africa. Sailors left their ships, salesmen their shops, men their wives – all to try their luck in the Namib sands. The town of Lüderitz expanded rapidly. Fine stone houses designed in the German Art Nouveau style replaced the village's corrugated-iron huts. A school and electricity plant were built, and streetlights installed. Churches sprang up. A stock exchange was founded. After World War I, the mining rights went to the powerful mining-house, the Anglo-American Corporation, and a new company was formed: the Consolidated Diamond Mines, known today as namdeb.

The rare descloizite on calcite, from the Tsumeb Mine.

A fossil of an ammonite (an extinct marine invertebrate).

Built in grand Art Nouveau style by a German diamond magnate, Goerke House is one of several diamond-rush houses to grace the little coastal town of Lüderitz.

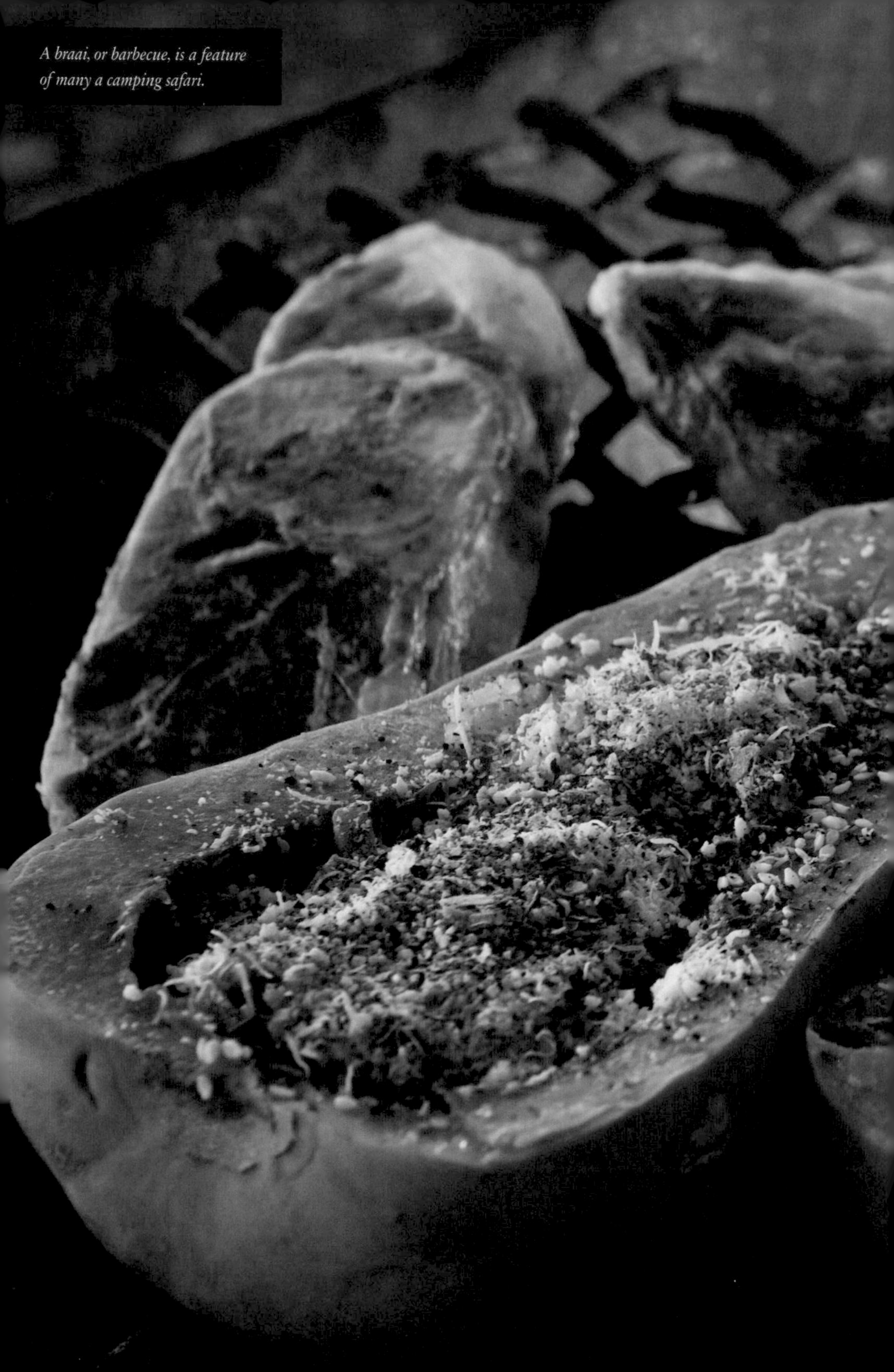

A braai, or barbecue, is a feature of many a camping safari.

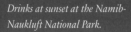

Drinks at sunset at the Namib-Naukluft National Park.

FOOD AND DRINK

With no shortage of restaurants in Windhoek and on the coast, the cuisine has a richness and diversity that reflects Namibia's cosmopolitan culture.

There's one word almost every Namibian understands: *brötchen*, the German word for "bread roll", which has penetrated every linguistic group in the country. Indeed, European visitors will find all sorts of familiar breads and pastries in the bakeries here, from dark, thinly-sliced pumpernickel loaves to apfel-strudel, feather-light Sachertorte, sumptuous Schwarzwaldkirschtorte (Black Forest cherry cake) and many others.

You'll find plenty of other German staples on Namibian menus, too, from frankfurters to *sauerkraut*. Not to mention the beer, of course, which is brewed strictly in accordance with German purity laws.

When it comes to local produce, carnivores have a field day. All sorts of exotic cuts – oryx (gemsbok), kudu, ostrich, springbok and croco-dile – are served as main-course steaks, roasts or stews. And Namibian beef is said to be the tastiest and healthiest in the world, because the cattle are free-ranging.

Seafood in Swakopmund.

A tangy type of cured meat made from spiced strips of beef or game, biltong originated as a way of preserving meat in the early days of European settlement, and is now a popular accompaniment to pre-dinner drinks around the braai.

Fish aficionados will not be disappointed either and can look forward to sampling some fresh *kabeljou* (cob), kingklip and sole, all caught off the Atlantic coast. Oysters farmed at Swakopmund are a much-prized local delicacy, as are the crayfish (rock lobster) fished in the Lüderitz area.

Other local specialities to look out for include the Kalahari truffle *(nabas)*, an indig-enous tuber with a slightly nutty flavour. Sliced thinly, it adds a delicious depth to salads, sauces and casseroles.

Also much in demand are the tasty white *omajovo* mushrooms which sprout on termite hills following the summer rains. They're deli-cious either sautéd in garlic butter, or served in soups.

South African influences

The South Africans have exported their national pastime, the *braai* (barbecue), to Namibia, which means that every weekend in summer, gardens turn blue with smoke as hunks of meat are grilled. Be sure to sample *boerewors* ("farmer's sausage"), which is made from beef or game and flavoured with spices and herbs. The pleasures of the palate are usually rounded off with wine from South Africa's Western Cape region.

On special occasions, Namibians like to prepare a delicious hearty South Africans stew called *potjiekos* or "small pot food". This is cooked outdoors in a traditional round, cast-iron cooking pot (the *potjie*). Into the mix can go anything from chicken, beef, seafood, tomatoes, onions, rice or potatoes, all of which are slow-cooked with a spicy sauce, which often has

O Portuga, on Nelson Mandela Avenue, is a good place to sample the distinctively spicy cuisine associated with the former Portuguese colony of Angola, as well as a wide selection of top-quality seafood dishes. Also renowned for its seafood, Luigi & the Fish on Sam Nujoma Drive is a popular place for a lingering dinner.

For lunchtime fare, the Mugg & Bean, with its first-floor balcony overlooking Post Street Mall, serves aromatic coffee as well as a wide selection of sandwiches and light meals. Other good options in the café style include

The Namibian Institute of Culinary Education's bar and restaurant.

"secret" ingredients. The pot itself often has to be heated using scanty amounts of wood and charcoal, or even twisted grass or dried dung – it can take anything from three to six hours to cook the stew.

Eating out in Windhoek, Swakopmund and Lüderitz

Namibia's capital is well-supplied with good cafés and restaurants, catering for most tastes and pockets. The ever-popular Gathemann Restaurant in Independence Avenue (on the first floor of the Gathemann Building) has prime balcony seating and is an excellent place for Namibian specialties. Vegetarians are well catered for, and there's an extensive wine list.

the Zoo Café in the central but surprisingly tranquil Zoo Park, the Craft Centre Café in the Namcrafts Centre on Tal Street, and the more out-of-town Jenny's Place on Sam Nujoma Drive.

Swakopmund is renowned for its fresh seafood. The best place to try it? Look no further than the award-winning restaurant at the Hansa Hotel, which also has an impressive selection of South African wines. Another fine place for seafood is The Tug, with a great setting down on the beachfront, next to an iron jetty (watching the sun dip down into the sea is an added bonus). Then there's Kücki's Pub, one of the liveliest and most popular restaurants-cum-bars in Swakopmund. You can sit inside or in a spacious courtyard, but either way, the food (which is traditional German) is very good.

Swakopmund is also renowned for its traditional German cafés. The Hotel Schweizerhaus's Café Anton on Bismarck Street is one of the best places to indulge in calorific cakes and pastries, and there are nice sea views, too.

Food-wise, Lüderitz is as much of a treat as Swakopmund. The speciality here is crayfish, although all the usual meat dishes are also available, too. There's no better place to try the local seafood than Ritzi's Seafood Restau-

> *Wine lovers should be sure to try Pinotage, a uniquely South African cultivar developed from a cross between Pinot Noir and Cinsault. The Beyerskloof and Zonnerbloem estates both produce easy drinking Pinotages widely available at restaurants.*

But what would the life of the desert nomad be without the *!nara?* This nutritious fruit grows on river-banks, its deep roots drawing up water; for the Nama it has become a multi-pur-

The Village Café in Swakopmund.

rant, which is now situated in the Harbour Square Mall.

Desert Delicacies

Here in this hot and largely arid land, the indigenous peoples have had to adapt their diet to the resources available – which they have done both imaginatively and inventively over the years.

Take the ostrich egg, for example, which is equivalent to some two dozen hen's eggs. The San (Bushmen) know many ways of preparing it; cooks will make a hole in the upper half of the shell and use a twig as a spoon to mix the yolk and the white. A hollow in the earth is filled with hot coals, the egg is poured in and an omelette produced.

pose staple. Pressed, the fruit yields up a sweet, thirst-quenching liquid, while the pulp can be made into cake. Baked into a dry breadstuff, it can keep for up to two years, while its roots are used to make medicine.

Meat is a special treat for desert-dwellers, whose poisoned arrows kill game on contact – even giraffe. Hunters expertly dismember the carcass on the spot; specially marked arrows leave no doubt as to whose property the game is. Some claim the head as their special portion. This is buried in a pit filled with glowing coals and left to cure for a day, after which it is removed and the skull broken open – thus exposed, the brain is the greatest delicacy one can hope for.

RELIGIOUS BELIEFS

Officially, Namibia is a Christian country.
In practice, many traditional African beliefs
maintain a powerful place in religious life.

Leutwein Cemetery.

Africa, the melting pot of many different cultures and languages, is also a meeting-point of religions. Namibia is no exception and, when considering local traditions, there is no question of speaking about a single, unified religion. The country's indigenous peoples have their own beliefs: for example, many vastly different taboos are observed by different Herero clans, while the Damara used to have many different names for their god.

Despite this wide diversity of religious forms, one can perceive common threads among the colourful fabrics of the various indigenous beliefs. Virtually every one of them espouses the view that God created the world and has guarded it ever since. Certainly, various clans have given different names to the supreme being, and developed wildly differing conceptions of this god. But ultimately, all Africans are referring to the same God when they speak of the Creator and Guardian of the Earth.

In their countless myths, Namibia's indigenous peoples also tell of the original link and covenant between God and Man, which was broken through some mistake committed by a man or a beast. But God did not cease to exist; his importance for the collective African peoples remained intact.

Missionary misapprehension

Time and again, Christian missionaries were astonished to find there were no formal religious services among the indigenous population; they took this as an indication of the lamentable degree to which heathen practices had spread.

But it was a mistake to make such judgements solely on the basis of European

The German missionary Heinrich Schmelen undertook the first translation of the New Testament into the Nama language, aided by his wife – herself a Nama.

tradition. For in Africa, God is a being so holy and so thoroughly above Man that one hardly dares to speak his name aloud. If his name is uttered, it must be very guardedly – just as one is reluctant to disturb one's king or chief with trivia or unimportant daily concerns. Men on earth contact the deity through the agency of beings nearer to him: the ancestors, more pithily termed "the living dead".

In traditional religion, the belief is that those who have died are not truly dead; they have taken on a new form of existence, but remain in contact with the living. They continue to belong to the family, even after their names have been forgotten.

European missionaries were quick to conclude that "true worship" was displaced, in indigenous cultures, by this human "ancestor cult". Again, this is to assess the situation in narrow European terms, leading to the wrong conclusions. For African traditions recognise no difference between the sacred and the pro-

Yet to conclude that the entire Namibian population follows Christianity as it is practised in the major churches of Europe would be false, for many old African traditions have permeated the Christian denominations.

Ancestors' Memorial Day

This celebration of the Hereros is a fine example of this religious "co-existence". Most indigenous traditions have, as a rule, remained closed to outsiders; but, in Namibia, the various Herero clans celebrate their national holiday with much fanfare and public display in

A church in Windhoek.

fane; religion and daily life form a single unified whole.

Traditional religion today

"Official" statistics declare that approximately 91 percent of Namibia's population is Christian. Which means only a small fraction of the population, it would seem, continues to observe traditional religious practices. Such traditionalists tend to be found more in the northern regions, among peoples such as the Himba in Kaokoland or the San people, or Bushmen. This fact demonstrates the incredible zeal with which the missionaries pursued their goal: to introduce Christianity into every corner of the land.

Gobabis, Okahandja and Omaruru. While these festivities may not adhere strictly to the letter of religious law, both traditional and Christian elements are clearly evident.

In the case of Gobabis, events focus on a farm cemetery just outside town, where important chiefs and leaders of the East Herero (Mbanderu) are buried. For Nikodemus' Day (named after one of the chiefs), Herero journey here from every corner of the land. If they arrive before sunset of the previous day, they must first visit the graves. Before doing this, their presence is made known to the ancestors, and they must undergo a test around the Ancestral Fire to determine whether or not their presence is also welcome to the ancestors. The cult priest pulls the visitor's fingers; if a joint cracks, the candidate has passed muster. If not, he had better keep his distance.

For those admitted, there follows a ritual purification: a master of ceremonies sprays a mouthful of water over the guests. Now they may have access to the graves. At the entrance to the cemetery, the master of ceremonies kneels to the ground and introduces every visitor; through his voice, the ancestors command the petitioner to draw nearer. Each person kneels by the grave of the oldest chief, lays his hand on a stone and gives his name and place of origin.

The first missionaries

In 1805 the London Mission sent two German brothers, Abraham and Christian Albrecht, to Namibia to begin missionary work among the Khoi-khoi (Nama). Only someone who has crossed the dry, infertile regions in the south of the country will fully appreciate the difficulties they faced; indeed, in order to do their job and survive, they had no choice but to move with the nomadic Nama. Abraham died in 1810, but Christian continued their work, eventually establishing the first Christian community in Warmbad. In 1814 another London

Traditionally, cattle skulls replace the Christian cross on Herero graves.

The other "living-dead" are greeted by touching their gravestone, or by laying small stones on the grave. Visitors can then move freely among the graves. On Sunday, this ceremony is repeated; then, gathered around the graves, worshippers hold a service as if in church.

The thinking is that people's sins determine the course of events. Anyone who has disregarded the commands and wisdom of the ancestors cannot have access to them. While Christianity concentrates on sins committed against God, the indigenous tradition addresses itself to the sins which men have committed against other men. It is for this reason that cooperation between the two traditions is seen as important.

DUALITY OF DEITIES

At least two groups of San (Bushmen), the !Kung and the G/wi, traditionally believe in two "great chiefs" or gods. Yasema is the powerful god of good who lives in the east. He makes the sun rise, created all things and is the stronger god, on whom one calls for healing. Chevangani is the lesser god, who lives in the west, makes the sun set, and causes evil, sickness and death. When the Dutch Reform Church (ngk) began to work among the Bushmen in the 1980s, missionaries reported that, while the San had no problem in identifying Yasema with God and Chevangani with Satan, converts to Christianity were few.

Mission-backed German missionary arrived in Windhoek. Heinrich Schmelen's achievements were many: not only did he found a station at Bethanie (his one-room house can still be seen there today), but he discovered a new route west to the coast in the course of his missionary work.

Variety of churches

It may sometimes seem to visitors that Namibia has churches at every turn. In fact, they fall quite neatly into three groups, one of which dates back to the missionary era. Origi-

Traditional healer at work.

nally nurtured by the Rhine Mission and the Finnish Mission, the Evangelical Lutheran Church has the largest following in this category today.

Then there are all those churches that developed when the white settlers came, such as the Roman Catholic Church, which also practises mission work – as does the Anglican Church – and the German Evangelical Lutheran Church.

The influence of the third group, the truly African, independent churches, cannot be judged by its church buildings alone: its congregations are based, for the most part, in black sections of the cities or on former reservations, where they remain unobtrusive and hidden. But if you pass through one of these areas on

a Sunday, you will run across people singing, clapping their hands, or dancing around a candle in front of a house, under a tree, or in a simple room. It is not only priests and bishops who work here: prophets and charismatics do as well, while prayer healing and talking in tongues are seen as signs of the efficacy of the Holy Ghost. Song plays an important role even in the large communities of the former mission churches. No organ is needed; the congregation always sings in four-part harmony.

Striving for unity

There is no question that the South African policy of apartheid also influenced church life in Namibia for years. The Catholic Church and the Anglican Church, at least, ignored the question of race and refused to segregate communities – unlike the South African Dutch Reform Church (NGK) – but on the whole their white adherents preferred not to align themselves directly with anti-apartheid action.

Under apartheid, the Lutheran Church split into three. Of the two 'black' churches, the Evangelical Lutheran Church in Namibia (ELCIN) dominated in the north while the Evangelical Lutheran Church in the Republic of Namibia (ELCRN) was more popular in the south. Most white Lutherans belonged to the German Evangelical Lutheran Church (GELK). After independence, unity proved to a elusive goal. Indeed, It was only in 2007 that the three Lutheran constituency formed the United Church Council of Namibia Evangelical Lutheran Churches, with the ultimate aim of becoming one national entity.

ISLAM IN NAMIBIA

A relatively recent presence in the country, Islam is now adhered to by an estimated 4,000 Namibians, most of whom are recent converts among the Nama, though there are also tiny enclaves of South African immigrants of Indian origin in some larger towns. The recent growth of Islam within Namibia was precipitated by the conversion of the Nama politician Jacobs Salman Dhameer at a 1980 conference in Lesotho. The country's first mosque was built shortly afterwards in Katutura, a suburb of Windhoek, and there are now at least a dozen mosques countrywide, half of them in Windhoek.

Bushmen performing a traditional trance dance.

THE ARTS

Contrary to most visitors' expectations,
Namibia's cultural scene is a flourishing blend
of myth, township art and modernity.

Most people think of Namibia as a country of wild landscapes and stunning scenery. Less well known, however, is the country's urban environment, which has given rise to a rich cultural scene. For decades, white immigrants particularly in Windhoek and Swakopmund – have worked to preserve their European culture and build up an art scene within the country itself. Since independence in 1991, black artists, too, have made their presence known.

Soon after World War II, artists and artistically-minded citizens and patrons of Windhoek and Swakopmund started to found cultural associations with their own exhibition spaces which presented a wide range of local and foreign works. Their aim was to promote local talent, as well as introducing it to the international art scene.

Neighbouring South Africa was a major force behind Namibia's artistic development – yet even in the days when apartheid was the

A work by John Muafangejo.

Sculptors are rare in Namibia. The best known is Dörte Berner from Dordabis, whose monumental works, sculpted from local soapstone, often depict lonely, scorned men, or families seeking protection.

status quo, local art societies were open to members of all races. Today, galleries and exhibitions display the works of black artists, as well as works about Africa, while the National Art Gallery of Namibia in Windhoek contains an extensive collection of Namibian art works old and new.

African crafts

Since independence in 1991, the country has been in a pioneering phase, artistically speaking. In Okavango, Ovamboland, Caprivi and in the south of the country, there has been a revival of traditional craft production, with locals being encouraged to create anew – without falling into the rut of mass-production.

Pottery and basketry – the latter traditionally woven with Makalani palm leaves – are practised by women in northern Namibia, from the Caprivians to the Ovambo and the Kavango. Woodcarving, too, is part of the northern tradition, although it's usually practised by men.

As for beadwork, the San (Bushmen) and the

Himba are traditionally the most skilled practitioners. Authentic San crafts (bags and clothing decorated with beads made from ostrich egg shells, seeds and porcupine quills) are easiest to find in the Tsumeb area; for Himba crafts you have to go to Kaokoland – or check out Windhoek's private galleries.

Tapestries woven from Karakul wool also occupy a special place in the local crafts scene. Wall-hangings and floor coverings from the large weaving establishments such as Ibenstein and Dorka near Dordabis (see page 160) can reach a very high standard.

tradition in Namibia before World War I of naturalistic depictions of nature; this school remained the major artistic force in the country until new stylistic conceptions and subjects came onto the scene in the 1970s.

The calligraphic brushstrokes in the works of Adolph Jentsch, a landscape painter acknowledged far beyond the borders of his own country, are meant to establish a mystical connection between one's own heartbeat and the rhythm of surrounding nature. Jentsch, strongly influenced by Far Eastern philosophies, often meditated for hours in the wilder-

Tapestries for sale in Swakopmund on Rakotoka Street.

Oil and watercolour landscapes

Namibia's scenery has fascinated European artists ever since colonial times. After all, even the most barren stretches of the Namib Desert can be bewitching, whether because of the bizarre light effects in the early morning or the unusual play of intense colours as evening approaches. From this land of stones and vast distances, artists have often created landscape images depicting unspoiled Edens and romantic panoramas.

Even the renowned colonial painter Ernst Vollbehr, in general a rather distanced observer, bathed his work *Lüderitz Harbour* in a gentle pink afternoon light. The oil landscapes of Carl Ossmann, exhibited in Berlin, started a

ness before starting on a watercolour. Other significant names to look out for in local galleries are Otto Schröder, Johannes Blatt and Jochen Voigts.

Animal subjects

Axel Eriksson, Zackie Eloff, Hans-Anton Aschenborn and other artists often include peacefully grazing antelopes in their depictions of nature: for them, wild animals – so remote from the rest of the world – are an important part of this tranquillity.

Fritz Krampe, however, who had sketched elephants and gorillas in the Berlin Zoo as a child, chose African wildlife as a central theme of his work, filling entire canvases with it.

Krampe spent much of his time exploring the Etosha region and other areas of Africa rich in wildlife. He was less interested in gentle gazelles or picturesque ostriches than in the large, threatening animals: lions, elephants, buffalo, hyenas and vultures. His trademark became the representation of action: his brushstrokes were quick, strong, often sketchy. The viewer almost recoils from these oil paintings, drawings and lithographs of fighting, hunting or fleeing animals – as if he or she could feel the hot winds of the steppe and smell the danger.

Focus on man

All of the above artists occasionally produced portraits or figurative works. But it wasn't until the 1980s, probably as a result of socio-political developments associated with the country's move towards independence, that man, his environment and his perceptions, were seen as challenging subjects for the visual artist. In retrospect, the discovery of the human figure can already be seen in the landscape paintings of Anita Stayn and François de Necker.

Photography, as well – an art which has reached a high level of technical development in Namibia – now tends to concern itself more with *Homo sapiens* than with the microcosmos of nature which it used to depict: the devastation of border wars in Kaokoveld, or the jubilation of independence ceremonies.

Black art

A new, vital artistic category is making headlines in Namibia, township art. This term, coined in the black slums of South Africa, describes the work of a new generation of artists in Namibia, who have been able to receive an artistic education at the Windhoek Academy, today the University of Namibia, or private art schools in Lüderitz Bay, with the help of grants and scholarships. Joseph Madisia, Andrew von Wyk and Tembo Masala have already attained renown.

In black parlance, "sharp" is the superlative form of "good"; and the drawings and paintings of these young artists, depicting existence in the crowded township huts, telling of suffering, poverty and protest, are sharp – as well as aggressive, funny, cynical and penetratingly realistic. Colours tend to be loud and jarring;

simple actions are magnified into lofty expressiveness. These are pieces which captivate the viewer by means of their unmitigated realism. At the same time, they present a balance between daily city life and African myth.

One of the best-known names on the modern Namibian art scene belongs to the Ovambo John Muafangejo. This artist, who died tragically young, remained impressively uninfluenced by European stylistic elements even after he had visited South Africa and travelled in Europe. His lino-cuts of traditional life among the Ovambos, and his visions of biblical his-

Karakulia weavers at work.

John Muafangejo, who died aged 44 in 1987, confined himself exclusively to black-and-white linoleum prints, and was the first black man to have his art exhibited in Namibian galleries.

tory are absolutely original and unique, and so unparalleled that they fetch high prices on the South African art market.

The Performing Arts

Song and dance were among the first artistic expressions of the Namibian indigenous peoples. As early as the late Middle Ages, Portuguese sailors to Africa witnessed local musicians play-ing reed flutes in settlements along the coast. Other travellers documented performances of vocal music in black *kraals* as early as 1668.

The Nama in the centre and south of Namibia possessed a whole range of handcrafted and technically advanced musical instruments which were taken over, in part, by the San and the Khoi-San: bowls covered with stretched hides to serve as drums; a stringed instrument called the "gora"; and the "ramki", a kind of gui-tar with three or more strings made from cattle tail-hair or plant fibres.

High drama at the National Theatre of Namibia.

Reed flutes were used to stimulate and arouse during traditional religious rituals – when worshippers imitated the movements of animals in order to summon spirits – bone rattles provided a rhythmic accompaniment. Indigenous clans also used hand-rattles made from gourds, as well as signal trumpets made of antelope horns. In the north of Namibia, the Ovambos and Kavangos used tall wooden drums. In Caprivi, xylophones were added to complete the rich sound texture. In Okavango, traditional drums and other instruments are still used today in ritual dances, and even in Christian services.

As for the indigenous dramatic tradition, song and dance have always played an integral role. Since independence, various cultural organisations have established programmes where actors are sent to outlying areas – not just to entertain, but also to involve members of the community in creating and acting out a story.

Even in traditional ceremonies, dramatic ele-ments have always been powerfully deployed. Sensations and experiences are elevated into a magical sphere through the use of dance, rhythm and music.

European influences

For decades, the official music and theatre scene of Namibia was dominated by European tastes and styles as an élite group of "culturally aware" Windhoek and Swakopmund residents attempted to transplant the cultural heritage of Germany, Britain and South Africa into the "wilderness". After World War II, the found-ing of artistic organisations meant that exhibi-tions, ballet and theatre performances could be arranged, and foreign artists brought in.

In 1902, the Swakopmund Men's Choral Association was established, followed by the Men's Choral Association of Windhoek and numerous other choirs (mixed as well as men's) throughout the country.

Since the abolition of South Africa's apart-heid system, black and white Namibians alike have begun to explore their joint cultural traditions. Deluged with critical acclaim on European and American tours, the mixed-race Cantare Audire Choir performs religious and classical European music, as well as spirituals, African and Namibian compositions.

THEATRE IN NAMIBIA

Namibia's formal theatrical tradition dates back to its earliest colonial days. Long before SWARUK, the Southwest African Council on the Performing Arts, was founded in 1966, talented laymen were stag-ing such difficult works as Goethe's *Die Mitschuldi-gen* or Tennessee Williams's *The Glass Menagerie*.

These days, in addition to the work of the National Theatre, sundry community theatres have formed in the townships. In its School of Arts, the University of Namibia has its own theatre depart-ment. The Warehouse Theatre is a live music venue and experimental where young Namibians can display and fine-tune their skills.

The First Artists

The ancient art that adorns the rockscapes of Namibia is the posthumous legacy of the hunter-gatherers who were once the region's sole inhabitants.

The rock art of Namibia is closely associated with shamanic trance experiences, which remain to this day a central ritual amongst the last few remaining San clans living in the Kalahari desert. During such dances, the women will clap and sing special "calling" songs named after things which they believe to be particularly powerful – the eland or the giraffe, for instance – while the men dance slowly and rhythmically around them.

The San believe that this singing and dancing activates a supernatural potency, and that it is the task of the shamans in the group – usually about half of the men and about a third of the women – to harness this energy in order to enter a trance state associated with the spirit world. Once in this world, the shamans are said to be able to cure the sick, resolve social conflict and control wildlife movements, including a legendary creature believed to bring rain.

Shamans entering a trance usually experience a variety of physical and visual hallucinations, and often use "death" and "underwater" as metaphors for their trance experience. In traditional rock art, this state of mind would often be depicted by a dying eland. Think of the similarities: both can bleed at the nose, froth at the mouth, stumble about and eventually collapse unconscious.

When you are attempting to decipher rock art, therefore, bear in mind that the commonest themes are trance dancing (women clapping and men dancing), those animals which symbolise supernatural potency (usually an eland), and the visual and physical hallucinations which shamans ritually undergo.

Influences

A recent interview with one of the last surviving descendants of a San artist – an octogenarian living in South Africa's Eastern Cape – has shed new light on the probable ritual use of the paintings. She told how eland were driven up the valley, where her (habitually nomadic) clan had temporarily settled, and killed at a spot near the cave where the family slept. Blood from the animals was mixed with paint in an effort to transfer the eland's power to the paintings which decorated the walls of the clan's cave.

In addition, if the clan shamans wanted to increase their potency level while dancing, they would face the freshly executed paintings to harness their powers. In other words, the paintings and engravings were not just depictions of things that happened in the spirit world or symbols of powerful creatures, they were also powerful things in themselves – storehouses of the potency that made contact with the spirit world possible.

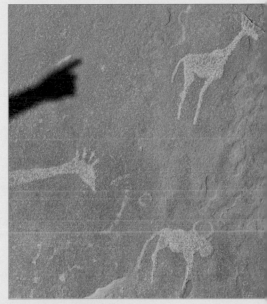

Rock pictograms at Twyfelfontein.

The San's way of life initially survived the arrival of the Khoi herders, who migrated down from the north of Africa some 2,000 years ago; indeed, they developed good relations with them and lived together in relative harmony. But their society came increasingly under pressure following the arrival of the Boers and the British at the Cape in the 17th century. These white colonists not only took over the San's land and hunting areas, they looked down on them as little more than vermin – and hunted them down accordingly.

Today, a very small number of San groups struggle to survive in Botswana, Namibia and South Africa, but their numbers are so few, they cannot really be said to represent a distinct social grouping any more.

THE ARCHITECTURAL HERITAGE

The combination of German colonial rule and
Namibia's extreme climate spawned a curious
but effective style of building.

An appropriate architecture for Namibia has to cope with a wide daily temperature range and intense solar radiation. Any functional building has to moderate the effects of daytime heating on the structure and the interior. For many centuries, the indigenous peoples responded appropriately by building a framework of poles sheathed with thick layers of mud and small openings.

The official architecture of the German colonial era found a different solution, adapting the building traditions of Germany to the altered demands of climate and building materials. The result was a verandah architecture – essentially a thick-walled core covered with a saddle roof and surrounded by a perimeter of lean-to roofs. The latter would shield the walls from the sun's rays, thereby retarding the passage of heat to the interior of the core.

The verandah genre

The verandah genre was promoted by missionaries who had encountered it all over South Africa and applied it to their buildings in Namibia since the early 19th century. The Imperial Directorate of Building Services – primarily under the directorship of Gottlieb Redecker, the first architect born in Namibia – developed verandah architecture based on contemporary classical interpretations. A good example is the modifications made to the Ludwig von Estorff House in Windhoek in 1902.

In colonial Namibia, the verandah came to serve additionally as the equivalent of a foyer or entrance hall, and as a congenial, cool, covered outdoor living space, especially if located on the southern part of the house.

German architecture in Lüderitz.

The verandah genre was applied to a wide range and scale of building types, achieving its logical conclusion and monumentality in the Parliament Building in Windhoek, the *Tintenpalast* ("Ink Palace") of 1913, essentially a double-storeyed verandah building with classical elements.

The foreign visitor to Namibia will not fail to see the Wilhelmenian influence in many of the colonial buildings. Obvious examples are the Railway Station, Prison and the Hohenzollernhaus in Swakopmund. The moderate climate here perhaps allows the Germanic architecture to blend in with the landscape rather more successfully than elsewhere in the country.

William Sander

The most prolific private architect was Wilhelm Sander, whose legacies are firmly imprinted on contemporary Windhoek; the Gathemann and Genossenschaftshaus in Independence Avenue are perhaps the first you will encounter. It was Sander who, inspired by a disused military post, recycled and remodelled it as a medieval castle, Schwerinburg, thereby setting the course for the "manor house" of Duwisib in the south of the country and two more castles in the capital by and for himself. Woermann House

Indigenous architecture is designed to provide shelter from the intense summer sun.

in Swakopmund, by the house architect of the shipping line, Friedrich Höft, is based on the design principles of the Arts and Crafts movement while making sparing use of Art Nouveau motifs.

Also Art Nouveau-inspired is the Windhoek landmark, the Church of Christ, completed in 1910. But the centre for Art Nouveau (*Jugendstil*) architecture is without doubt Lüderitz, the southern harbour town which developed after 1908 when diamonds were found at Kolmanskop.

The town, in a majestic setting focused on the harbour and Shark Island, has the homes of the magnates located on the Diamantberg,

the paradigm of which is the well-preserved Goerke House of 1909.

South Africa and apartheid

After the German era, development was hesitant, hampered by political indecision, prolonged droughts and the depression in the 1930s. Things changed in the 1950s when the priority became the incorporation of Namibia into South Africa, which made available massive development aid. The infrastructure was developed and Windhoek matured into today's modern city.

> Namibia's most important office block is Windhoek's glass-clad Namibia Diamond Corporation (formerly cdm) Building whose distinctive faceted south façade provides the glare-free conditions required for diamond sorting.

But the ideology of apartheid was packaged along with economic assistance. To architects, that meant that they had to design into public buildings separate facilities for each of the two races. Examples are the Main Post Office and the terminal buildings of Windhoek's two airports.

A major development was the Windhoek Library, Museum and Archives Building, the result of an architectural competition won by Hellmut Stauch, son of the discoverer of the Namibian diamond fields, August Stauch. A proponent of modern architecture as developed in Brazil, the younger Stauch reaffirmed in his buildings the need to adapt design to the Namibian climate.

With rising urban land values came the inevitable demand for taller buildings. Stauch's penchant was the external filigree of louvres to shade the core of the building without impeding daylight – in principle a continuation of the verandah traditions of colonial Namibia. The Carl List Haus of 1964 was the prototype.

Architecture since Independence

German colonial buildings are being preserved and renovated on a large scale; for example, the Alte Feste, Kaiserkrone, and

Orban Schule (Conservatoire). This particular style of architecture, termed historicist because it drew upon historical prototypes, initiated the very idea of conserving old buildings.

The architecture being realised at the dawn of independence in 1990 again drew upon historical sources relating the two periods of the country's past.

The hipped gable roof composition of the Wernhil Park Shopping Centre and the mansard roof and clock tower of Mutual Platz echo the roofscapes of the Wilhelmenian past.

In Lüderitz, similar historical motifs have been revived in recent years.

Brave new architecture

Bold architectural responses are being made to the country's problems. In such a harsh landscape, the normal set of value judgements hardly applies. The new buildings complete the urban landscape, perhaps more by similarity than by contrast; nevertheless they add to the totality, its richness and diversity, while the old structures remain relevant to everyday contemporary life throughout Namibia.

Old and modern architecture in Windhoek.

MISSION AND CHURCH BUILDINGS IN NAMIBIA

Many of Namibia's oldest buildings are associated with early Christian missions. The first European-constructed building, a house built by Wesleyan missionaries in Warmbad in 1806, was destroyed six years later by the Nama leader Jager Afrikaner (father of Jonker). Generally regarded to be the oldest standing building in Namibia is the stone house built by the Lutheran missionary Reverend Schmelen at Bethanie in 1814, gutted by fire a few years later, and rebuilt and expanded upon by the Reverend Knudsen in the 1840s. The mission church at Bethanie dates to 1859, and there are also 19th-century churches at Otjimbingwe (1867), Okahandja (1876), Keetmanshoop (1895) and Olukonda (1899). For the most part, these are simple and unadorned stone or whitewashed structures, whose lack of architectural pretensions match the austere conditions under which they were constructed.

The early 20th century saw the construction of more elaborate churches in major centres of colonial settlement. Among the most charming is the small Catholic cathedral erected in Tsumeb in 1913–14, and dedicated to St Barbara (patron saint of miners). Far more imposing are Windhoek's neo-Romanic Catholic Cathedral (1904–30), the striking Lutheran *Felsenkirche* ("Church on the Rocks") in Lüderitz and its counterpart in Swakopmund, and the Lutheran Christus Church in Windhoek.

A balloon rides over the Namib
Naukluft Park at sunrise.

ACTIVE PURSUITS

For lovers of the Great Outdoors, there are few places on earth more "outdoors" than Namibia's sparsely populated wilderness.

Enjoying the white water.

Namibia's desert climate, with clear skies and sunshine throughout the year, together with its wealth of unspoilt wilderness areas and few crowds, makes it an expansive playground for outdoor enthusiasts who can enjoy a diverse range of activities.

Hiking and climbing

During Namibia's winter months, between April and October, hiking and climbing give an opportunity to experience the Namibian landscape's spectacular views and really feel the freedom of space in a natural environment. Walking is mainly done in the early morning and evening, with a rest during the heat of the day. One of the main pleasures is that, even on the most popular trails, it never gets crowded.

Hiking trails extend from the Brandberg, Spitzkoppe, Pondok and Naukluft mountains to the Waterberg Plateau and Fish River Canyon. They vary in length, from short walks to

> For testing rock climbs, head to the Spitzkoppe in the northwest – its highest peak, Groot Spitzkoppe (1,728 metres/5,670ft), has been called "the Matterhorn of Namibia".

serious eight-day hikes across rugged terrain, where you need to carry your own equipment.

It's important to be suitably fit, to carry enough water and to wear proper walking boots. Trails need to be booked in advance with the Namibia Wildlife Resorts office in Windhoek (see Travel Tips, page 267) and a party must consist of between three and 10 hikers.

The Brandberg granite massif rises to Königstein, at 2,573 metres (8,440ft) the highest mountain in Namibia. It's a strenuous three-hour return hike to see the "White Lady of the Brandberg" painting, but there's a network of other trails, and guides can be hired from the local community. The mountain presents a number of technical climbs for serious mountaineers.

Among Namibia's many walking trails, the Naukluft mountains are the setting for one of Africa's toughest hikes – the 120km (72 mile) eight-day Naukluft Trail. It follows the Naukluft river before ascending the escarpment, from which there are expansive views across the plains. Two circular trails – the Waterkloof

(17km/10 miles) and Olive (10km/6 miles) – provide challenging day hikes.

The steep ascents encountered on each day's hike and the rocky terrain underfoot are physically demanding and the trails are not recommended for beginners or the unfit.

Considered one of the top five hiking trails in southern Africa is the Fish River Canyon. Following an 80km (50-mile) stretch of the river, from Hiker's Point to Ai-Ais, it involves rough walking – scrambling over rocks, ploughing through loose sand and sustaining soaring temperatures – but solitude, spectacu-

to become absorbed in learning about wildlife issues and the natural environment while staying in camps surrounded by sandstone cliffs.

Take to the water

Canoeing the Orange river along the South African border is very different from canoeing on the Zambezi. Five-day trips in Mohawk two-man canoes traverse a 75km (47-mile) stretch of the river. There are no hippos or crocodiles, so swimming in the scorching midday temperatures while gently drifting downstream, is particularly relaxing. The river

Hiking in the Waterberg National Park.

lar scenery and the magnificent colours of the canyon make up for any discomfort. There are no facilities whatever, though, so backpackers must aim to be totally self-sufficient.

The Waterberg Plateau Park has nine short wilderness trails, open throughout the year. Of the longer trails, which require advance booking, there is an unguided, 42km (26-mile), four-day hike around sandstone kopjes at the southern end of the plateau.

But the park's main appeal is the guided Okarakuvisa Trail, a three- or four-day trek. Here walkers track animals (white and black rhino, and sable and roan antelope, amongst others) through the bush in a pristine wilderness area away from roads and other people,

> For an adrenalin rush, try white-water rafting on the Kunene River, which borders Angola. The best rafting is a 120km (72-mile) stretch between Ruacana and Epupa Falls.

meanders through stark, arid scenery, interspersed with rapids. At night, with no unnatural light in the sky, the stars are particularly awesome, and you can experience the eerie silence of the desert.

In contrast, there are game-viewing trips by *mokoro* (dugout canoe) on the northern rivers. At the coast there's sea-kayaking among seals and dolphins around Walvis Bay, and boat excursions to see dolphins, seals and pelagic birds.

Riding

Namibia has a strong horse-riding tradition, based on the farming community, and riding is widely available to visitors at lodges and on private farms, where it's often possible to see game such as oryx and kudu from horseback.

One of the most exciting options, giving a flavour of the scale and variety of the Namibian countryside, is the set of 6 to 10 night trails organised by the Namibia Horse Safari Com-

Namibia's Professional Hunters' Association follows a strict ethical code, with all trophy hunters being accompanied by an experienced professional hunter or registered guide.

Angling

Fishing is a popular Namibian pastime, with a choice of deep-sea fishing and surf angling off the Atlantic coast, and freshwater fly-fishing in the northern rivers of Zambezi, Chobe, Kunene and Kwando, or on the dams. Prime surf angling spots are found along the blustery Atlantic coastline north of Swakopmund to the

Recreational fishermen on the coast near Swakopmund.

pany. Most challenging of these is the Namib Desert Trail, which involves up to 70km on saddleback daily, starting at Sossusvlei then descending into the arid lands of the Namib Desert, with its gravel plains and dunes, before arriving at the coast at Swakopmund.

Hunting

Hunting is part of an everyday way of life for many Namibian farmers who regularly shoot game for the pot. In the 1980s, as cattle and Karakul prices fell, many farmers diversified into offering trophy hunting on their farms, and consequently hunting now attracts a high proportion of international visitors, too – particularly Germans and Americans. Encouragingly,

UNDERWATER ATTRACTIONS

The shipwrecks that litter the Skeleton Coast are the prime attraction for divers, the best dive sites being between Lüderitz and Spencer Bay, further north, where visibility is good – between 3 and 10 metres (10–33ft). December to May are considered the best months for diving. Arrangements can be made through the Namibian Underwater Federation (NUF, see Travel Tips page 268).

Inland, for experienced cave-divers, there's the chance to swim subterranean lakes – including the crystal clear water of Dragon's Breath Cave, which was only discovered in 1986, and contains the largest underground lake in the world.

mouth of the Ugab river, while deep-sea fishing trips can be arranged from Swakopmund. Shark fishing here compares with the best in the world, with some copper sharks weighing in at around 180kg (400lb). Other species like west-coast steenbras, cob, blacktail and white stumpnose are a regular catch, although what you end up with on your hook will largely depend on what bait you use. Red bait is considered a good, all-purpose choice, as are fresh pilchards. Steenbras are partial to shrimps, while cob will readily take white mussels. The season runs from November to March.

Many fly-fishermen gravitate to the Chobe and Zambezi rivers in eastern Caprivi, lured by the ultimate freshwater challenge, the tiger fish. Here a serious quest for large specimens – over 9kg (20lb) – involves fishing the rapids from a dugout canoe (*mokoro*). Fishing lodges like Impalila can also organise boat excursions, complete with guides and fishing equipment. Tiger-fishing is generally most rewarding between the months of August and December. Bream, barbel and African pike are among the staggering 81 fish species found in these waters.

Many remote areas can only be reached by a four-wheel-drive vehicle.

SANDBOARDING

Swakopmund has developed as a centre for desert adventure enthusiasts. The sand dunes of the Namib provide an exciting variation on snowboarding called sandboarding. Most sandboarding is carried out between Swakopmund and Walvis Bay, which boasts some of the tallest dunes in the country. A popular site, the prosaically named Dune Seven, 10km (6 miles) out of Walvis Bay, is the tallest on the coastal belt at 130 metres (425ft). Quadbiking is also popular here, motorised four-wheelers making it possible to take picnics and sundowner trips in the desert. It's important to go on organised trails, as birds nest in certain areas.

Sky adventures

Thanks to the near-perfect atmospheric conditions prevailing in Namibia, it's a popular destination for air sports enthusiasts.

Ballooning across the Namib desert at dawn, followed by a traditional champagne breakfast, is a wonderful way to experience the size and emptiness of the desert. Recreational flights over Sossusvlei from Swakopmund give expansive views of the Kuiseb river canyon, star and crescent dunes stretching to the horizon, the pan at Sossusvlei and wreck of the *Eduard Bohlen* which ran aground in 1910.

Bitterwasser, southeast of Windhoek near Uhlenhorst is renowned for its world record-breaking gliding conditions, with some of the best thermals in the world. Microlighting takes place around Windhoek, the Brandberg and the coast and the season usually stretches from October to January.

Four-wheel-drive trails

Namibia's rugged terrain has always attracted 4x4 enthusiasts who relish the wilderness experience, testing their wits and their vehicle's performance against the elements. However, with the rise in 4x4 clubs, more people are venturing into remote areas, where their enthusiasm has not been matched with care for the environment. Gravel plains are most at risk, as vehicle tracks can last for centuries.

There are a number of recognised 4x4 trails. Among these are the Windhoek to Okahandja Trail travelling through several farms in the Khomas Hochland; the Dorsland Trail, which marks the Namibian section of the 1878 Dorsland Trek, from South Africa through Namibia to Angola; and the Kalahari-Namib Trail which opened in 1999. They present a driving challenge, but the routes are not advisable to those who have no experience of African 4x4 driving conditions.

Tswalu Kalahari Reserve, Namibia

THE SKY AT NIGHT

With its cloudless skies, low pollution levels, and sparse sources of artificial light, Namibia offers some of the world's finest conditions for star-gazing. On a clear night, about 2,500 individual stars, down to the sixth order of magnitude, can be discerned with the naked eye, along with and up to five planets.

The brightest star in the sky is Sirius, the so-called Dog Star. The planets Saturn, Jupiter, Mars, Mercury and Venus (the latter also known as the Evening Star), can often be seen on occasion, depending on their location relative to Earth. You may also see magnificent shooting stars and satellites on a clear night.

Many constellations are easily identifiable. The famous Southern Cross, named after the shape made by its four brightest stars, has long been the compass of mariners and other wanderers in the southern hemisphere. Orion is distinctive, too, with three stars in his belt. Taurus is clearly visible from November to May. Virgo can be seen from March to August, Aquarius from August to January, and Leo from February to July. You can spot Scorpio, the brightest zodiac constellation, from May to November.

Also prominent is the Milky Way, a hazy luminous band comprising unknown billions of stars, and which Namibia's Bushmen call the "backbone of the night".

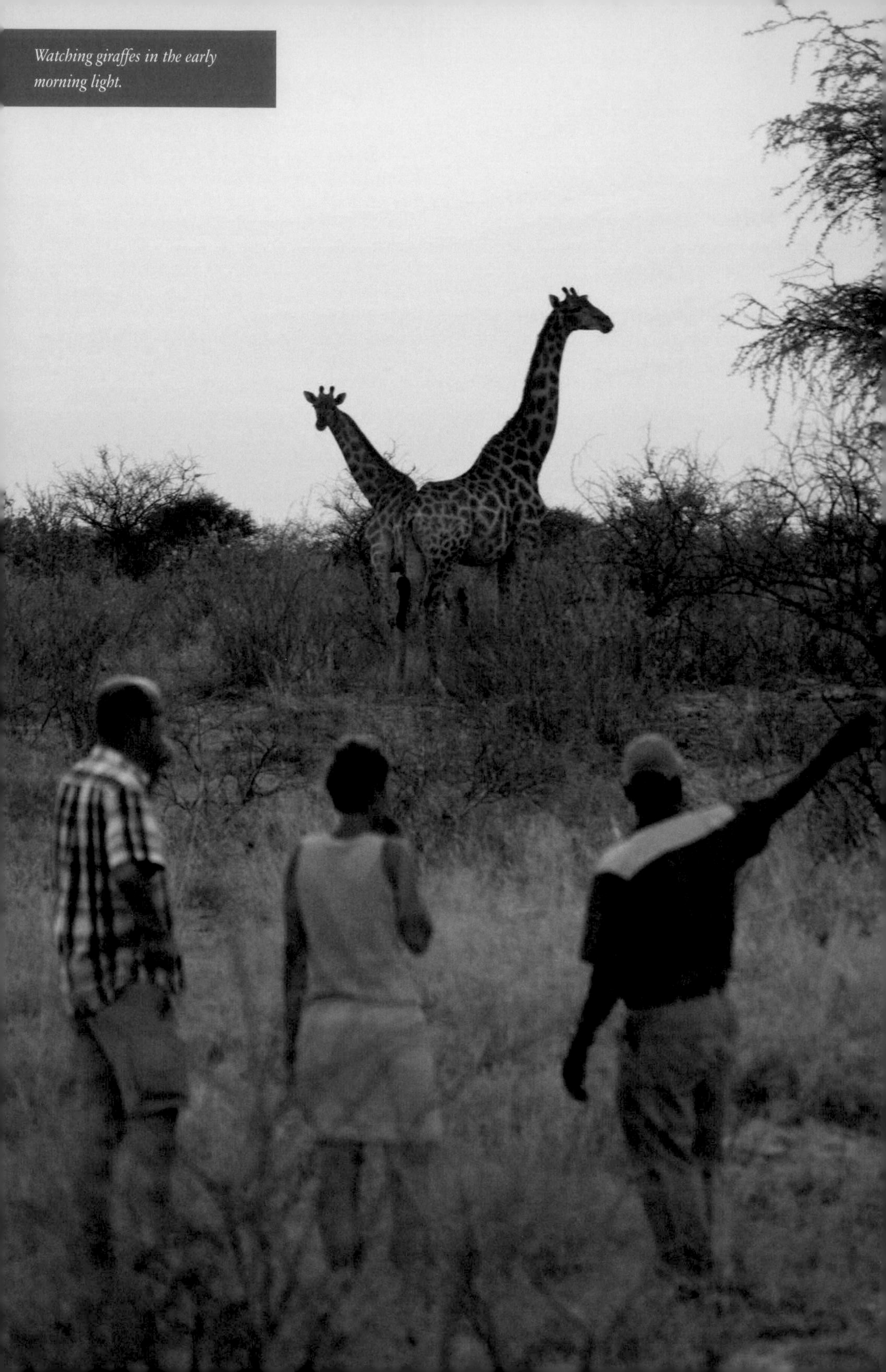

Watching giraffes in the early morning light.

ON SAFARI

**Namibia's extraordinary landscape and
extensive conservation areas make a wildlife
safari a unique and memorable experience.**

Lunch break on the way to Lüderitz.

Shimmering expanses of white at Etosha Pan, apricot and coral dunes in the Namib desert, verdant waterways of the Caprivi, empty, bleached beaches along the Skeleton Coast, barren terracotta mountains in Damaraland, ochre rock faces of the Fish River Canyon and cloudless azure skies all paint vivid, lasting impressions of the Namibian landscape.

The country is big, raw, wild and often bleak. There's an overwhelming feeling of space, timelessness and distant horizons. It's a desert land of extremes, where even during the winter months, between April and October, temperatures are known to regularly soar to 30°C (86°F) during the middle of the day, dropping to near freezing at night.

Wildlife viewing against this backdrop is a very different experience from other safari destinations in Africa. What makes Namibia particularly special is the number of large mammals found in a desert environment, and the fact that the animals are not restricted to designated parks.

Put safety first: if you are driving yourself on safari, do stick to the speed limits – many accidents result from speeding on gravel roads and losing control of the vehicle, or swerving to avoid a crossing animal.

In hostile terrain, sightings of species such as desert elephants, Hartmann's mountain zebra or the elusive black rhino are particularly gratifying, while the renowned Etosha National Park compares with the best game parks in Africa and has sizeable herds of the endemic black-faced impala. The clown-faced oryx (gemsbok), with its distinctive black and white mask and rapier horns, is a desert specialist, and is often seen in the sand dunes.

Birdlife is surprisingly diverse, thanks to the variety of habitats, with more than 700 recorded species. Raptors are numerous, and it's common to see pale chanting goshawk perched on telephone posts at the roadside, or eagles soaring on the afternoon thermals. In the arid regions of Damaraland, the guttural croak of Rüppell's korhaan can be heard echoing along the valleys in the early morning, mingling with the mewing of Karoo long-billed larks.

Plant life is equally intriguing and often bizarre, such as the quaint *Welwitschia mirabilis* (an underground tree with "pine" cones), elephant's foot or the aptly named bottle tree.

Namibia is geologically rich, and much of its ancient history is well preserved. There are dinosaur footprints, fossilised trees, and magnificent sites of stone age rock art, the most famous being at Twyfelfontein. Remarkably, the descendents of these early artists, the San (also called the Bushmen), still live in the Kalahari today. Other indigenous peoples, like the Himba pastoralists of the Kaokoveld, also still pursue a traditional lifestyle.

more comfortable in October and November when it's cooler, but if you want to see baby animals or migrating birds, the summer months are best.

The scheduled tours generally cover the most popular and accessible highlights of the country, a typical 10-day itinerary travelling from Windhoek to Sossusvlei, Swakopmund, Damaraland, Etosha and returning to Windhoek. Special interest safaris and mobile camps give the flexibility of travelling on different routes and at a more relaxing pace, with time to appreciate the scenery and to learn about the environment.

Scanning the horizon for game.

Choosing a safari

Namibia does not have a safari heritage like its counterparts elsewhere in Africa. But there is a distinctive Namibian safari style, characterised by well-organised efficiency and a comprehensive variety of options, ranging from budget tours on scheduled coaches and minibuses, to more expensive special interest tours and mobile 4x4 camping safaris complete with knowledgeable local guides, fly-in safaris with a pilot-guide, self-drive trips or train travel.

Combined with some of the active pursuits described in the preceding chapter, a uniquely Namibian safari can be designed to suit most tastes and budgets. Travelling is

Few people will have time to visit all corners of the country, so it is worth giving some thought to which safari destinations suit you best. Etosha, for instance, is the ideal destination for serious wildlife photographers, first-time safari-goers, or anybody else looking to see large volumes of wildlife. By contrast, the Damaraland reserves host relatively low volumes of wildlife, but on the other hand offer the opportunity to track the rare desert-adapted elephants and rhinos in one of the world's most thrillingly empty landscapes. For dedicated hikers, meanwhile, the Waterberg Plateau, though it hosts less variety than Etosha, is the perfect place to track wildlife on foot.

If you plan to travel in remote areas, bear in mind that even the more upmarket tours do not offer the camping luxury found in countries such as Tanzania or Kenya; logistically, it's impractical to travel with so much equipment – so the camping is comfortable rather than luxurious. And don't confuse mobile camps (where your tents travel around with you) with permanent tented camps, which are among the best in Africa. In areas like Damaraland and the Kaokoveld, the road scarcely exists in places, so these safaris will only appeal to the most adventurous.

Fly-in safaris are ideal for those on a tight time schedule. They provide a wonderful way to experience the diversity of Namibia, and with such clear flying conditions, they are the best way to appreciate the scale and geological complexity of the country.

Going on a self-drive safari holiday is easy to arrange, as the country has an excellent road network with well-maintained tarmac and gravel roads. There's a good choice of accommodation, from camping to guest farms, lodges and hotels. Tourism literature on the main attractions in each region is readily

On a day-long drive to see the Big Five.

NAMIBIA'S NATIONAL PARKS

Namibia's 20 or so state-owned national parks and reserves are managed by the Ministry of Environment and Tourism (MET). They range in size from the 59,768 sq km (23,076 sq miles) Namib-Naukluft Park to the tiny Popa Falls Game Reserve. The best known and most visited park, 22,270 sq km (8,600 sq miles), Etosha was established in 1907 and supports 114 mammal and 340 bird species. The best time for game watching is May–September, when you can expect to see many antelope species, elephant, rhino, giraffe and lions.

The vast Namib-Naukluft Park, Africa's largest wildlife reserve and the fourth largest in the world, embraces flat gravel plains, rugged mountain ranges (the Naukluft),

steep river gorges, the dunes of the Namib Desert (including Sossusvlei) and the lagoons of Sandwich Harbour and Walvis Bay. The Skeleton Coast Park is a true wilderness area, a narrow strip stretching 16,390 sq km (6,330 sq miles) along the Atlantic Ocean from the Ugab River all the way north to Angola. Namibia's smaller parks are no less remarkable. They include the Cape Cross Seal Reserve, with its immense breeding colony of Cape fur seals, as well as the Fish River Canyon (a spectacle second only to America's Grand Canyon) and the Waterberg Plateau Park, where you can see endangered species such as white and black rhino, and roan and sable antelope.

available. When selecting a car-hire company for a safari, it pays to scrutinise insurance cover details, especially the Collision Damage Waiver (CDW).

The ideal safari vehicle is a 4x4 such as a Land Rover or Land Cruiser, which can get you through pretty much any terrain, and also has excellent elevation for wildlife photography. Unfortunately, however, 4x4 rental is generally twice as expensive as taking an ordinary saloon car, and the latter option will get you around most parts of Namibia without any problem, though it will restrict access to very

oryx, kudu, ostrich and succulent seafood from the coast, a speciality being Walvis Bay oysters. South African wines and Namibian-brewed beer are readily available.

Train travel for tourists has recently come of age, with the introduction of the Desert Express in 1998. A luxury service, it travels between Windhoek and Swakopmund, with several stops on the way, including a sunrise excursion to the Moon Valley in the Namib desert. Other trains are the Shongololo Express and Rovos Rail (see Travel Tips, page 245).

Okaukuejo Camp in Etosha National Park is one of the best places to see black rhino.

sandy areas, or to places that become muddy after rainfall.

Namibia offers a wide range of accommodation, from international standard hotels to lodges, tented camps, guest farms, guesthouses, rest camps and campsites. When selecting accommodation from one of the tourism publications, bear in mind that standards are based on the physical infrastructure – number of rooms and facilities offered – rather than on the ambience or quality of service.

Namibian cuisine generally gives excellent value for money, except perhaps at some of the rest camps. The main centres have superb restaurants, serving Namibian beef, mutton,

GEARING UP

If you are serious about getting decent pictures on safari, it is worth investing in a reasonable SLR camera and at least one high-magnification lens. Most people opt for a zoom lens, for instance 70-300. First-time safari-goers seldom realise the importance of supporting your camera to prevent camera shake. To obtain the sharpest wildlife shots from a stationary vehicle, rest your camera on a beanbag, something you can make before your trip.

Binoculars are essential for viewing distant wildlife and for close-up views of birds. An 8x magnification is the minimal requirement, but birdwatchers may prefer 10x or 12x.

It's all about the wait.

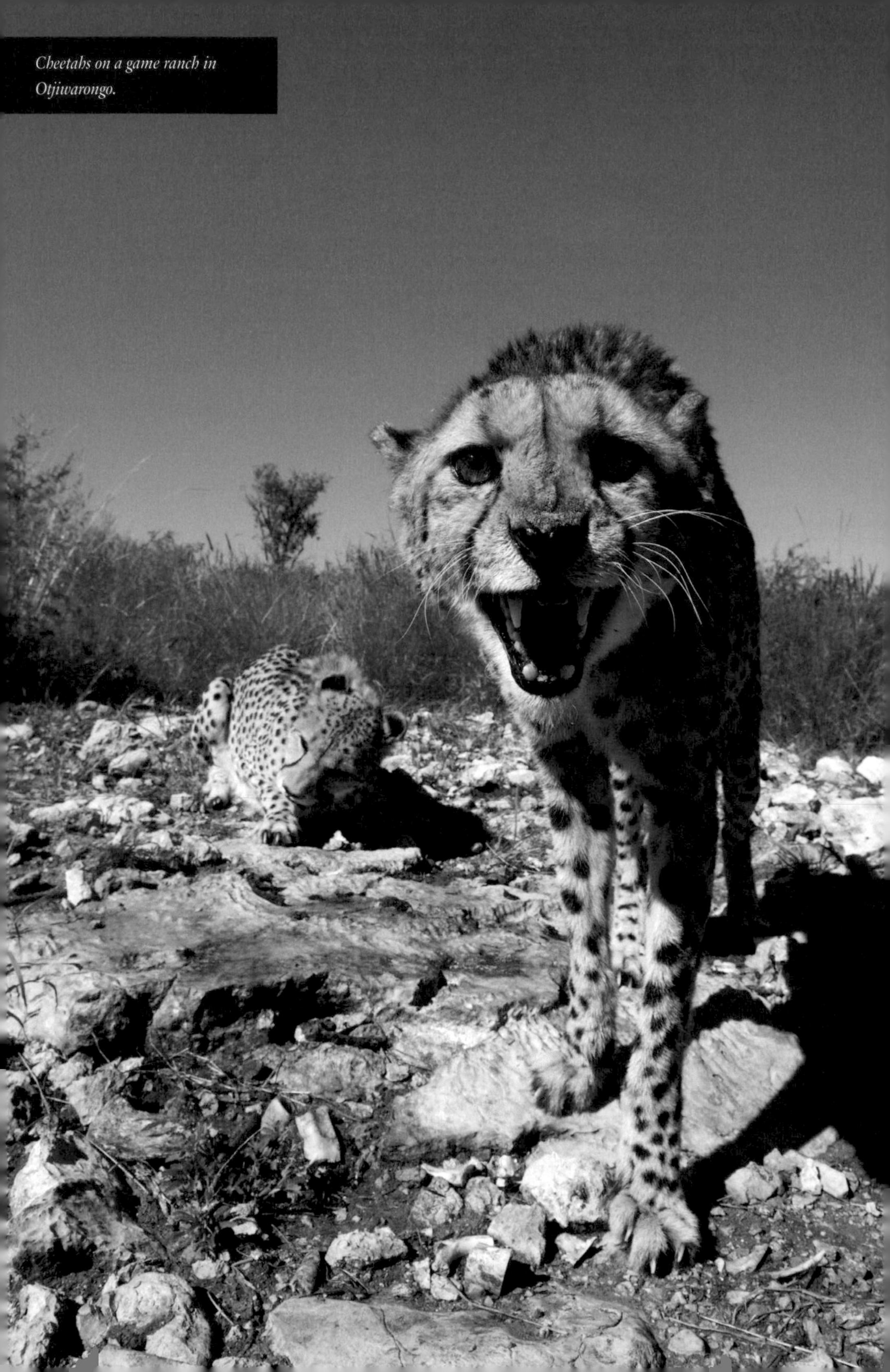

Cheetahs on a game ranch in Otjiwarongo.

THE PREDATORS

There are cats, there are dogs, there are relatives of the weasel – and plenty of other creatures besides – all aiming to stay alive by hunting and killing.

Namibia's wildlife survives despite the harsh regimes nature dictates in this largely arid country. Fourteen major vegetation zones support at least 134 species of wild mammals in niches where they feed, establish territories and reproduce. Some are "Namibian specials", endemic animals which live nowhere else. Most have developed unique and interesting adaptations which help them survive in their dry and hot environment.

All of Africa's "Big Five" (elephant, rhinoceros, buffalo, lion and leopard), plus the well-known prey animals, are present in Namibia. Some are specifically adapted to the desert; others display unique survival mechanisms.

The **lion** *(Panthera leo)* is by far the largest African predator: an adult male may weigh anything up to 240kg (530lb). Lions are unique among the cats in that they live in social groups or prides, which hunt cooperatively. There is also greater sexual dimorphism (differences between sexes) than in other species.

A pride consists of a coalition of males, generally two or possibly three brothers who defend and hold a territory, up to 15 females who are usually related, and usually some youngsters. Females do the hunting, bringing down prey as large as buffalo and young elephants.

Like other big cats, lions hunt by ambushing prey and then sprinting after it for a short distance. They have little stamina, so unless their quarry is close when they break cover, they have little chance of success. Once lionesses have killed, the males and the cubs feed first.

Occasionally, lions make their way down the river valleys into the Skeleton Coast National Park, where they struggle to make a living, scavenging the tide line and occasionally hunting Cape fur seals. They are likely to be shot as soon

A spotted hyena scavenges a carcass.

as they leave the park. Resting lions will barely flick a tail or twitch a foot for hours at a time. Only if you come across playful young cubs or a mating pair are you likely to witness any activity. Lions are more active after dark and you may see them on a spotlighted night drive from a private lodge or at a floodlit water hole.

The next largest African cat is the **leopard** *(Panthera pardus)*, about 2 metres (6ft) from nose to tail, with a male weighing 60kg (130lb) or more. This muscular and solitary nocturnal hunter is one of the most secretive of cats.

Leopards creep up on their quarry in the darkness, only making a dash at the very last moment. In order to prevent lions or hyenas from stealing their prey, these powerful beasts will haul their food up into a tree and cache it there, sprawling over a nearby branch in the shade of the dense foliage during the day. Alternatively, they will crawl into impenetrable thickets or deep grass.

Only the very fortunate will spot a leopard in daylight in Etosha – although waterhole watchers may be rewarded by one coming to drink at night. Nevertheless, it is always worth checking any likely looking trees, where a luxuriant bell-rope of a tail is frequently a giveaway.

Leopard and **cheetah** (*Acinonyx jubatus*) are both persecuted by Namibian farmers for steal-

> *The spotted hyena, with the strongest jaws of any mammal, can eat large bones – a source of nutritious marrow. Its droppings are usually white because of all the calcium they contain.*

alone, defending and feeding her litter until the cubs are almost full-grown and have learned to hunt for themselves.

Cheetahs cover long distances and have extremely large territories, generally centred around a number of play trees which they scent-

A serene lion in Etosha National Park.

ing stock. They are snared, trapped and shot – and for cheetahs this is a significant problem. Namibia has around 2,500, the largest population in the world, but they live mainly on farmland where they constantly come into conflict with man.

The cheetah differs from true big cats in that it has semi-retractable (as opposed to fully retractable) claws. The fastest land mammal, this lithe cat, weighing around 50kg (115lb), can achieve speeds of 100kph (60mph) over short distances.

As with lions, coalitions of brothers hold territories but they do not consort with the females except to mate with them, and take no part in rearing the young. The female does this

mark with both faeces and urine.

Next on our list is the **spotted hyena** (*Crocuta crocuta*), the second largest carnivore in Africa. Standing 90cm (3ft) tall and weighing around 65kg (140lb), it is a formidable animal with powerful forequarters and a massive and heavily muscled head. It has a spotted coat and a comparatively short tail. Although often seen individually, in pairs and in threes, hyenas live in large clans, which defend a territory.

Though they have a reputation for scavenging, hyenas are extremely competent cursorial hunters, employing their considerable reserves of stamina and often cooperating to run down prey, such as wildebeest, over long distances.

They will steal prey from other predators, including lone lions, and will eat all manner of carrion, making more efficient use of prey than any other carnivore. They are found mainly in Etosha and in the Caprivi Strip area.

The much smaller **brown hyena** *(Hyaena brunnea)* weighs about 40kg (90lb). It tends to be a specialist of arid areas and survives throughout the Namib Desert in western Namibia. It is much the same shape as the spotted hyena, but has long, coarse, light or dark brown hair. It spends its nights foraging individually, feeding mainly on small mammals, birds, insects, reptiles and wild fruits such as melons.

It is often possible to find the tracks of the brown hyena, showing where it has wandered hither and thither during the night in search of food. In spite of its solitary nature, the brown hyena also holds territories with others in its group of males and females.

The dog family

The **African wild dog** or painted dog *(Lycaon pictus)* is found in the northeast of Namibia. It is a rangy animal, similar in size to a domestic Alsatian, with a short coat randomly patched with black, white and gold. The wild dog lives in a close-knit pack of 10 to 15, which roams a very large territory up to 2,000 sq km (770 sq miles), living a nomadic lifestyle unless rearing puppies. The pack is a highly specialised and efficient hunting team, pursuing and attacking prey as large as buffalo.

Throughout Africa, the wild dog population is dwindling. It suffers from the same fatal diseases as domestic dogs (notably distemper and rabies), is often a road casualty, and is also heavily persecuted by farmers, being both shot and snared. Attempts to reintroduce the dogs to Etosha have unfortunately failed in the past, and with a wild population estimated at between 3,000 and 5,000, the animal is now IUCN-listed as an endangered species.

The black back and black bushy tail of the **black-backed jackal** *(Canis mesomelas)*, make it unmistakable. Its flanks and long legs are chestnut, it has pointy ears, stands about 38cm (15ins) at the shoulder and weighs about 8kg

A black-backed jackal in Etosha.

NAMIBIA'S SMALLER CATS

The lynx-like **caracal** *(Felis caracal)* is found throughout the country except for the Namib coastal strip. It is a robustly built cat, over a metre (3ft) in length and weighing around 16kg (35lb). It varies in colour from sandy brown to silvery grey, with very distinctive ear tufts and a fairly short tail.

The caracal is nocturnal, solitary and a very swift and adept hunter, even catching birds in the air as they take off. As well as mainly ground-living birds, it also eats mammalian prey up to the size of an impala.

The **serval** *(Felis serval)* is much the same size as the caracal but slighter, weighing only around 11kg (25lb). It has long legs, a small head, upstanding ears and a fine black-spotted coat on a gold background. Mostly found in the north of Namibia, it hunts at night, either by itself or in pairs, and feeds mainly on small mammals although it will also take birds and reptiles.

The **African wild cat** *(Felis lybica)* looks very much like a pale domestic tabby, but with distinctive reddish-brown ears. It lives throughout the country, except for the Namib coastal strip, and feeds on mammals up to the size of a spring hare, as well as on birds, reptiles and invertebrates. Although it is largely a nocturnal animal, you may see a wild cat during the daytime at quieter watering holes in Etosha, when it might try hunting doves coming down to drink.

The bat-eared fox has very acute directional hearing: it can pinpoint termites moving underground, and digs furiously to unearth them before they can burrow away.

(18lb). It is capable of living throughout the country and may be seen anywhere from the Namib Desert to the Caprivi Strip.

It is probably the most commonly seen carnivore and may be spotted trotting singly or in pairs through the national parks such

summer months, the bat-eared fox is mostly seen by day during winter, when the cold desert nights keep insects inactive.

The silvery buff **Cape fox** *(Vulpes chama)* is a small fox (3kg/7lb) with a dark, bushy tail. Generally solitary and nocturnal, it lies up during the day in cool shade or in an underground den. It is an omnivore and takes a range of small prey and fruits.

Like some other foxes it caches food, and you may spot a hungry Cape fox out in daylight excavating a hidden larder. It lives throughout the drier parts of Namibia. Keep a look out for

The endearing bat-eared fox.

as Etosha. It is frequently seen at floodlit waterholes, and large numbers gather around coastal seal colonies, where they are known to suffer from mange from time to time. An omnivore, the jackal eats insects, small mammals, fruits and nuts, and often scavenges around campsites. Its high-pitched screaming cries are one of the characteristic sounds of the African night.

The little **bat-eared fox** *(Octocyon megalotis)* has unmistakable huge rounded ears thick buff grey fur, and the legs, muzzle and the tip of its bushy tail are black. The long front claws are used to dig for insects, its primary prey. It will also take other invertebrates, small mammals, birds and reptiles. Nocturnal during the

Cape foxes at dusk, when you may see one or even a pair emerge from a den.

The weasel family

Namibia has two otters but very little permanent water, so both species are confined to the Caprivi Strip. The larger **Cape clawless otter** *(Aonyx capensis)* grows to 160cm (5ft) in length and weighs up to 18kg (40lb). It is a typical otter with a dense, dark brown coat, flat streamlined head and a broad tapering tail. Its white chin is characteristic. Each foot has five toes and those on the hind feet possess rudimentary claws and are also webbed. It is able to manipulate food with its feet and hold it while it feeds. Although most of its diet is aquatic creatures, the Cape clawless otter takes a range of prey including insects, reptiles and even birds.

The **spotted-necked otter** (*Lutra maculicollis*) is much smaller (1 metre/3ft long and 4.5kg/10lb in weight). It too is chocolate-brown but with a mottled creamy white throat and upper chest. Like the Cape clawless, its hind feet are webbed but in this species they have white claws. The diet of the spotted-necked otter contains a greater proportion of aquatic prey as this species is more tied to water than the Cape clawless. Look out for it swimming low in the water, tail emerging as it dives.

Like the honey badger, the **striped polecat** (*Ictonyx striatus*) is almost entirely nocturnal. It is a black and white striped animal weighing just under a kilogram (2lb) and is found throughout Namibia. It is a solitary insectivore and uses a highly distasteful secretion from its anal glands in self-defence. You may see this animal beside the road at night when it is out foraging.

The **small-spotted genet** (*Genetta genetta*) weighs in at just under 2kg (4lb). Its buff-coloured body is covered with small dark spots while its tail is ringed with black and has a white tip. It lives throughout almost all of

Grant's golden mole attacks a locust.

The **honey badger** or **ratel** (*Mellivora capensis*) is slightly larger and heavier than the Eurasian badger – 1 metre (3ft) in length and weighing in at about 12kg (26lb). It is black with a broad silvery-grey saddle stretching from the top of its head to the tip of its tail. This gives it a rather ghostly appearance at night when the legs are almost invisible and the animal appears to float along.

It is powerfully built with long sharp claws on its front feet. It is a nocturnal animal, usually seen alone or in pairs foraging for small mammals, invertebrates, birds, reptiles, bee larvae and honey. Its tough, thick skin helps considerably in its defence and it is fearless and aggressive in its dealings with other creatures in the bush.

SAND-SWIMMER

Many Namibian mammals have developed unique adaptations for survival in their dry, hot environment. One of the most fascinating is **Grant's golden mole** (*Eremitalpa granti*), a totally sightless yet ferocious predator only 8cm (3ins) long, endemic to the arid Namib Desert. Aided by its streamlined coat of silky pale yellow fur, this nocturnally active mole "swims" beneath the loose sand, covering up to 5km (3 miles) a night. This adaptation enables the mole to live without burrows in the sliding dune slipfaces, and also to sense through the sand the movements of its favourite prey – webfooted geckos, crickets and beetle larvae.

Namibia, apart from the desert regions, and preys on rodents, small birds, invertebrates and reptiles, hunting and foraging for fruit alone at night. It prefers to live in areas of bush, so that it can climb a tree if disturbed.

Varieties of mongoose

Finally, there are a number of mongooses in Namibia of which the best known is the **suricate** *(Suricata suricatta)* or meerkat. This small mongoose weighs just less than a kilogram (2lb) and is characterised by a silvery coat with dark bands across the back, a dark

diurnal animal and though it lives in warrens with others of its species, it forages individually, hunting for small mammals, invertebrates and sometimes birds.

Yellow mongooses are often seen crossing roads, and may also be spotted at some of the waterholes in Etosha, where they sometimes share the holes of ground squirrels.

The **slender mongoose** *(Galerella sanguinea)* often appears black when it is glimpsed running for cover. In fact it is reddish-brown, with short legs, a long sinuous body and a tail with a black tip. Like the yel-

A honey badger in the Kalahari.

burglar's mask, and rounded ears on the sides of its head. It is a diurnal animal, living co-operatively in a family of up to 30 in dens with many entrances.

When they first emerge in the morning, suricates take some time to warm up, standing on their hind legs and facing the sun. The group tends to forage as a pack, feeding on invertebrates and small reptiles. Baby-sitters look after any young in the den and look-outs warn the rest of the group if danger threatens.

Sometimes **yellow mongooses** *(Cynictus penicillata)* live alongside suricates, their slightly larger cousins. This mongoose is yellow with a white-tipped tail in the southern part of the country, which is greyer in the north. It is a

low mongoose, it is a solitary animal, hunting mainly insects during the day, and is often seen crossing roads.

Both the **banded mongoose** *(Mungos mungo*, weighing 1.4kg/3lb) and the **dwarf mongoose** *(Helogale parvula*, just 250g/8oz) live in the north of the country and both live in groups. The former is grey with dark bands on its back. It hunts during the day, foraging in open woodland under logs and bark in search of invertebrates and wild fruits. Dwarf mongooses are black or very dark brown and tend to live in old termite mounds scattered throughout the group range. Like many other mongoose species, it feeds on invertebrates, reptiles and small mammals.

An alert yellow mongoose in Etosha.

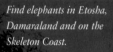
*Find elephants in Etosha,
Damaraland and on the
Skeleton Coast.*

GRAZERS AND BROWSERS

Namibia's vegetarians include the largest land
mammal, the world's tallest animal, aquatic antelopes
and rodent-like creatures related to the sea-cow.

Despite Namibia's aridity, it supports a splendid variety of herbivores. Foremost among these, the **African elephant** (*Loxodonta africana*) is probably the animal that gives wildlife watchers in Africa the most pleasure, thanks to its dextrous trunk, high level of intelligence and complex social system. It is also the biggest land mammal: weighing up to 6 tonnes and with a shoulder height of up to 4 metres (13ft). By standing up on its hind legs – something seen only occasionally – a big bull can reach higher than a giraffe.

The trunk can do most of the same delicate tasks as a human hand, as well as more strenuous work such as lifting logs or ripping bark. It is also used for sucking up water for drinking and bathing. Most adult African elephants have tusks, which are incisor teeth composed entirely of dentine and continue to grow throughout the animal's life. The large ears, rich in blood vessels, act like car radiators – waving them back substantially reduces the body temperature.

Elephants live in family units led by an elderly matriarch, with sisters, daughters, granddaughters and their offspring. Male elephants tend to live individually or in loose aggregations and are calmer and easier to approach than breeding herds with their vulnerable calves. Only when a bull elephant is in a mating condition (called *musth*, a state similar to oestrus in females) does it tend to be unpredictable. Bull elephants in this state are normally found within breeding herds where they seek out receptive females.

Elephants eat almost any vegetable matter and they often spend time by water, grazing the lush water plants growing there. The elephant's digestive system is very inefficient, so they have

A blue wildebeest in the morning sun at Etosha.

ELEPHANT MANAGEMENT

In some areas of Namibia's wilderness, desert-adapted elephants have come into conflict with local tribespeople. The elephants damage windmills, leaving people without access to water, then angry locals feel justified in shooting the animals. Fortunately, there are now volunteer projects set up to help local farmers build walls around their windmills which protects them but still allows the elephants to drink. Research by these volunteer groups can provide the government with invaluable information on elephant numbers and identifications, so they can manage desert elephants and lessen their chances of conflict with tribespeople.

The black rhinoceros is not black, any more than the white rhino is white. Zoologists today prefer to use the terms "narrow-lipped" or "hook-lipped" for the former, and "wide-lipped" for the latter.

to cram in as much food as possible, and sometimes feed for 16 hours out of 24. They also drink a great deal. A bull elephant will consume 230 litres (50 gallons) of water a day, taking on board 100 litres (22 gallons) at a time.

Giraffes are found in the north of the country.

Elephants are generally easy to see in Etosha, especially around many of the waterholes. You should also look out for them in the Caprivi Strip, where you may come across some of the big herds for which Botswana and Zimbabwe are well known. Namibia is noted, too, for its desert-adapted elephants, which live in Damaraland and the Skeleton Coast. Well adjusted to a desert existence, these animals sometimes go without water for four days.

Endangered giant

Another large mammal adapted to desert life is the **black rhinoceros** (*Diceros bicornis*), which stands 1.5 metres (5ft) at the shoulder and weighs up to a tonne. It is a large grey beast

with two horns, each a dense mass of hair (not attached to the skull), and ears in the shape of funnels. This is a browsing animal, using its prehensile upper lip to grasp food, which it cuts from shrubs with its premolars, giving bushes a rounded appearance in areas where it feeds frequently. The black rhino is short-tempered, and prone to charging.

Rhinos have been heavily poached in the past, both for traditional Asian medicine and for dagger handles for Yemenis. Fortunately the latter market is now in decline as other materials have become fashionable but poaching

Burchell's zebra (mountain zebra have a fold of skin on the throat).

continues, particularly in neighbouring South Africa, where the more common and conspicuous white rhino accounts fir the vast majority of killings. The global black rhino population hit its nadir in the 1980s, since when it has climbed back to around 4,500. Anti-poaching schemes in Namibia, pioneered by Save The Rhino Trust Fund, have included intense monitoring, involving local communities in helping to protect the animals and cutting off their horns to remove temptation. Namibia made controversial headlines in 2014 when it auctioned a hunting permit for an elderly 'surplus male' for US$350,000 to raise money for conservation efforts. Etosha is one of the easiest places to see black rhinos in the wild. They are often spotted at the floodlit waterholes at the rest camps and may be seen at dusk or daybreak moving to and from water in the coolness of the day.

Zebra and giraffe

The **Hartmann's mountain zebra** *(Equus zebra hartmannae)* is a Namibian endemic that thrives in arid places. It lives mainly in the mountainous hinterland between the coastal desert and the plateau in the interior. This is a tall, lean zebra, 1.5 metres (5ft) tall at the shoulder and weighing 300kg (660lb). It

numbers congregate at waterholes in Etosha National Park and the Caprivi Strip.

It is impossible to confuse the **giraffe** *(Giraffa camelopardalis)* with any other animal in Namibia. The tallest creature on earth, a male can measure over 5.5 metres (18ft) and weigh up to 1,200kg (1.2 tons). The giraffe lives in the north of the country where there is sufficient savannah woodland to provide its essential browse, but it is not unusual to see giraffe some distance away from trees of any size.

Giraffe live in loose aggregations and, because of their great height, are able to maintain visual

The springbok is the most common antelope in Namibia.

> *The giraffe's black tongue is the longest of any mammal's – 45cm (18ins) – and mobile enough to curl round the tips of branches.*

lacks the "shadow stripes" of Burchell's zebra and is more nomadic, moving on when food is scarce.

The **Burchell's zebra** *(Equus burchelli)* is smaller, standing 1.3 metres (4ft 3ins) at the shoulder and weighing around 315kg (700lb). Its stripes are wider than the mountain zebra's and there are grey "shadow stripes" between the black stripes. It lives in the north, thriving in open woodland or grassland, and significant

contact over much greater distances than other mammals. They are plentiful in Etosha and can also be seen in the Caprivi Strip.

Antelopes large and small

The **oryx** *(Oryx gazella)* is frequently known by its Afrikaans name of **gemsbok** (pronounce the "g" like a guttural "h"). It is a heavily built antelope, weighing up to 240kg (530lb). The upper parts of its body are buff, its belly white, and a broad black line divides the two. It also has a black band down the centre of its back and a black tail. Its distinctive face is black with a broad mask of white and a white nose. Both sexes of the creatures have long, straight horns, which form a V-shape on the top of the head. It is generally seen in small groups in the desert, but it forms larger herds at waterholes in Etosha, where fighting between males is a fairly frequent occurrence.

Like many of Namibia's desert-dwellers, the gemsbok is well adapted to arid conditions, and it may be seen climbing sand dunes where there is not a speck of green. Mainly a grazer, it also digs up succulent roots and eats wild melons for their water. It grazes at night, when lower temperatures lead to an increase in the vegetation's water content. (Even dead grass that has been baked by the sun all day can absorb 40

In Etosha they may form very large herds and can often be seen during the heat of the day when they are least active, crowded into what little shade the thorn trees offer.

The handsome **kudu** *(Tregalaphus strepsiceros)* is 1.4 metres (4ft 6ins) at the shoulder and weighs up to 250kg (55lb). It has a buff grey body with a few vertical off-white stripes, a white V-shaped marking on the face, large, veined ears and, on the male, a wonderful pair of spiral horns. A creature of scrub and savannah woodland, it possesses an uncanny ability to hide in the sparsest of cover, and is

A greater kudu bull; kudus are adept at hiding in sparse cover to avoid enemies.

percent of its weight in airborne moisture during the night.) The gemsbok also produces concentrated urine, to preserve fluid, and allows its body temperature to rise without sweating. It can, quite simply, survive without drinking.

The **springbok** *(Antidorcas marsupialis)* is another desert antelope, standing about 75cm (30ins) at the shoulder and weighing 37kg. It has a chestnut back, a white belly and a darker brown band dividing the two. Its face is largely white with a black band running through its eyes towards its muzzle. Its ears are long and both sexes carry lyre-shaped horns.

Springbok are both browsers and grazers but they only drink when water is available, surviving on the moisture in their food at other times.

sufficiently athletic to clear a 2-metre (6ft) fence with ease. It lives in small groups and is most active in the cooler times of the day.

The **impala** *(Aepyceros melampus)* is an elegant, lightly built antelope, found in the Caprivi Strip area. It stands 90cm (3ft) at the shoulder and weighs around 50kg (110lb), a browny reddish animal with a pale belly and black markings around the tail and on the heels. The male has a pair of gracefully curved lyre-shaped horns.

A distinct subspecies, near-endemic to Namibia, is the **black-faced impala** *(Aepyceros melampus petersi)*, found exclusively around Etosha. It is heavier and darker than the common impala and, as its name suggests, has a dark blaze on its face.

Namibia's smallest rodent is the desert pygmy mouse (Mus indutus), which measures 10cm (4ins) from nose to tail, and weighs just 6 grams (0.25 oz).

The **red hartebeest** (*Alcelaphus buselaphus*) is a chestnut-coloured antelope with whitish flanks measuring 125cm (4ft) at the shoulder and weighing around 150kg (330lb). Both sexes have horns that grow upwards and then backwards from the forehead. It occurs in northeast Namibia, preferring fairly open country, and often drinks at waterholes on the western end of the Etosha Pan.

An inhabitant of rocky areas, the **klipspringer** (*Oreotragus oreotragus*) is a small, stocky antelope that grows to about 60cm (2ft) at the shoulder. It walks on the tips of its hooves like a dancer on points. These dainty feet allow it to move through its habitat with grace and ease. Generally living in pairs, it is sometimes visible in the river gorges of the Namib-Naukluft National Park.

An even smaller antelope, the **Damara dik-dik** (*Madoqua kirkii*), is no bigger than a medium-sized dog – only 38cm (15ins) at the shoulder, and 5kg (11lb) in weight. It is yellowish grey in colour with a tuft of hair on its forehead, a long, shrew-like snout and large glands below the eyes. This species is endemic to Namibia and is found in the central and northern areas in thick scrub. Look out for it in Etosha, where it is quite common, but difficult to spot.

Squirrels and mice

The **ground squirrel** (*Xerus inauris*) is a common resident of Namibia's most arid areas. Its kidneys are among the most efficient in the animal kingdom when it comes to conserving water, and because of this it can survive without drinking throughout the dry season, which can last up to a year in the desert.

It is a small grey rodent with a single white stripe along its sides and a bushy tail, which it can use as a sunshade when necessary. Colonies of up to 30 animals live in burrows which are sometimes shared with mongooses, a partnership that benefits both species – while the vegetarian ground squirrel is the pioneering type, given to digging extensive warrens, the mongoose is an alert predator with a dislike of snakes, which it will attack fearlessly.

The **tree mouse** (*Thallomys paedulcus*) is a small grey-yellow rodent with white underparts and dark rings of fur around the eyes. Its other distinguishing feature is a tail that is longer than the head and body together. As the name suggests, tree mice are totally arboreal, living in holes in trees or abandoned birds' nests. Although they prefer acacia trees, they live throughout Namibia's savannah woodlands.

The **rock hyrax** or **dassie** (*Procavia capensis*) is a curious brown animal that resembles a large guinea pig, about 60cm (2ft) long and weighing in at 4kg (9lb). Scientists, at a loss to

Ground squirrels live in burrows.

classify this unusual creature, have placed it and its close relatives in their own order, the Hyracoidea. Their evolutionary development is quite distinct from the rodents they resemble – in fact, unlikely as it may seem, their closest living relatives are probably the elephant and the dugong or sea cow.

Hyraxes live in colonies among rocks and feed on whatever vegetation grows nearby. You have a good chance of seeing them in rocky areas in the south of Namibia, such as around Hardap Dam. White urine stains on the rocks are a sure sign that dassies are around.

Hippos spend all day in the water.

Water-loving mammals

A number of mammals are found only in the Caprivi area. These usually demand wetter conditions than are generally available in the rest of Namibia and consequently tend to overlap into neighbouring Botswana's Okavango Delta. The largest and most obvious of these is the **hippopotamus** (*Hippopotamus amphibius*), a 1.5-tonne barrel-shaped herbivore. It spends its days semi-submerged in rivers and waterholes and likes these to be deep enough for it to sink out of sight if danger threatens. Hippos emerge in the evening to graze, returning to the safety of water during the day. Dominant bulls mark their territories by scattering dung with a vigorous flicking of the tail. Being large and lying

around in "schools" of around 12 or more, hippos are easily seen in the rivers of the Caprivi.

The **African** or **Cape buffalo** (*Syncerus caffer*) is a massive, black, ox-like animal that weighs about 750kg (0.75 tonne). It has impressive horns, especially on the male. Buffaloes need abundant grass, shade and water to survive and live in large herds, often several hundred strong. They seek shade during the day, and move to and from water at dawn and dusk. They love to wallow, especially the old males which often live in a solitary state and are notorious for being dangerous if disturbed accidentally, charging blindly at the perceived danger.

The **red lechwe** (*Kobus leche*) is limited to the Okavango and surrounding areas. It is a chestnut-coloured water-loving antelope, about 1 metre (3ft) to the shoulder and weighing 100kg (22lb). The male has elegant lyre-shaped horns, but its special distinction is elongated hooves to assist it when walking in muddy places. Lechwe are generally seen resting on dry ground during the day but feed in shallow water, and will flee into the water if disturbed.

An even more specialist water antelope is the **sitatunga** (*Tragelaphus spekei*), slightly larger than the lechwe and confined to almost the same region. It has a long, coarse brownish coat with white markings on the face, neck, chest and feet, and the male has spiralling horns. The most aquatic of antelopes, it spends most of its time in dense reed beds, in water up to 1 metre (3ft) deep. Widely splayed hooves enable it to walk on mats of reeds and other floating vegetation, and it often lies up in reed beds, trampling down the stems to form a platform.

WARTS AND ALL

No African scene is complete without at least one **warthog** (*Phacochoerus aethiopicus*). Often described as grotesque, but not without appeal, this grey, bristling pig weighs around 100kg (220lb) and has large wart-like protuberances on the sides of its face. An adult's canine teeth develop into curved tusks. A group or "sounder" of warthogs usually consists of sows and their young, or unattached bachelors. They are active during the day, feeding on grasses and roots, often kneeling to graze, but will scuttle away when you approach, their thin tails held erect. They spend their nights underground, generally in aardvark holes.

How to Spot Wildlife

Whether you are on an organised safari or driving yourself through Namibia's game reserves, it pays to take a proactive role in spotting wildlife.

For lions and other predators, early morning and late afternoon are best for game drives. Most predators are largely nocturnal, but they tend to remain quite active for an hour or so after dawn, and may also start moving about a short while before sunset. These cooler hours of the day are also when you are most likely to witness action and interaction, such as cubs playing together or adults grooming. Other good reasons to be out and about at this time of day are the high level of avian activity, and superb photographic light (except in overcast weather).

In a sunny climate like Namibia's, animals generally prefer to lie or stand in the shade. In open country, always scan the ground below isolated trees, and in thicker vegetation make an effort to look into the dense bush rather than letting your eyes follow openings through it. Most animals drink at least once daily, usually from mid-morning onwards so it's worth stopping at any accessible watering point in the hope it might attract thirsty wildlife. If things look quiet at first, switch off the engine and wait for a few minutes to see what happens.

In some private reserves, or parks where dangerous animals are thin on the ground, it is possible to track wildlife on foot. This is an exciting way to see animals, far more involving than game drives, since the slower pace and silence allow you to tune into to sounds, smells and textures, and to focus on birds and insects.

Animals that are habituated to vehicles might be a lot less relaxed when they encounter human pedestrians, so try to blend in – wear neutral colours such as green, grey or khaki, remove brightly coloured accessories, avoid applying artificial scents, and talk as softly as possible, or keep silent.

Whether in a car or on foot, experienced trackers often locate predators by using indirect clues. Circling vultures often point towards a recent kill, while baboon or impala alarm calls might indicate that a lion or leopard is lurking somewhere out of sight. Likewise, a freshly steaming pat of roadside dung combined with torn-off branches and other destroyed vegetation is a telltale sign of recent elephant activity. And if you locate a trail of fresh predator paw prints on a muddy or sandy road, it is probably worth following, as lions and other animals frequently follow roads as they would a natural animal trail.

For the novice, picking out a predator's spoor might be easier said than done. Dirt roads are often criss-crossed by a profusion of animal tracks, the majority of which are made by antelopes or other cloven hoofed ungulates. Typically, these look like an inverted elongated heart, split

The African elephant, an impressive sight.

lengthwise down the middle, and they might be anything from 2cm (1.3 inches) long in the case of a duiker to 20cm (8 inches) for a buffalo.

Predator prints also comprise an inverted heart shape, but there is no central split, and it is topped by four oblong or circular toe marks. To identify what made the print, look at the size – 10cm (4 inches) or longer, for instance, would narrow the option to a lion or spotted hyena – and check for the triangular claw marks that are present in the case of any mongoose, dog or hyena, but absent in genets and all cats other than cheetah.

For the uninitiated, it is possible to confuse primate and carnivore prints, but the former more closely resemble a human footprint and have five clearly defined toes.

NAMIBIA'S BIRDS

From seashore to arid desert, from savannah to riverine forest, the varied landscape is home to a wide diversity of birds.

The diversity of habitats in Namibia is reflected in the number of birds found there. A total of 706 bird species have now been recorded in the country, of which one, the dune lark, is endemic (found nowhere else in the world) and 14 are near endemic (more than 95 percent of their range lies within Namibia). More than 500 species breed locally, the remainder being migrants.

Coastal habitats include rocky and sandy shores, lagoons and saltworks (the latter are found in all of Namibia's major coastal towns, and have a pronounced effect on the local bird populations). These give rise to some remarkable birds, from the **great white pelican** *(Pelecanus onocrotalus)*, so characteristic of the coastline round here, to the **greater** and **lesser flamingos** *(Phoenicopterus ruber and Phoeniconaias minor)* which occur in very great numbers along these shores, and whose sonorous honking can be heard all night when the tides are right for night-time foraging.

The dramatic plumage of the crimson-breasted shrike.

A distinctive bird of prey found in the semi-desert is the bateleur. It has the shortest tail of any eagle, so rocks from side to side as it flies, hence the name: bateleur is French for an acrobat of sorts.

Birdwatchers in these coastal regions can also expect to see large skeins of **cormorants** *(four species)*, accompanied by **Cape gannets** *(Morus capensis)* flying offshore. Closer inshore, enthusiasts are quite likely to encounter several species of terns and gulls, the most common of which are the **kelp gull** *(Larus dominicanus)* and **Hartlaub's gull** *(Larus hartlaubii)*.

One of the most interesting birds of the Namib coast is the tiny **Damara tern** *(Sterna balaenarum)*, whose world population numbers only about 7,000 individuals. They breed along the Namib coast in summer and migrate northwards to Nigeria in autumn. Their nest consists of a shallow scraper on the gravel plains of the desert, usually a couple of kilometres (1 mile) inland. Only one egg is laid; shortly after hatching, the chick leaves the nest and wanders about, probably to avoid predators such as black-backed jackals which are common in the region. Parents and offspring keep in touch through contact calls. The main threats to the survival of the Damara tern are habitat loss and the large number of thoughtless off-road drivers who crush the eggs.

African penguins (*Spheniscus demersus*) are occasionally seen near the shore, but these delightful birds prefer to forage out to sea, breeding on islands off the coast. Their call is a loud, donkey-like bray.

Desert habitats

The gravel plains north of the Kuiseb River and the sand dune complex to the south support a small but distinctive bird population. The most obvious of these is the **ostrich** (*Struthio camelus*), the world's largest bird, which occurs in large numbers in even the most barren habitats,

display in the breeding season. It inflates its throat to fan out white neck feathers, arches its tail up along its back and emits a deep "oom-oom-oom" call.

Rüppell's korhaan (*Eupodotis rueppellii*), found almost exclusively in the Namib desert, is nicknamed the desert frog because of its strange croaking call.

A number of raptors including the lovely little **red-necked falcon** (*Falco chicquera*) turn up in this area. So too do several species of larks, buntings and chats which are of particular interest to keen birdwatchers since many of the

White pelicans are numerous on the coast.

and may often be spotted in the distance, running elegantly through the desert mirage. They are usually seen in pairs or groups, sometimes with large crêches of young birds.

Equally memorable, though much smaller, is the **Namaqua sandgrouse** (*Pterocles namaqua*), huge flocks of which can be seen making spectacular daily visits to desert waterholes. This little bird is related to the pigeon, but it has a longer tail and lovely sand-speckled markings.

Other birds found in these areas include the stately bustards and korhaans. Frequently seen in Etosha is the **kori bustard** (*Ardeotis kori*), reputedly the largest flying bird in the world – although it is reluctant to take to the air unless threatened. The male has a dramatic

DRINKS CARRIER

The Namaqua sandgrouse is well adapted to its arid environment, having evolved a method of collecting water for its young and transporting it over long distances. (There is precious little liquid to be obtained from the bird's usual diet of dry seeds.)

The adult sandgrouse's breast feathers are specially modified to absorb and hold moisture. The bird visits a waterhole in the early morning and completely immerses its breast in water, then flies back to the nest site – up to 50km (30 miles) away – laden with precious liquid, which the chicks then release by nibbling at the parent's breast feathers.

creatures are extremely specialised and limited in their distribution.

The semi-desert escarpment

An important area for near-endemics in Namibia is the transition zone between the desert and the arid savannahs. These include the **Damara hornbill** *(Tockus damarensis)*, a plain-faced form of the charismatic red-billed hornbill that was recently elevated from sub-specific status to be listed as a full species.

Other birds found here include a small green and pink-marked member of the parrot family

The martial eagle (Polemaetus bellicosus), *one of the largest birds of prey.*

much loved by cage bird enthusiasts, the **rosy-collared** or **rosy-faced lovebird** *(Agapornis roseicollis)*, which is generally found in small and quite noisy groups and, because it needs to drink regularly, is never too far from water.

Also look out for that striking, self-assured little harlequin, the **white-tailed shrike** *(Lanioturdus torquatus)*, and the **rockrunner or Damara Rock-jumper** *(Achaetops pycnopygius)*, a small brown bird with an enchanting liquid call, which scuttles around rocky outcrops like a mouse, darting for cover into grass. Other species you may see here include **Hartlaub's francolin** *(Pternistis hartlaubi)*, often seen in small groups scurrying over rocks, **Bradfield's swift** *(Apus bradfieldi)*, the cackling **violet**

wood-hoopoe *(Phoeniculus damarensis)*, and the tiny **Herero chat** *(Namibornis herero)*.

The arid savannah

The southern Kalahari, the central highlands and the north-central regions reaching as far north as the Etosha National Park all comprise a number of acacia-dominated vegetation types. One of the most striking species of birds found in places in these regions is the **sociable weaver** *(Philetairus socius)*. This species is noticeable mainly for its communal nests, which are enormous structures woven from twigs into the

Violet-eared waxbills (Uraeginthus granatinus).

shape of a dome. Straw is then used to fill in the gaps, giving the nest a thatched appearance, and to make separate chambers inside the communal nest. You'll often come across them weighing down substantial branches of sturdy trees, or even wrecking telephone poles; some nests have been in continuous use for up to 100 years. These nests can attract squatters, too. Other bird

The African skimmer gets its name from its fishing technique – flying low with its bottom jaw dipped just below the water. If it sees a fish, the bird snaps its bill closed, neatly trapping its prey.

species who use them include rosy-faced love-birds and tiny grey **pygmy falcons** *(Polihierax semitorquatus)*, whose entrance holes can be distinguished from those of the weavers by their coating of white droppings. Telephone poles are also good places to spot a **pale chanting goshawk** *(Melierax canorus)*, a light grey bird with long orange legs and orange base to the bill, which uses these poles as hunting perches.

Keep an eye out for dramatically marked **crimson-breasted shrikes** *(Laniarius atrococcineus)*, black and white above, with an improbably scarlet breast (or, rarely, a buttercup yellow *monteiri)*, all characterised by long, heavy, downward-curving bills, some with a casque on the upper mandible.

The dry woodlands

The northeast of Namibia comprises one of the country's smallest habitats, but it does contain spectacular species of deciduous trees, growing from a substrate of deep sand. In these areas you can expect to see interesting raptors, from the **little banded goshawk** *(Accipiter badius)* to its cousins the **gabar** *(Micronisus gabar)* and the **dark chanting goshawk** *(Melierax metabates)*.

Rosy-faced lovebirds are found in semi-desert areas.

one), and dainty **violet-eared waxbills** *(Uraeginthus granatinus)*, with distinctive violet cheeks.

Other residents of these parts include **helmeted guineafowl** *(Numida meleagris)*, noisy grey birds with blue faces and red caps which live in flocks and look especially comical as they bustle along in single file, and the enchanting **lilac-breasted roller** *(Coracias cordata)* and **purple roller** *(Coracias naevia)*. The former is more conspicuous than its quieter cousin, but both perform spectacular and noisy display flights of rolling aerobatics – hence the name.

These areas are also very much characterised by **hornbills** including the **African grey** *(Tockus nasutus)*, **southern yellow-billed** *(Tockus leucomelas)* and **Monteiro's** *(Tockus*

HORNBILL HIDEAWAY

The hornbills have unusual nesting habits. The female lays her eggs in holes in trees, then seals herself completely into the nest with a mixture of mud and sticks, cemented together with saliva – presumably to ensure maximum safety while the eggs are incubated. She must then rely totally on the male to feed her through a small slit in the nest, and while incubating the eggs she moults all her wing and tail feathers.

Later, when the eggs have hatched, the female breaks out of the nest, and helps the male to feed the young. The young repair her escape-hole and remain incarcerated until they are ready to fly.

Then there are the **kingfishers**, including the **woodland** *(Halcyon senegalensis)* and the **grey-hooded** *(Halcyon leucocephala)* varieties; the latter's wings in flight are as brilliant in colour as the European kingfisher's, and take you by surprise in this waterless environment.

In forested areas, birds often rely heavily on vocalisation to locate other members of their species. Some of the birds in these dry woodlands have beautiful calls, for example, the liquid whistles of the **African golden oriole** *(Oriolus auratus)* and the **black-headed oriole** *(Oriolus larvatus)*, and the musical twitter of the **orange-**

Typical birds of the riverine forests include brightly coloured fruit-eaters like **Schalow's turaco** *(Tauraco schalowi)*, **Cape parrot** *(Poicephalus robustus)*, and **black-collared barbet** *(Lybius torquatus)*, and some attractively marked insectivores such as the **Natal or red-capped robin-chat** *(Cossypha natalensis)*, **tropical boubou** *(Laniarius bicolor)*, **grey-headed bush shrike** *(Malaconotus blanchoti)*, and the spectacular red and green marked **Narina trogon** *(Apaloderma narina)*, which has a booming hoot of a call.

Other remarkable birds include the handsome **African skimmer** *(Rynchops flavirostris)*, a

The Goliath Heron (Ardea goliath) is the world's largest heron.

breasted bush shrike *(Telophorus sulfureopectus)*.

The riverine forests

Namibia's inland wetlands consist of a varied collection of systems, ranging from perennial to episodic rivers, and from large man-made dams to ephemeral pans and small springs. The riverine forests here form a link with the tropical and eastern regions, where rainfall is higher.

A host of large and obvious birds are found by water: giants like the **goliath heron** *(Ardea goliath)*; smaller but wonderfully plumaged egrets such as the **great white egret** *(Egretta alba)*; and odd-looking species such as the **hamerkop** *(Scopus umbretta)* which builds a round haystack of a nest 2 metres (6ft) across.

large tern-like bird with dark brown upper parts, white underparts and a large orange-red bill. It can often be seen flying low over rivers with slow, leisurely wing beats.

Lucky birdwatchers may also be treated to a view of the magnificent **Pels fishing owl** *(Scotopelia peli)*, a gentle-looking giant of a creature which feeds on a diet of fish and crabs, along with the occasional small mammal. Look out for it on riverside tree branches, where it likes to roost and forage from.

Finally, no list would be complete without the **African fish eagle** *(Heliaeetus vocifer)*, which is common near water all over southern Africa, and whose haunting cry is powerfully evocative of the whole region.

The side-winding adder lives up to its name, leaving very distinctive tracks.

AMPHIBIANS AND REPTILES

From mighty crocodiles to tiny sand frogs – not to mention garish tortoises and lethal snakes – Namibia has no shortage of cold-blooded inhabitants.

Namibia's great variation in altitude, geomorphology, regional rainfall levels and associated vegetation are reflected in its extraordinary reptilian diversity. Species associated with the tropics are found in the northern Kunene and Kavango Rivers, notably the impressive **Nile crocodile** *(Crocodylus niloticus)*, which can reach 6.5 metres (20ft) in length and weigh 1 tonne (2,200lbs), feeding mainly on fish when young but taking larger mammals as an adult.

The **Nile monitor** *(Varanus niloticus)*, the longest African lizard at 2 metres (6ft), shares the same habitat as crocodiles, and is known to dig up their nests to feed on the eggs. The **African soft-shelled turtle** *(Trionyx triunguis)* is also found in the Kunene River, and **green turtles** *(Chelonia mydas)* collect in the warm river mouth to escape the cold Benguela current.

Travelling by car, especially after rainfall, it's not unusual, to come across a large **leopard tortoise** *(Geochelone pardalis)* on the road. It is a good idea to stop and move it off the tarmac into some roadside grass where it cannot be seen, for many Namibians regard it as a delicacy. While the leopard tortoise is widespread throughout Africa, the **Nama padloper** tortoise *(homopus sp.)* is endemic to Namibia.

Chameleons and geckos

If you are lucky, you may spot a **Namaqua chameleon** *(Chamaeleo namaquensis)*, one of 55 endemic reptile species, moving stealthily through the desert to which it is adapted. Entirely terrestrial, this chameleon feeds on insects and even lizards. The fact that it can actually run for a short distance is just one of its peculiarities.

A blue-headed agama basks on a rock.

The arid parts are particularly rich in specially adapted species. There are a great number of geckos, many with a very restricted range. Most unusual are the two species of **web-footed gecko** *(Palmatogecko sp)* that inhabit the wind-blown Namib sands. The webbed toes of these delicately marked nocturnal animals enable them to walk nimbly up the slip-face of shifting dunes and, in particular, to dig burrows in the fine sand to escape the deadly heat of the day.

Six species of diurnal geckos are commonly found in the Namib. Their perfect camouflage enables them to remain unnoticed most of the time but, if they are spotted, they will quickly dive under a rock for shelter. Come sunset, the clicking chorus of the nocturnal common barking gecko (*Ptenopus garrulus*)), calling from their burrows, help make those nights under the Southern Cross ever so memorable.

A variety of snakes

Other Namib endemics include Peringuey's side-winding adder (*Bitis peringueyi*), which has evolved a number of characteristics to enable it to thrive in a desert environment. Its eyes are on the top of its head so that, when it sinks into the sand to escape detection or the

Aggressive Cape cobra (Naja nivea) with flattened hood in the Kalahari desert.

heat of the sun, it still has a view of the world. It also has a lateral "side-winding" motion that enables it to move up sand dunes as steep as 45°. Other species of dwarf adders also occur, some, such as the **horned adder** (*Bitis caudalis*), with horn-like scales above their eyes. None is seriously poisonous, but they are in great demand from snake-lovers, who like to keep them in their terrariums.

Snakes that are more dangerous or even fatal to humans, such as the **puff adder** (*Bitis arietans arietans*), **Cape cobra** (*Naja nivea*), **zebra spitting cobra** (*Naja a nigricincta*) and **black mamba** (*Dendroaspis polylepis*) are seldom encountered. The last three will

> *When cornered, the spitting cobra discharges its venom, aiming at the eyes of the presumed enemy. It is acutely painful and, unless you wash your eyes out quickly, can cause lasting damage.*

generally make themselves scarce if you approach them, but puff adders often lie on or beside paths, relying on their camouflage to escape detection, and it is then that the unwary may be bitten.

Like the leopard tortoise, snakes are most commonly seen on roads, either crossing as swiftly as the flitting shadow of a passing bird, or coiled up in the evening on the tarmac when they relish the warmth stored in the blacktop during the day. Many are killed at this time and their crushed bodies at the roadside offer the opportunity to inspect these often beautifully marked reptiles in safety – but do make sure they are dead before going too near!

The rare and infrequently seen **Angola dwarf python** (*Python anchetae*) lives in the mountainous areas from the northwest of Windhoek into Angola. In the same habitat lives a very active endemic, the diurnal **western rock agama** (*Agama anchietae*). The male, with its orange head and tail and black or blue body, tends to sit in a dominant position on a rock, from where, with bobbing head, it scans its territory for a yellow-headed female or other males which might want to challenge him.

DESERT AMPHIBIANS

You wouldn't expect arid Namibia to be thriving with amphibious life, and for most of the year you'd be right. But in wetter years, ephemeral pools formed after rain give frogs a brief window to lay eggs and for tadpoles to metamorphose into the adult form, an unusually rapid process enhanced by the sun-warmed water. These include the pugnacious African bullfrog (*Pyxicephalus adspersus*), the world's second-largest amphibian, and Lelande's sand frog (*Tomoptema delelanii*), whose melodious trilling call, combined with the snoring croak of the guttural toad, provide the aural backdrop to summer nights around a Namibian campfire.

Cool chameleon.

Quiver Tree Forest, Keetmanshoop.

PLANT LIFE

A wide range of curious plants thrive in Namibia's diverse habitats, including species that manage to live where there is minimal rainfall.

In the dry season, a visitor might have the impression that Namibia is almost barren and its vegetation is monochromatically drab. Broad expanses of golden-brown grass, rugged mountainsides and plains dotted sparsely with scrub are characteristic of many regions of this desert land. But as spring begins, in August and September, acacias such as the **camelthorn** *(Acacia erioloba)* deck themselves out with mimosa-like bunches of flowers. After months without rain, this reawakening always seems like a miracle.

When the first rainfall comes, generally in October, broad, dusty plains are transformed overnight by a covering of green fuzz. In a few days, this has developed into a thick yellow carpet of **morning stars** or **devil's thorn** *(Tribulus zeyheri)* mainly on disturbed ground, especially roadsides and around waterholes, while countless bulbs and buds quickly unfold colourful flowers. Annual plants suddenly appear, ornamented with magnificent flowers of every

Acacia erioloba.

Although most acacias are trees, the waterthorn Acacia nebrownii grows in small bushy clumps. In the evenings its yellow balls of blossom waft a sweet fragrance across the savannah.

colour and transform the veld. Some 2,400 flowering plants, along with 345 different grass species, have been recorded in Namibia.

The cold Benguela Current, which runs along the entire coast, prevents rainfall from the west. The result is a strip of desert running northwards from the Orange River on the southern boundary to the Kunene River on the border with Angola – the Southern, Central and Northern Namib. This can be further split into the 56km- (35-mile-) wide coastal belt, which receives almost no rainfall but obtains some moisture from coastal fogs, and the eastern semi-desert, which gets a meagre 50–100mm (2–4ins) of rainfall annually.

In the transition area between the two, the famous **welwitschia** plants *(Welwitschia mirabilis)* sprawl across the sand, their twin leaves shredded by the wind. Some of these living fossils are over 1,000 years old. Other desert dwellers include several species of **stone plants** *(Lithops spp.)*, also known as Bushmen's buttocks, which look like stones until their beautiful flowers emerge.

More humble but tremendously important for the desert ecosystem are the two species of **ganna** or **brack-bush**: *Salsola aphylla*, which grows in seasonal riverbeds, and the dune-loving *Salsola nollothensis*. Apparently growing on top of a dune, ganna actually grows first and the dune forms around it, helping to retain moisture and protect it from the wind.

In dune areas, especially around Sossusvlei, you should come across that staple of the Namib desert, the **!nara melon** (*Acanthosicyos horridus*), a Namibian endemic. It has protective stems with long, bare, evil-looking thorns

the western half of Ovamboland. Here, **mopane** (*Colophospermum mopane*) appears as shrubs or trees. Although apparently providing welcome shade in the middle of the day, the mopane often fools the innocent traveller for its paired leaves fold together to save moisture, thus casting little shade, while small black mopane bees descend on any source of moisture and collect, irritatingly, around the eyes and nose. The dry river beds, or *arroyos*, are lined with white-flowering **ana trees** (*Faidherbia albida*) which can easily reach heights of 15 metres (50ft).

Stone plants look more like pebbles than plants – until they bloom in the rainy season.

but somehow oryx, brown hyena and porcupine penetrate its defences in order to get to the watery melon.

Slightly further inland are two more noteworthy plants. One is the **elephant's foot** (*Adenia pechuelii*), which grows among rocks and has a thick grey-green stem about a metre (3ft) tall with woody twigs on top. The second is *Euphorbia damarana*, quite a large plant with many individual, grey-white stems whose milky latex is poisonous to man – although black rhino and gemsbok eat it without ill effect.

In the north of Namibia, the semi-desert gives way to the mopane savannah, which characterises mountainous Kaokoland and

Among the dark red rocks and kopjes in this area, **sterculia** trees (*Sterculia quinqueloba*) are common. Their thin, light grey, bark is made even whiter by a white bloom that covers it as an adaptation to the dry climate. They stand out in graphic contrast to the dark, rocky background. In the same general habitat are what appear to be small baobab trees. In fact they are **moringas** (*Moringa ovalifolia*), whose bloated trunks and branches resemble the general pattern normally made by roots – giving rise to the legend that they have been planted upside-down.

In many areas where there is enough water, especially on the Kunene, tall **makalani palms** (*Hyphaene petersiana*) with their odd but strangely appealing scent grace the landscape. In the rainy season, the area is regularly flooded, and various beautiful water plants spring up, including water lilies, different types of *Aponogeton*, and the mimosa-like *Neptunia oleracia*, whose feathery petals close at the slightest touch.

The northern Kalahari consists for the most part of an open dry forest, which reaches all the way to the Caprivi Strip. In the Kavango region the **false mopane** *(Guibourtia coleosperma)* or oshivi tree and others are harvested and used by the Kabangos for their woodcarvings.

> The hard fruits of the makalani palm are known as vegetable ivory. They are frequently carved into ornaments with animal motifs.

Bordering on southern Ovamboland, Etosha National Park is dominated by the eponymous pan, a salt desert that supports almost no vegetation. Only in the west, after the rainy season, is it lightly bedecked with a species of salt-loving grass. To the north and west, this basin is bordered by grassy plains and to the south, by a savannah of small shrubs.

Here, at the beginning of the rainy season, **omuparara** trees *(Pettophorum africanum)* explode into yellow blossom; in autumn, the **purple-pod terminalia** *(Terminalia prunioides)* leaves large red blotches of colour on the landscape. **Marula** trees *(Sclerocarya birrea)* produce fruits that are a particular favourite of elephants. It is probably a myth that they become drunk by eating them when they are fermenting, although marula fruit is turned into a creamy liqueur for human consumption.

Further east in Bushmanland you may come across the **poison grub tree** *(Commiphora africana)* under which are found *Diamphidia* beetles. The Bushmen dip the shafts of their arrows in the deadly juice of these insects but keep the tips clean in case they stab themselves accidentally.

The central highlands, with altitudes of up to 2,000 metres (6,560ft), are the highest part of Namibia. Characteristic plants here include the **mountain thorn** *(Acacia hereroensis)* and **wild sage** *(Pechuela loschea-lubnitzia)*. In the spring, the **worm-bark tree** *(Albizia antheimintica)* is thickly covered with large yellow blooms which resemble downy chicks.

South of here, once you leave the mountains at Rehoboth, the broad expanses are covered by dwarf shrub savannah. Here, large trees can only be found in dry riverbeds in small stands. The **quiver-tree** *(Aloe dichotoma)* is an exception. An aloe rather than a true tree, it grows to a reasonable size, and its branches, hollowed of their cellular interiors, were once modified by Bushmen to make quivers. It is possible to make out its distinctive mushroom shape on plains and stony hillsides, especially in May when it has shining yellow blossoms.

The succulent desert plant Phyllobolus digitata.

SAUSAGE TREES AND BAOBABS

Two of Africa's most spectacular trees are common in northeast Namibia. Most noticeable in the Caprivi Strip, the sausage tree *(Kigelia africana)* has exquisite blood-red, velveteen flowers, but is named after the large elongated fruits that hang from the branches and occasionally drop to the ground, to be eaten by the likes of rhino and baboon. No less striking are the baobab trees *(Adansonia digitata)*, ancient bulbous giants whose enormously thick trunks have an edible pulp eaten by elephants. Even when they are totally hollow, baobabs somehow survive, supported by their shell of bark.

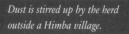
*Dust is stirred up by the herd
outside a Himba village.*

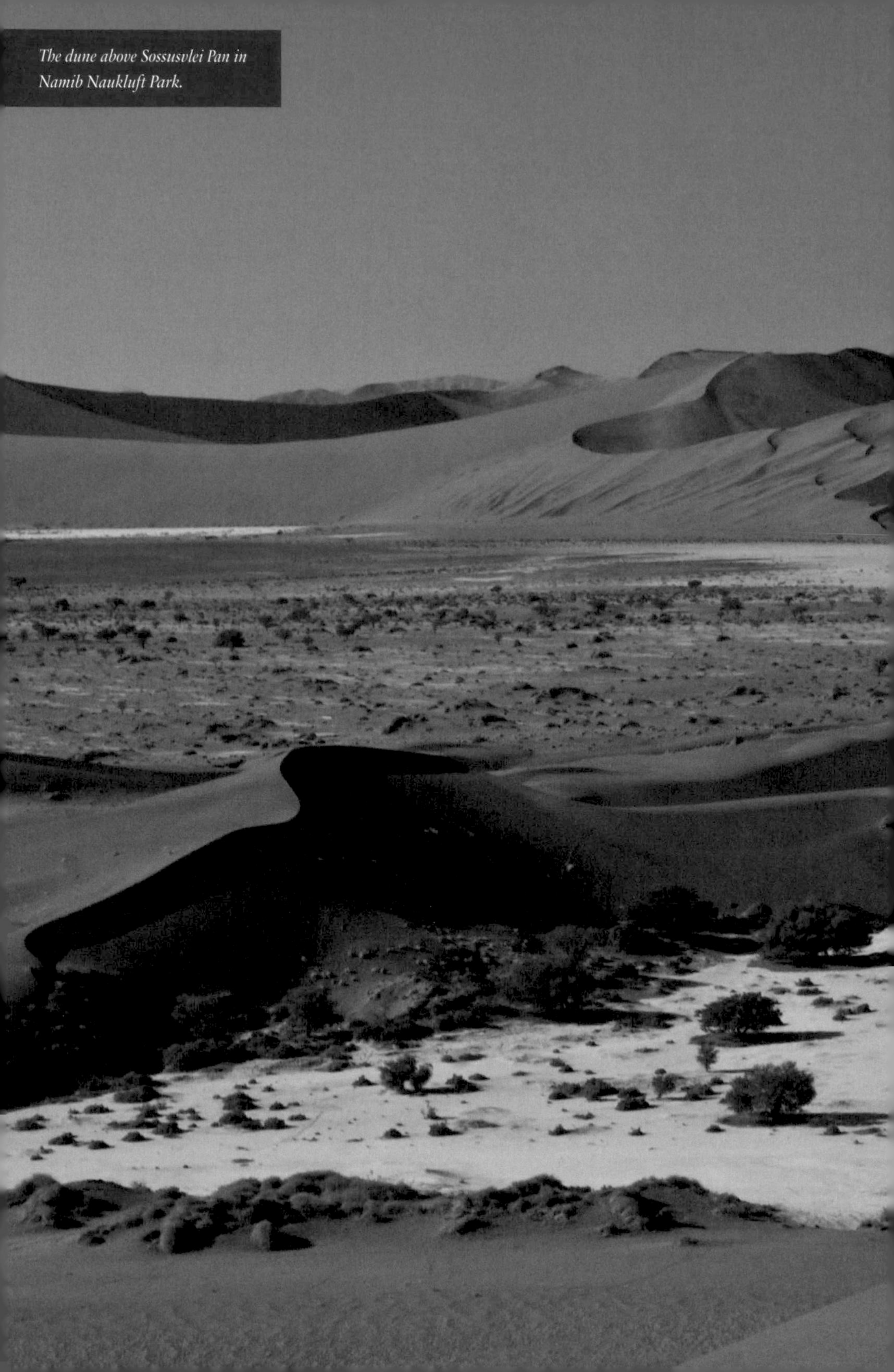

The dune above Sossusvlei Pan in Namib Naukluft Park.

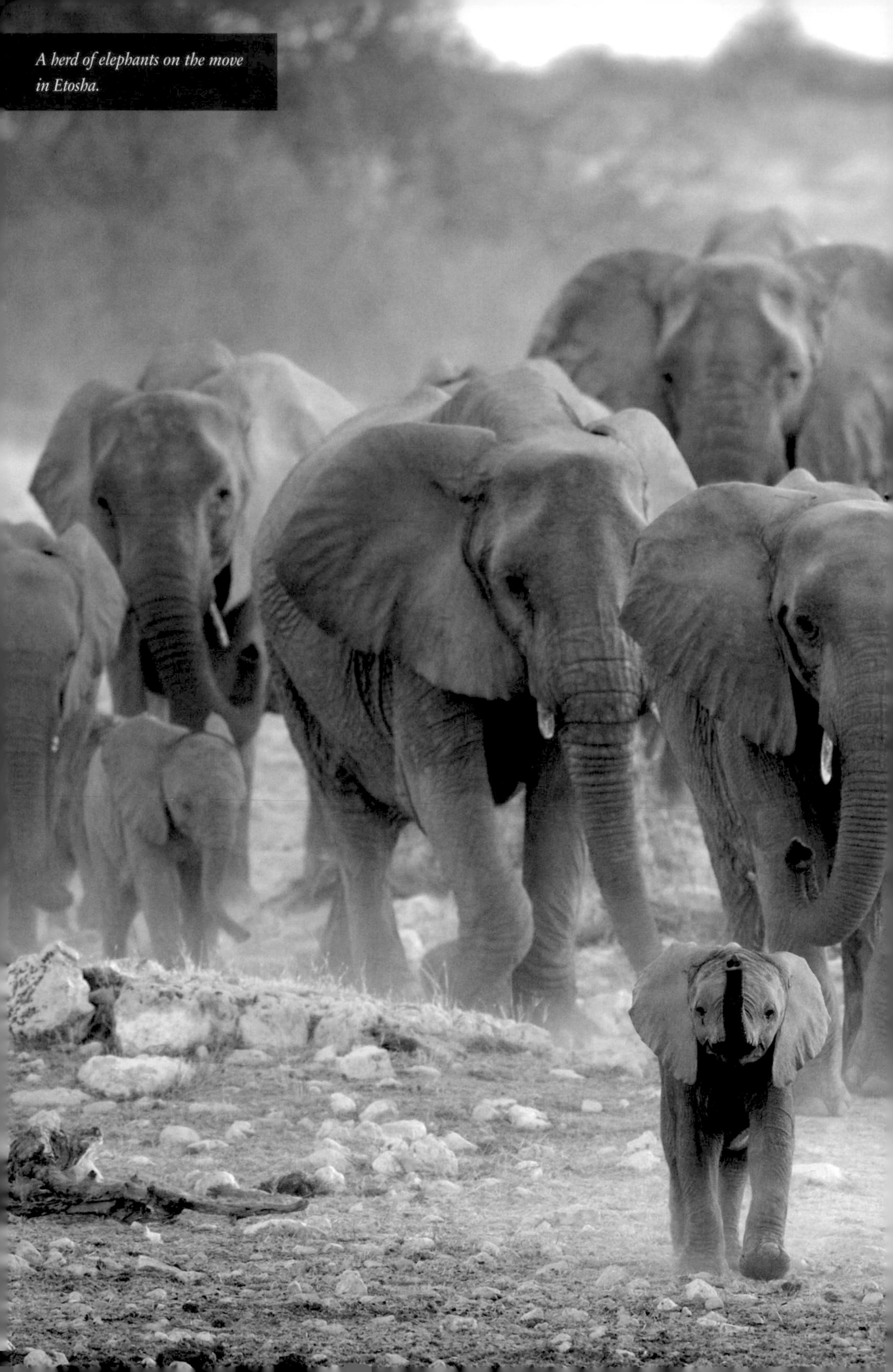

A herd of elephants on the move in Etosha.

INTRODUCTION

A detailed guide to the entire country,
with principal sites clearly cross-
referenced by number to the maps.

Quiver Tree Forest, Keetmanshoop.

Named for the ancient desert that stretches the length of its Atlantic coast and dominated by thousands of square miles of sand and rock, Namibia has a landscape that is always extreme. Yet while it may not seduce with the bountiful charms of neighbours like cosmopolitan South Africa, or Botswana with its profusion of wildlife, it is Namibia's desert with its extraordinary flora and fauna, gutsy people and vast distances that brings visitors back – and back again – for another taste of an untamed wilderness.

There's more to this enormous country (it's nearly as big as France and Italy combined) than just the desert, too. Its northern borders are well-watered by rivers, while other parts of the country offer landscapes of spectacular, rugged mountains, deep canyons and wide-open plains.

Fish River Canyon as seen from the air.

The Namibian adventure usually begins in Windhoek, a city still dominated by the graceful buildings erected at the turn of the 19th century when the great scramble for African territory brought a sudden influx of German missionaries and colonists to this wild land. The capital acts as a useful jumping-off point for a range of intriguing journeys into the interior, including the majestic Fish River Canyon in the south and the mysterious Skeleton Coast to the west.

Wildlife fans will most probably already have heard of the Etosha National Park, one of the finest game reserves in the world, where the huge diversity of southern Africa's wildlife (including all of the "Big Five") can be viewed at close range. Heading to the northwest, the Kaokoveld is home to some extraordinary desert-adapted flora and fauna as well as the proud Himba people. Then there's remote Damaraland, strewn with archaeological finds dating back to Stone Age times. While it's only accessible to expeditions with four-wheel-drive vehicles, the lush wilderness of the Caprivi region, on the other hand, is easily explored by car.

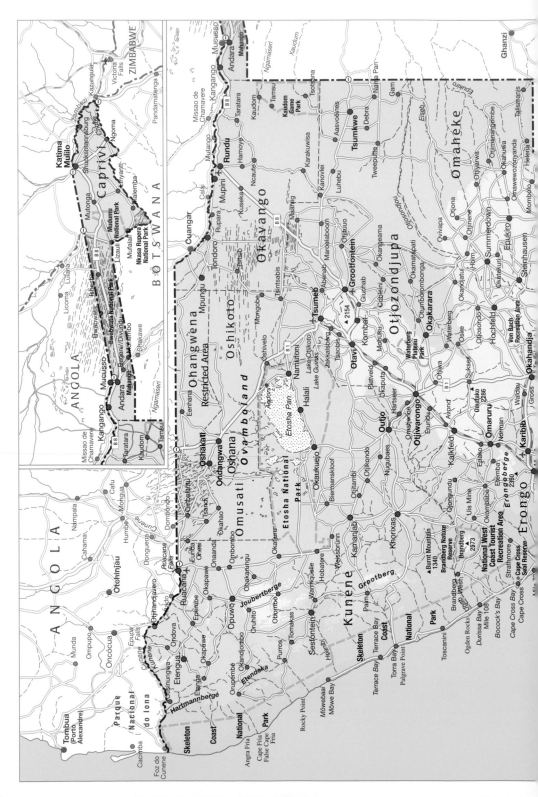

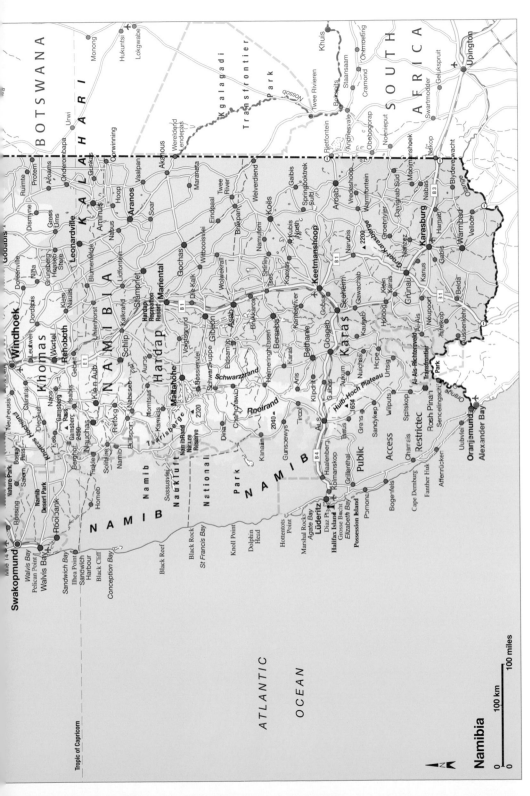

Namibia

WINDHOEK

Set at the geographical heart of the country in the rolling Central Highlands, Namibia's cosmopolitan capital is a sprawling African city with a marked Teutonic flavour.

Cupped in a valley bounded by the Auas Mountains to the south, the **Eros Mountains** to the northeast and the hills of the **Khomas Hochland** ("Highland") to the west, **Windhoek** is Namibia's capital and its commercial, financial and administrative hub. Yet it's not just a busy transit point. The town and the surrounding countryside have plenty to offer visitors, too.

At first glance, the place seems unusually small for a capital city, but appearances are deceptive – several outlying suburbs are tucked away in the surrounding valleys. Windhoek's population, which stood at 332,300 in the 2012 census, is a colourful ethnic mix of Europeans, Ovambos, Hereros and Damaras, with smaller numbers of Nama, San and "Coloured" (mixed-race) people as well.

Despite its name, which translates as "Windy Corner", the place is not particularly windy – in fact, thanks to its relatively high altitude (about 1,650 metres, or 5,400ft) it enjoys a dry and pleasant highland climate most of the year round. However, high summer (January–February) can be very hot and humid, with temperatures often hitting the 35°C (94°F) mark. What's more, nearly two-thirds of the city's average annual rainfall (365mm/14.4ins) is recorded in the first three months of the year, with occasional

showers in November and December. Summer gardens, in other words, can be spectacular.

A town of many names

Although Windhoek itself is little more than a century old, the hot springs in the area have attracted settlers in one form or another for many thousands of years. The original site (in today's Klein Windhoek valley) was called *Aigams* ("fire water") by the Nama and *Otjimuise* ("place of smoke") by the Herero, although since

Main Attractions
Post Street Mall
Owela Museum
National Art Gallery of Namibia
Katutura
Daan Viljoen Game Park

Chief Hosea Katjiku-Ru-Rume Kutako outside the Houses of Parliament.

then it has also been known as Elbersfeld, Concordiaville, Esek and even Queen Adelaide's Bath – although it's unlikely that the blue-blooded one ever set foot here.

In around 1840, the Nama chief, Jan Jonker Afrikaner settled at the springs with his followers and renamed the site Wind Hoock – apparently a corruption of the name Winterhoek, after the South African mountain range where he had been born. This name stuck and, by 1850, "Windhoek" was in general use.

In 1890, during the German colonial occupation, a military outpost was established in the town to house the headquarters of the German *Schutztruppe* (Defence Force) under Major Curt von François, whose brief it was to broker a peace between the warring Nama and Herero. That same year, Windhoek was declared the administrative capital of German South West Africa and in 1909 it became an independent municipality with its own mayor, since when it has evolved into the busy commercial and financial centre it is today.

A walking tour

Thanks to the city's compact size, it's easy to take in all the main sights on a self-guided, two-to-three-hour-long walking tour. Set out early in the morning or late in the afternoon to avoid the hottest temperatures, and wear a pair of good walking shoes (and a sun-hat).

Our walk begins at the bus terminal at the corner of **Fidel Castro Street** and busy **Independence Avenue**, slicing through the heart of the city centre (the Kalahari Sands Hotel, which dominates the skyline here, is a useful orientation point).

A short walk north from this intersection, past a pavement market selling Namibian indigenous arts and crafts, is tranquil **Zoo Park** Ⓐ (daily; dawn–dusk; free). Although you won't find animals at the park any more, there was a small zoo here from German colonial times right up until the early 1960s, along with an elegant café where an orchestra played classical music. There is still is a very agreeable café here, but the only sign of wildlife is a sculpted column commemorating a Stone Age elephant hunt which took

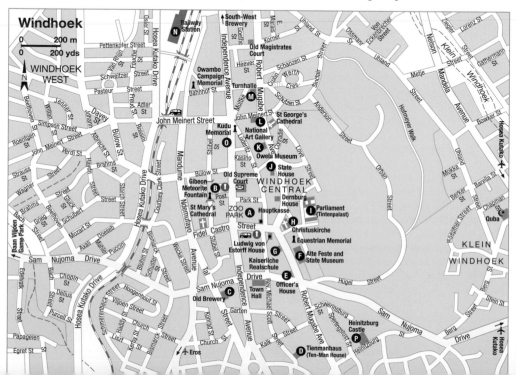

place here some 5,000 years ago. Relicts of this ancient hunt include the fossilised tusks, jaws and other bones of two elephants, and the quartzite tools used by their human pursuers to carve up the meat, all of which were unearthed during municipal excavations in 1962. Nearby to the south, the **Kriegerdenkmal**, or War Memorial, is a white obelisk topped with a gilt eagle, unveiled in 1897 and dedicated to the memory of German soldiers who fell in the 1893–94 Nama wars.

The park also offers a good view of three fine old colonial buildings, set just across the street on the west side of Independence Avenue. The Erkrath Building (1910), the Gathemann House (1913) and the Kronprinz, built in 1902 as an hotel, were all designed by renowned local architect Willi Sander and are known collectively as the **Old Business Facades**.

Around Independence Avenue

A short step north up the avenue takes you to Windhoek's main post office, past the **Post Street Mall** on your left (the striking Clock Tower near the top of this street is a replica of a turn-of-the-century structure which once crowned the Deutsche-Afrika Bank). The mall itself is a good place to shop for souvenirs, with its profusion of curio shops, craft stalls, chain stores and street cafés. Its centrepiece is the curious **Gibeon Meteorite National Monument** Ⓑ, an open-air display-cum-fountain housing 33 relics of the largest known meteorite shower ever to have hit the earth – probably about 500 million years ago, when it scattered debris over an area of 360 by 110km (210 by 65 miles) centred on the small town of Gibeon. The individual stones on display, which weigh up to 555kg, were collected over the period 1911–3, but the meteorite shower was first documented by the explorer J.E. Alexander in 1838, prior to which the metallic rocks (an iron-nickel alloy) were used by local hunter-gatherers to shape into tools.

Now retrace your steps down Independence Avenue; walk south as far as Sam Nujoma Drive and turn into it, heading west. A left turn from here into Tal Street takes you to the **Old Brewery** Ⓒ, where Namibia's favourite tipple, Windhoek Lager, was once produced – it's now home to a thriving arts complex, including the trendy Warehouse Theatre, the Namibian Craft Centre and the Craft Café.

After a break for refreshments at the café, turn left into Garten Street to find Independence Avenue once more. Cross it and head east for one block to reach the Rev. Michael Scott Street, leading south to the H-shaped, fortress-like **Tienmannhaus (Ten-Man House)** Ⓓ. Built by Hobe, Hoch and Matheis in 1906 to provide accommodation for ten unmarried government officials, it's another fine example of the local colonial style.

Historic heart

The next section of the walk takes in some of the most interesting German-era architecture Windhoek has to

The Gibeon Meteorite fell in prehistoric times. Pieces of the meteorite were used by the Nama people to create tools and weapons.

Craft sellers inside the Old Brewery.

offer, as well as some great city views. Head north up Rev. Michael Scott Street back to Sam Nujoma Drive and turn right onto Robert Mugabe Avenue, the city's colonial heart. The **Officer's House ❸** (closed to the public), on the corner, with its decorative Putz-style brickwork, was built in 1906–7 to house senior officials, while just up the road is Windhoek's oldest building, the whitewashed **Alte Feste ❺**. Built over 1890–93 as the headquarters of Captain von François' *Schutztruppe*, and extended in 1901, it now houses the historical section of National Museum of Namibia (tel: 061 2934437; Mon–Fri 9am–6pm, Sat–Sun 3–6pm; free). Exhibits include a particularly well-thought-out display on Namibia's struggle for independence.

Just north of the Alte Feste stands an **Equestrian Memorial** (actually, it's pretty hard to miss), erected in 1912 to commemorate the German soldiers who fell in the Herero and Nama Wars of 1904–9. The turreted structure opposite is the **Kaiserliche Realschule ❻**, built in 1907 as the

first German primary school in Windhoek. Later it became the city's first German secondary school, then an English school; it now houses government offices.

Immediately north of the equestrian memorial is the graceful German Lutheran **Christuskirche ❼**, or Christ Church. Designed by Gottlieb Redecker in an adventurous blend of neo-Gothic-meets-Art Nouveau (*Jugendstil*), it was built between 1907 and 1909 using sandstone transported from a farm 30km (18 miles) distant, and remains one of Windhoek's best-known landmarks.

Across the street is the **Ludwig von Estorff House**, named for a *Schutztruppe* commander who lived here between 1902 and 1910. Originally built in 1891 as a canteen for military artisans, it was subsequently used as a residence for senior officers such as von Estorff. One block north lies the equally impressive **Hauptkasse**, once the colonial government's revenue office – it, too, now houses government offices, namely the Ministry of Agriculture.

The Alte Fest, or Old Fort, is the oldest surviving building in Windhoek.

Another Gottlieb Redecker design crowns the hill behind Christuskirche to the east. The imposing **Parliament Buildings ❶** (tel: 061 2882605; www.parliament.gov.na; guided tours run between 9am–noon and 2–4pm, and take up to two hours; free) with their splendid gardens once housed the colonial government's administrative headquarters and were nicknamed the **Tintenpalast**, or "Ink Palace" – a sly reference to the vast quantities of ink the toiling bureaucrats seemed to get through.

Back on Robert Mugabe Avenue, a short stroll north takes you past **Dernburg House**, built especially to accommodate the German Secretary for the Colonies when he paid a visit to Namibia in 1908 (it was subsequently used as government offices). **State House ❶**, the official residence of Namibia's President, is a little further on. The graceful colonial governor's mansion which once stood here was flattened in 1958 to make way for this modern building; all that remains today is a section of garden wall.

More city-centre sights

While the walk outlined above offers a basic tour round the core of Old Windhoek, there are plenty of other interesting buildings to explore nearby. A short walk north of State House on Robert Mugabe Avenue is where you'll find the **Owela Museum ❸** (tel: 061 2934358; Mon–Fri 9am–6pm, Sat–Sun 3–6pm; free), containing the National Museum of Namibia's worthwhile albeit slightly timeworn natural history section. It offers some information on Namibia's diverse local cultures, but the excellent displays on cheetah conservation are the biggest draw here. Worth a quick look, too, is the church in Love Street, a block away from the museum to the east – known as **St George's**, it's the smallest cathedral in southern Africa.

Back on Robert Mugabe Avenue, heading north as far as the junction with John Meinart Road, the **National Art Gallery of Namibia ❶** (tel: 061

231160; www.nagn.org.na; Mon–Fri 8am–5pm, Sat 9am–2pm; free) is definitely worth a visit. Temporary exhibitions complement the permanent art displays, which themselves cut across a broad range of styles and periods.

Look out particularly for the outstanding linocuts by John Muafangejo, and paintings by the colonial artist Adolph Jentsch. Immediately next door, the **National Theatre of Namibia** (tel: 061 374400; www.ntn.org.na) hosts regular theatrical and other productions, usually in the evening.

On the corner of Robert Mugabe Avenue and Bahnhof Street you'll find the **Turnhalle ⓜ**, built in 1909 as a gymnasium. In the 1970s it was turned into a conference centre, springing to fame in 1975 when the South African government staged the first Constitutional Conference on Independence for South West Africa here. This historic gathering brought a range of white and black Namibian political leaders and groups together for the first time to discuss the country's future; it subsequently became known simply as "the Turnhalle Conference".

The Owela Museum in Windhoek displays items from the San, Herero, Nama, Damara, and Ovambo peoples.

KATUTURA

Situated on the northwest outskirts of Windhoek, Katutura is a bustling residential district whose Herero name means "the place where we do not wish to go". It's a reference to the area's former incarnation as a blacks-only township, established in 1960 by the South African administration, who forcibly evicted Windhoek's black residents from their homes in the Old Location (now Hochland Park) and moved them here. Since independence, of course, apartheid policies such as these have been swept away and, increasingly, Windhoek's urban areas are becoming differentiated along economic lines, rather than race. As a result, Katutura is now the site of several important landmarks, notably the Sam Nujoma Stadium, built in 2005, and the Katutura State Hospital. Hochland Park's Old Location Cemetery – a national monument – makes a worthwhile, if poignant, excursion. There's a mass grave here where 13 people are buried, shot dead by the South African police on 10 December 1959 during protests against the forced removals to Katutura. The day of the killings, 10 December, is known as International Human Rights Day and is a public holiday. Now home to around 200,000 people (almost two-thirds of Windhoek's total populace), Katutura is safe to explore independently by day, but you may feel more secure, and will certainly gain more insight, on a guided bike tour organised through Katu Tours (tel: 061 210097 or 081 303 2856; www.katutours.com).

The Herero

Survivors of the harshest excesses of German rule, the pastoralist Herero have a social order based on an unusual system of double descent.

The Herero (OvaHerero) migrated to what is now Namibia some 500 years ago. According to oral tradition, they came from the Great Lakes of East Africa, travelling through present-day Zambia and southern Angola and arriving at the Kunene River in about 1550.

After a sojourn of some 200 years in Kaokoland, many migrated further south. Towards the middle of the 18th century their vanguard reached the Swakop River Valley; by the 19th century, the Herero were established firmly in central Namibia. Today, they number around 250,000 and are still regarded as expert cattle breeders.

The Herero nation includes a number of sub-divisions:

The Herero proper, including the traditional chiefdoms of Maherero (Okahandja region), Zeraua (Omaruru), Kambazembi (Waterberg) and others. In

A Herero woman and child near Brandberg.

Kaokoland, the Ndamuranda and the Tjimba Herero also belong to this subgroup.

The Mbanderu in the east of Namibia (especially in the district of Gobabis).

The Himba and other smaller factions living in northern Kaokoland and in southwest Angola.

A striking feature of their social order is that every individual belongs not only to a matrilineal (eandag) clan, but also to a patrician (oruzo) clan. Traditionally, the matriclans exert control over property, especially cattle, and supervise the application of inheritance laws. The patriclans take responsibility for sacred objects and holy cattle (ozohivirikwa), the exercise of authority in the family, succession of chiefs, priesthood, ancestral fires, and ritual food taboos.

Genocide

The Herero were victims of the first genocide of the 20th century. Perpetrated in retaliation to an anti-colonial uprising led by Samuel Maharero in January 1904, the killing climaxed in August of the same year when a German military expedition led by General Lothar von Trotha killed at least 3,000 Herero combatants. The Germans then rounded up and killed all women, children and other Herero non-combatants in the vicinity. Survivors elsewhere in Namibia were herded into camps. The death toll remains speculative, but it's been estimated that the Herero of Namibia decreased from 80,000 to 16,000 over the course of 1904-5. The German government issued a formal apology in 2004.

As a result of the colonial wars, traditional culture suffered greatly, not only through population decrease, but also the confiscation of tribal land, a prohibition on cattle breeding, and restrictive labour regulations. But, even during this bitter period, there were attempts to revive the bonds of family life and tribal solidarity. In the beginning, the Herero made use of the means of communication offered by Christian congregations to keep in touch with their fellow tribesmen. Later they established their own organisations including burial societies, religious fraternities and paramilitary associations.

Before independence in March 1990, much of Herero political life centred around the so-called Herero reserves where headmen and councillors were elected. Since 1950 "Herero tribal meetings" have been held annually under the chairmanship of a "Chief's Council" led for decades by the revered Chief Hosea Kutako, who directed petitions at the UN calling for Namibian independence.

Castles and kudus

Walking westwards along Bahnhof ("Station") Street, you'll find Windhoek's gracious old **Railway Station** , built by the Germans in 1912 and later expanded in the same Cape Dutch architectural style by the South African administration. If you're planning to catch the Desert Express to Swakopmund, this is where it departs from (see Travel Tips page 245) but, even if you're staying put, the building is still worth a look round. Train buffs should head for the upper level and the little **Trans-Namib Transport Museum** (tel: 061 2982186; Mon–Fri 9am–noon and 2–4pm; charge), which covers the history of train travel in Namibia.

Diagonally across from the station, at the entry to the car park, stands a large stone obelisk. The **Owambo Campaign Memorial** was erected in 1917 to commemorate those South African and British soldiers who fell in the fight to bring down Mandume, king of the Kwanyama, the biggest Owambo tribe; Mandume himself was also killed during the campaign.

Other interesting buildings nearby include the **Kaiserliche Landesvermessung**, the old colonial surveyors' offices, on the corner of Independence Avenue and John Meinert Street. Diagonally across the street is the bronze **Kudu Memorial** , donated by a wealthy Namibian businessman in the wake of the terrible *rinderpest* epidemic of 1896, in which thousands of kudu (and cattle and sheep) perished. The statue, by Professor Behn of Munich, was erected in 1960.

Also within walking distance of the city centre – but only just – are Windhoek's three turreted castles, **Heinitzburg**, **Schwerinsburg** and **Sanderburg**. Designed by the ubiquitous Willi Sander in the early 1900s and set high on a ridge overlooking the city, these quirkily romantic buildings are much-loved landmarks, although only Heinitzburg Castle (now the Hotel

Heinitzburg; tel: 061 249597; www.heinitzburg.com) is open to the public – the other two are private homes. A firm favourite with the locals, thanks to its lavish afternoon teas, the Hotel Heinitzburg Garni is worth the effort it takes to walk there. Head south down Robert Mugabe Avenue to the corner of Heinitzburg Street, from where it's a short, steep climb up the hill to the castle at No 22.

Excursions further afield

There's a distinct lack of inexpensive, reliable public transport in Windhoek, which can be a source of frustration for visitors who want to branch out and explore beyond the city centre. There are, of course, plenty of companies offering city tours (see Travel Tips page 274) and taxis abound, too – although they are fairly pricey.

The **Aloe Trail** (formerly **Hofmeyer Walk**) is an hour-long hiking trail winding south through unspoilt countryside along the ridge that separates Windhoek from the Klein Windhoek valley. It's particularly rewarding during March and April, when the

The TransNamib Transport Museum contains memorabilia from the railway age in Namibia.

The Kudu Memorial in downtown Windhoek.

mountain aloes (*Aloe littoralis*) are in bloom – their bright red flowers attract plenty of birds. At any time of year, the views back over the city are stunning.

You can pick up the trail in Orban or Anderson streets, just east of the Parliament building, then follow signs to the finishing point in Uhland Street (be aware, though, that recently there have been reports of hikers being mugged along the trail; if you decide to embark on it, don't carry any valuables).

Also well worth a visit is the little-known National Earth Science Museum (1 Aviation Road; tel: 061 2848150; www.mme.gov.na/gsn/earth museum.htm; Mon–Fri 8am–1pm and 2–5pm; free) which is operated by the Geological Survey of Namibia in the Ministry of Mines and Energy Building close to Eros Airport. Of greater interest to most visitors than the geological displays here is the excellent collection of dinosaur and hominoid fossils, including that of the Otjiseva skeleton (Otavipithecus namibiensis), the first Miocene hominoid from southern Africa.

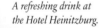

A refreshing drink at the Hotel Heinitzburg.

Festivals

A particularly good time to visit the city is during the main **Windhoek Carnival** (often abbreviated to **WIKA**; tel: 081 679 8921; www.windhoek-karneval.com), which usually falls in March or April. The city's best-known knees-up since the 1950s, it's also the one with the strongest Teutonic flavour. Summer's end is celebrated in true German tradition with oompah bands, much good humour and vast quantities of beer.

If, on the other hand, you prefer something rather more African, the AE//GAMS Arts and Culture Festival (tel: 061 2902493), usually held in September, is an eclectic mix of traditional dance and music, live bands and choral events, held at various venues in central Windhoek and Katutura. Also worth checking out is the Bank Windhoek Arts Festival (www.bankwindhoek arts.com.na), an ongoing event that stages several varied events monthly.

Wildlife

Windhoek, like most African cities, is not known for its wildlife viewing possibilities. Nevertheless, there are

a couple of worthwhile possibilities within easy day tripping distance of the city centre. Foremost among these is the **Sun Karros Daan Viljoen Game Park and Lifestyle Resort** (tel: 061 232 393; www.sunkarros.com daily sunrise–6pm; charge), a former government property that recently reopened as a private reserve.

Of greater interest, perhaps, for its network of day hiking trails rather than its game viewing, this mountainous area is nevertheless a good place to seek out the localised Hartmann's mountain zebra, giraffe and large antelope such as greater kudu, oryx and blue wildebeest.

Largely because it is permitted to walk freely, and to get out of your car at whim, Daan Viljoen is an excellent place to tick near-endemics such as Monteiro's hornbill, Damara rockjumper and white-tailed shrike alongside the striking crimson-breasted shrike, shaft-tailed wydah and violet-eared waxbill.

The game park lies 20km (12.5 miles) west of Windhoek, is accessible by a good tar road. In addition to game-viewing roads and hiking trails,

the reserve is also serviced by an excellent upmarket chalet resort, camping site, and restaurant.

The larger species

To encounter larger species of wildlife, a somewhat more contrived – but nevertheless worthwhile – experience can be had at **Okapuka Horse Safaris** (www.okapuka-safaris.com), set in a private game lodge some 40km (25 miles) north of Windhoek alongside the surfaced road to Okahandja.

Aimed primarily at horse-riders, it also welcomes overnight visitors (it would make a convenient first stop heading northward to Etosha or Caprivi), and non-horseback facilities include walking trails, game drives and a good restaurant.

A pride of captive lions is fed daily at 5pm, while free-ranging wildlife includes giraffe, gemsbok, greater kudu, blue wildebeest and (somewhat rare elsewhere in Namibia) the beautiful sable antelope.

This is also a rewarding spot for birdwatchers, protecting a similar selection of species to Daan Viljoen.

Although small, the Daan Viljoen Game Park presents a good collection of wild game.

View over the capital from Daan Viljoen Game Park.

Wood carver in Okahandja.

A safari camp.

CENTRAL NAMIBIA

Often overlooked by visitors thanks to its proximity to Etosha, this region is rewarding in its own right too, from its rolling hills and river valleys to its abundant historical sites.

A ll too often, the area north of Windhoek is seen by visitors merely as something to "get through" en route to northern Namibia's big draw, the Etosha National Park. Yet not only does north-central Namibia hold many attractions of its own which repay closer attention, it's also well set up for a self-drive tour. Most roads are tarmac or well-graded gravel, while provisions, banking facilities and fuel are available at all the main towns and most rest camps along the way. Bear in mind, though, that many of the attractions round here are on private land, and require advance booking.

Exploring the highlands

Heading north from **Windhoek** ❶ on the B1 highway, you'll pass through the hilly farmland of the **Khomas Hochland**, flanked on the east by the Onyati mountains. **Okahandja** ❷, 71km (44 miles) north of Windhoek, was founded by the Herero leader Tjamuaha c.1800. In 1827, the German priest Heinrich Schmelen became the first European to visit the town, leading to the establishment of a permanent mission in 1844. On 23 August 1850, nearby **Moordkoppie** (Murder Hill) was the scene of the massacre of 700 of Tjamuaha's followers by their Nama rivals. This event instigated a seven-year war in which the Herero

eventually conquered the Nama under the leadership of Tjamuaha's son Maherero,

A Rhenish school was founded at Okahandja in 1870, and six years later the **Rhenish Mission Church** was consecrated. Situated on Kerk Street, this is now the oldest building in town, and several prominent figures including Maherero's son William, the Nama leader Jonker Afrikaner, and the pioneering nationalist Hosea Kutajo – are either buried in the churchyard or in a separate cemetery opposite it.

Main Attractions
Erongo Rock Art
Otjihaenamaparero
  Dinosaur Prints
AfriCat Foundation
Waterberg Plateau National
  Park
Ibenstein Weavers

The German war cemetery, Waterberg Plateau.

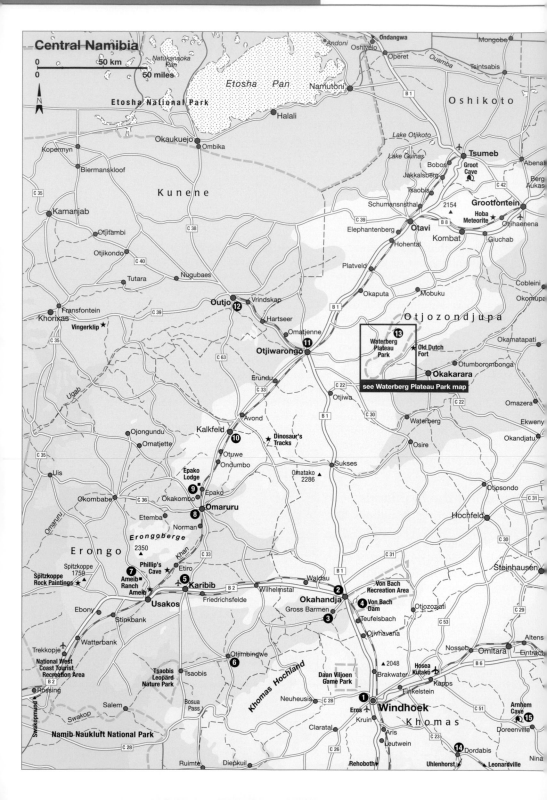

Central Namibia

0 — 50 km
0 — 50 miles

N

Natukanaoka Pan

Etosha Pan

Etosha National Park

Andoni
Oshivelo
Ondangwa
Mongobe
Operet
Quamba
Tsintsabis

Namutoni

O s h i k o t o

Halali

Kopermyn
Okaukuejo
Ombika

Lake Otjikoto
Lake Guinas
Tsumeb
Bobos
Abenab

Biermanskloof

Groot Cave
Berg Aukas
Jakkalsberg
C 42

K u n e n e
Tsaobis
Schumannsthal
2154
Grootfontein

Kamanjab
C 35

C 39
Elephantenberg
Otavi
Hoba Meteorite
Otjihaenena
Kombat

Otjitambi
Hohental
Giuchab
B 8

Otjikondo
C 40
Platveld

Tutara
Nugubaes
C 38

Cobleini
Fransfontein
Outjo
Vrindskap
Okaputa
Mobuku
Okomupa

Khorixas
C 39
Hartseer
B 1
O t j o z o n d j u p a

Vingerklip ★
Omatjenne

Otjiwarongo
Waterberg Plateau Park
Old Dutch Fort
Okamatapati

C 35
Erundu
C 63
Otumborombonga

Ojongundu
C 33
Okakarara

Omatjette
Kalkfeld
Avond
Otjiwa
Waterberg
Omazera

Uis
Otuwe
Dinosaur's Tracks
B 1
C 30
Ekweny
Okandjatu

C 35
Ondumbo
Sukses
Osire

Epako Lodge
Omatako 2286

Økombabe
C 36
Okakombo
Epako
Otjosondo
C 31

Etemba
Omaruru
Hochfeld

Norman
C 30

Erongoberge
2350
Khan
C 33

E r o n g o
Phillip's Cave
Steinhausen
C 31

Spitzkoppe
Spitzkoppe 1759
Ameib Ranch
Etiro
Waldau
B 1

Spitzkoppe Rock Paintings ★
Ameib
Karibib
Wilhelmstal
Von Bach Recreation Area

Ebony
B 2
Friedrichsfelde
Okahandja
Von Bach Dam
Otjozotjati
C 29

Stinkbank
Usakos
Gross Barmen
Teufelsbach
C 53

Watterbank
Ojivhavana
Altens

Trekkopje
Otjimbingwe
Nossob
Omitara
Eintract

National West Coast Tourist Recreation Area
B 2
Tsaobis Leopard Nature Park
Tsaobis
Daan Viljoen Game Park
2048
Hosea Kutako
Kapps
B 6

Rössing
Salem
Bosua Pass
Brakwater
Finkelstein

Swakop
Neuheusis
C 28
Eros
Windhoek
C 51
Arnhem Cave
Doreenville

Namib Naukluft National Park
Claratal
Kruin
K h o m a s
Nina

C 28
Ruimte
Diepkuil
Aris
Leutwein
C 23

Rehoboth
Dordabis
Uhlenhorst
Leonardville

Khomas Hochland

Kamdasberg
Von Bach Dam

see Waterberg Plateau Park map

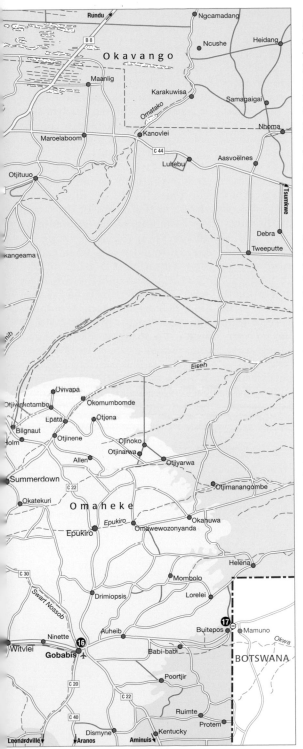

Okahandja is the main Herero administrative centre, and a place of great historical significance for these people as a whole, too. The **Green Flag Herero** or **Mbanderu** assemble here each June to pay homage to their forefather, Kahimemua Nguvauva, executed in Okahandja on 13 June 1896 for his involvement in a revolt against the German administration. On **Maherero Day,** which falls on the last weekend in August, the streets come alive as the **Red Flag Herero** march to honour the memory of their fallen chiefs, the men in military-style uniforms, the women in billowing red dresses.

Lining the southern and northern approaches to the town are curio markets run by the Rundu-based Namibian Carvers Association, which are well worth a visit (daily). There's also the **Ombo Rest Camp** (tel: 062 502003; www.ombo-rest-camp.com; small fee), 12km (7 miles) northwest of Okahandja on the C31, which doubles as a crocodile and ostrich farm, and offers 45-minute tours packed with facts about these two extraordinary creatures, which are respectively the world's largest species of reptile and of bird.

Okahandja has a limited selection of hotels, but there is plenty of accommodation just outside town. Although this is some of the best farmland in Namibia – prime cattle-ranching country, in particular – in recent years many farmers have restocked their land with game and opened up as guest farms catering for the tourist trade.

Apart from these, other good stopover places in the vicinity include **Gross Barmen ③** (tel: 062 501091; www.nwr.com.na; daily), another old mission station built round a dam on the Swakop River some 24km (15 miles) southwest of town on the C87. The main attraction here is a hot mineral spring, feeding a glass-enclosed thermal hall and an outdoor swimming pool. The water has a constant temperature of 65°C (150°F), but is cooled to a more bearable 40°C (104°F) for the thermal pool.

Closed for renovations in 2014, the spa has always been popular with weekending locals and visitors passing through en route to Etosha, and there are also some excellent walks and birdwatching in the surrounding wooded hills.

Stocked with carp, bream, barbel and bass, **Von Bach Dam** ❹ (tel: 061 400 205; www.tungeni.com), which lies just off the B1, some 3.5km (2 miles) south of Okahandja, is a big hit with water sport enthusiasts and fishermen. Game-viewing opportunities are limited, but kudu, Hartmann's mountain zebra, springbok, eland and ostrich are all present in the surrounding park. There's also a recently privatised and renovated resort on the lakeshore.

Outside Okahandja, the B2 turns off in a westerly direction to the coastal resorts of Swakopmund and Walvis Bay. Take this road and at first you'll pass through predominantly featureless bush farmland before the ochre-pink granite mass of the Erongo mountains come into view in the north, just outside **Karibib** ❺. This little ranching town (112km/70 miles from Okahandja), is best known for its high-quality marble produced at the Marmorwerke quarry nearby; examples can be seen on floors in the Houses of Parliament in Cape Town and even on wall panels at Frankfurt Airport.

The useful **Henckert Tourist Centre** (38 Hidipo Hamutenya Road; tel: 064 550700; 8am–5pm Mon–Fri) should be your first stop here; it began as a gem and curio shop back in 1969 but now houses a modern tourist information facility, a money bureau and a coffee shop too.

From Karibib, you can take a detour south to Otjimbingwe, or continue 30km (18 miles) along the B2 to Usakos to visit the Ameib Rock Paintings. Sleepy **Otjimbingwe** ❻ lies 51km (32 miles) along the D1953; founded as a Rhenish mission station in 1849, it remained a quiet little place until the early 1880s when – thanks to its strategic position halfway between Windhoek and Walvis Bay – it enjoyed a brief stint as German South West Africa's administrative capital. In 1890, however, the capital was transferred to Windhoek, and Otjimbingwe sank back into small-town torpor once more. It does have some interesting

A cheetah stares into the lens.

buildings, however, including the Rhenish church (the oldest place of Christian worship for the Herero, built over 1865–7), and the 1872 powder magazine erected to protect the locals against Nama attacks.

Erongo rock art

The Erongo massif is best known for its rock art sites, of which the vast **Phillip's Cave** – home to a famous engraving of a "white elephant" – is the most rewarding. It's situated on land belonging to an upmarket guest farm, the **Ameib Ranch** ❼ (tel: 081 857 4639; www.ameib.com), lying some 27km (17 miles) from **Usakos**: to get there, take the D1935 for 11km (7 miles) before turning right on the D1937. The cave is a short drive and then a 40-minute walk from the ranch house. There are also several good walks to the curiously-shaped rock formations scattered around the farm, too – the group of round granite boulders known as the **Bull's Party**, some 5km (3 miles) from the house, is one of the most picturesque.

Back in Karibib, it's a 65km (40-mile) drive north through undulating bush farmland to pretty little **Omaruru** ❽ on the C33. Set on the banks of the Omaruru River – dry and sandy for the best part of the year – this former Rhenish mission station came under repeated attack by Herero forces at the turn of the last century and in 1904 was finally besieged. But the day was saved by a German officer, Captain Victor Franke, who petitioned the then Governor for permission to march north with his company from their garrison in southern Namibia and lend their efforts to the fight. After a 19-day trek, he galloped into Omaruru and relieved the siege. **Franke Tower** on Omaruru's eastern outskirts was built in his honour; it's usually kept locked, but ask at the nearby **Central Hotel** if you want to get hold of a key.

If you're keen to see more rock art, there's a very well-preserved site with both paintings and engravings outside Omaruru on a farm owned by the Hinterholzer family. Follow the D2315, 3km (2 miles) south of Omaruru for 24km (15 miles) and then turn south on the D2316 for 19km (12 miles). Allow approximately an hour to reach **Erongo Lodge** (not to be confused with the Erongo Wilderness Lodge). It's a short drive to the site from here, along a road that climbs steeply into the thinly-wooded hillsides of the Erongo Mountains, past white-trunked moringa trees striping the ochre rock faces. Visiting arrangements can be made through Erongo Lodge (tel: 064 570852; www.erongo lodge.iway.na).

The road to Etosha

Like Okahandja, Omaruru is well served by guest farms, many of which stock game. Luxurious **Epako Lodge** ❾ (see page 250), 18km (11 miles) north on the C33, is a particularly good stopover choice if you don't have time to visit Etosha – the wildlife here includes elephant, leopard, white

Wood carving in Okahandja.

FACT

In Herero, Omaruru means "sour milk", after the milk their cows gave when they'd been grazing on a local shrub, known as the bitterbush.

rhino and giraffe, as well as over 180 species of bird. It also has some rock art, although the paintings aren't of the same quality as those found near Erongo Lodge.

Keep going north along the C33 for some 64km (40 miles) from Omaruru and you'll reach the village of **Kalkfeld** . The only reason for stopping here is to visit the fossilised dinosaur tracks on the nearby (and extraordinarily named) **Otjihaenamaparero Farm** (tel: 067 290153; www.dinosaurstracks.com; daily; charge). The most striking imprints here, made by a two-legged, three-toed dinosaur can be followed for about 25 metres (80ft). From Kalkfeld, follow the clearly signposted D2414 southeast for about 25km (15 miles), then turn left into the D2467 and follow it for another 1.5km (one mile) to a parking area, from where it is a short walk to the tracks.

A 70km (43 miles) drive northeast from Kalkfeld leads to **Otjiwarongo**, a rather unremarkable ranching town that has adequate tourist facilities and serves as a popular springboard for eastern Etosha and the Waterberg. The only attraction in the town centre is the **Otjiwarongo Crocodile Ranch** (tel: 067 302121; daily 9am–4pm; charge), a CITES-registered facility that breeds crocodiles for their skins, which are exported to make shoes, handbags and other goods, and also has a small café serving crocodile steaks and snacks.

A more popular stop-off than the town itself is the guest farm called **Okonjima**, which is signposted west of the B1 trunk road about 35km (22 miles) south of town. Serviced by several luxury lodges and a camping site, this vast and in parts mountainous acacia-studded farm is also home to the **AfriCat Foundation** (www.africat. org), whose pioneering work in the rescue and release of big cats has earned it numerous international ecological and ecotourism awards since it started operating in 1997.

A one- or two-night stopover at one of Okonjima's exceptionally comfortable lodges is the ideal way to break up the drive from Windhoek

Karakul pelts strung out to dry.

PRECIOUS PELTS

Soft, smooth, silky and supple, Karakul pelts are "Namibia's Persians", and the carpets and coats made from them fetch a high price both at home and abroad. Dordabis in the eastern part of Central Namibia is the heart of the Karakul industry; in these dry lands on the fringes of the Kalahari Desert, the hardy Karakul sheep enable many people to make a living where it might otherwise be impossible. The sheep's grazing habits stimulate the growth of many local plants and shrubs, while by treading grass stems into the ground, the herds also prevent erosion; the top level of soil, usually endangered by the wind, is thus saved.

There's only one thing that neither man nor beast can force from nature: rain. When there's a drought in these already arid regions, it has dire consequences on the Karakul industry. Lack of food and water drastically cut down the size of the herds.

The first sheep were imported from Germany in 1907; there are now over 1 million in Namibia, bred in black, grey, brown and white. In 1978, some 2,500 Karakul breeders produced 4.66 million pelts. Drought and reduced demand pushed the industry into decline in the 1990s, when production dropped to 120,000 pelts annually. More recently, while volumes remain low by comparison to the 1970s, a sharp rise in prices has done much to resuscitate the industry.

to Etosha, while also offering some superb close-up encounters with habituated leopard, captive lion and rehabilitating cheetah. Ask to be shown around the clinic and information centre for further insight into this multi-faceted organisation, which rescues an average of 70 "problem" cheetahs and leopards annually, and has been able to release more than 85 percent of these handsome creatures back into the wild. AfriCat also plays an important role in educating youngsters about big cats (tens of thousands of children and young adults have passed through its education centre or outreach programme since 1998) whilst also giving refuge to "welfare" animals which for one or another reason cannot safely be released back into to the wild.

Outjo ⑫, a further 68km (42 miles) northwest of Otjiwarongo along the C38, is an attractive little place set amidst low, grassy hills (the name means "small hills" in Herero) with views of the Paresis mountains. It was first established in 1897 as a *Schutztruppe* control post, although development pretty much ceased during the Herero War (1904–5). There's not really much to see here although, as it is just 96km (60 miles) from here to Etosha's Andersson Gate, it could serve as a good overnight stop if you're heading on to the park.

Waterberg Plateau National Park

The jewel of central Namibia, situated about 100km (60 miles) east of Otjiwarongo, is undoubtedly the **Waterberg Plateau Park** ⑬. An island of red sandstone cliffs lushly thatched with green, rising majestically above the surrounding savannah, the park was proclaimed in 1972 as a sanctuary and breeding-ground for threatened species such as white rhino, roan and sable antelope, and tsessebe. The scheme has been very successful, with some species now being translocated to other areas.

Other animals you might spot here include leopard, brown hyena and caracal, together with over 200 bird species, from the rare Rüppell's parrot and Verreaux's (black) eagle to Namibia's only breeding colony of Cape vultures.

This is not a park for self-drive tours. Instead, you can explore the nine short **nature walks** which have been laid out around the camp area, or book yourself onto one of the organised **game drives** which the park operates twice a day, visiting hides and waterholes. But perhaps the best way to experience the park's diverse landscapes – from woodland and grassland to thick acacia bush – is by joining one of the four-day organised **wilderness trails** which run in the dry season (between April and November), where you follow game trails with a qualified guide, and learn about ecology and wildlife issues.

Waterberg Camp (formerly Bernabé de la Bat Rest Camp; www.nwr. com.na) has accommodation in pink sandstone bungalows spread along the

Cheetahs are a conserved and protected species in Namibia, and many groups work to protect the animals.

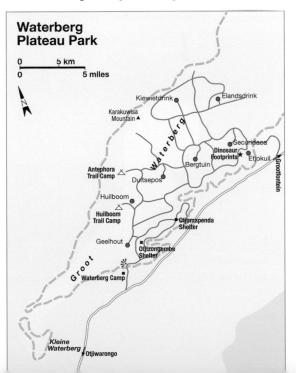

Waterberg Plateau Park

0   5 km
0   5 miles

N

Kiewietdrink
Elandsdrink
Karakuwisa Mountain ▲
Securidaca
Dinosaur Footprints
Etjokuil
Antephora Trail Camp
Bergtuin
Duitsepos
Huilboom
Huilboom Trail Camp
Otjomapenda Shelter
Geelhout
Otjizongombe Shelter
Waterberg Camp
Kleine Waterberg
Otjiwarongo

plateau's wooded slopes, along with a restaurant and shops, a petrol station and swimming pool. To reach the park from Otjiwarongo, it's a 27km (17-mile) drive south on the B1, followed by 58km (36 miles) east on the C22, before turning north onto the D2512 for 17km (10 miles).

East of Windhoek

Compared to the rest of the country, central Namibia's eastern section has relatively few tourist attractions. The main draw here is the region's tranquillity and unspoiled scenery – striking camel-thorn savannah vegetation on red Kalahari sand. It's best explored on a day trip from Windhoek, or as part of a route south following the fringes of the Kalahari to **Mariental** or **Keetmanshoop** via the C15 and C17.

Pretty little **Dordabis** ⓮ surrounded by rounded hills, is the centre of Namibia's Karakul industry, and farms have workshops offering rugs and wall-hangings for sale. One of the best to buy from is **Ibenstein Weavers** (tel: 062 573524; www. ibenstein-weavers.com.na), 3km (2 miles) south of Dordabis on the C15.

Other attractions include the **Arnhem Cave** ⓯ (tel: 062 581885; www. arnhemcave.com; open daily, charge), the longest cave system in Namibia with a total length of 4.5km (3 miles). An underground trail takes you past various kinds of mineral deposits and six bat species – including the giant leaf-nosed bat (*Hipposideros commersoni*), one of the world's largest insectivorous bats. As the cave is dusty, old clothes and a good torch are required. There's a small rest camp here, too.

To get there, take the B6 from Windhoek to the airport. Follow the D1458 southeast for 66km (41 miles), then turn north on the D1506 for 11km to a T-junction, when you should turn south onto the D1808 for 4km (2.5 miles).

Busy **Gobabis** ⓰, 200km (124 miles) east of Windhoek on the B6, is a cattle-ranching centre and – with the border at **Buitepos** ⓱ just 120km (190 miles) east – the main jumping-off point if you're heading east to Botswana.

The pools at Waterberg Park.

The Nama

Of slight build and delicate features, the Nama are the most populous surviving ethnic group to speak one of Africa's ancient click-based Khoikhoi languages.

The Nama form a subgroup of the indigenous Khoikhoi (previously referred to by the derogatory term "Hottentots"). Most Khoikhoi within the boundaries of Namibia belong to the Nama and Oorlam groups. Their original territory was centred on the Orange River, along the border with South Africa, but over the course of the 19th century, a rapidly advancing white farming community pushed them continuously northwards.

Led by Chief Jan Jonker Afrikaner, the Nama settled in the vicinity of Windhoek and Okahandja in the mid-19th century, where they soon came into conflict with the Herero who already inhabited the area. Setting aside past differences, however, the Nama, led by the septuagenarian Hendrik Witbooi, a grandson of Jonker Afrikaner, joined the Herero in taking up arms against the Germans in 1904. It is estimated that around 10,000 Nama – half of the entire population at that time – died over the next three years, many of them children and women interned in concentration camps.

Internecine quarrels in the past and wars against the advancing intruders brought great suffering to the Nama; under the South Africans their living space was confined to a number of so-called reserves. In spite of their heroic resistance against colonialism and strenuous efforts to preserve their identity, their culture has been greatly eroded. But their heroes still live on in tales and praise poems of chiefs and other prominent personalities.

Certain distinctive features make the Khoikhoi easily recognisable. The women's small and slender hands and feet are the subject of traditional praise poems. High and prominent cheekbones combined with a tapering chin and markedly platyrrhine noses add to the general flatness of the facial profile. Faces are animated by beautiful dark eyes which seem to be almond-shaped on account of a particular fold of the upper eyelid. In common with the Bushmen, the women have an extraordinary accumulation of subcutaneous fat over the buttocks.

The present-day Nama population numbers around 100,000. As pastoral nomads, the Nama traditionally had little need of permanent structures – their beehive-shaped rush-mat houses were perfectly suited to their lifestyle. The concept of communal land ownership still prevails among most clans today, except for the Aonin or Topnaars, whose fields are the property of individual lineages.

Nama tribes at the coast have always considered the sea an important source of food. Occasionally the people have taken to gardening and, in a small way, even to agriculture. Recently, communal agricultural projects have been established at Hoachanas, Gibeon, Berseba and other places.

A tribe of music and poetry

While their decorative art is somewhat poorly developed, the Nama possess a natural talent for music and poetry; no visitor to a Nama village at Sesfontein valley will easily forget the soft, lilting sounds of reed-flutes on a moonlit night. The literary talent of the people, meanwhile, expresses itself in prose and verse. Numerous proverbs and riddles, tales and poems have been handed down orally from generation to generation, while several hundred folk-tales are known and still told – some with as many as 40 different versions.

The Nama possess a natural affinity with music.

On the road to the Hoba Meteorite.

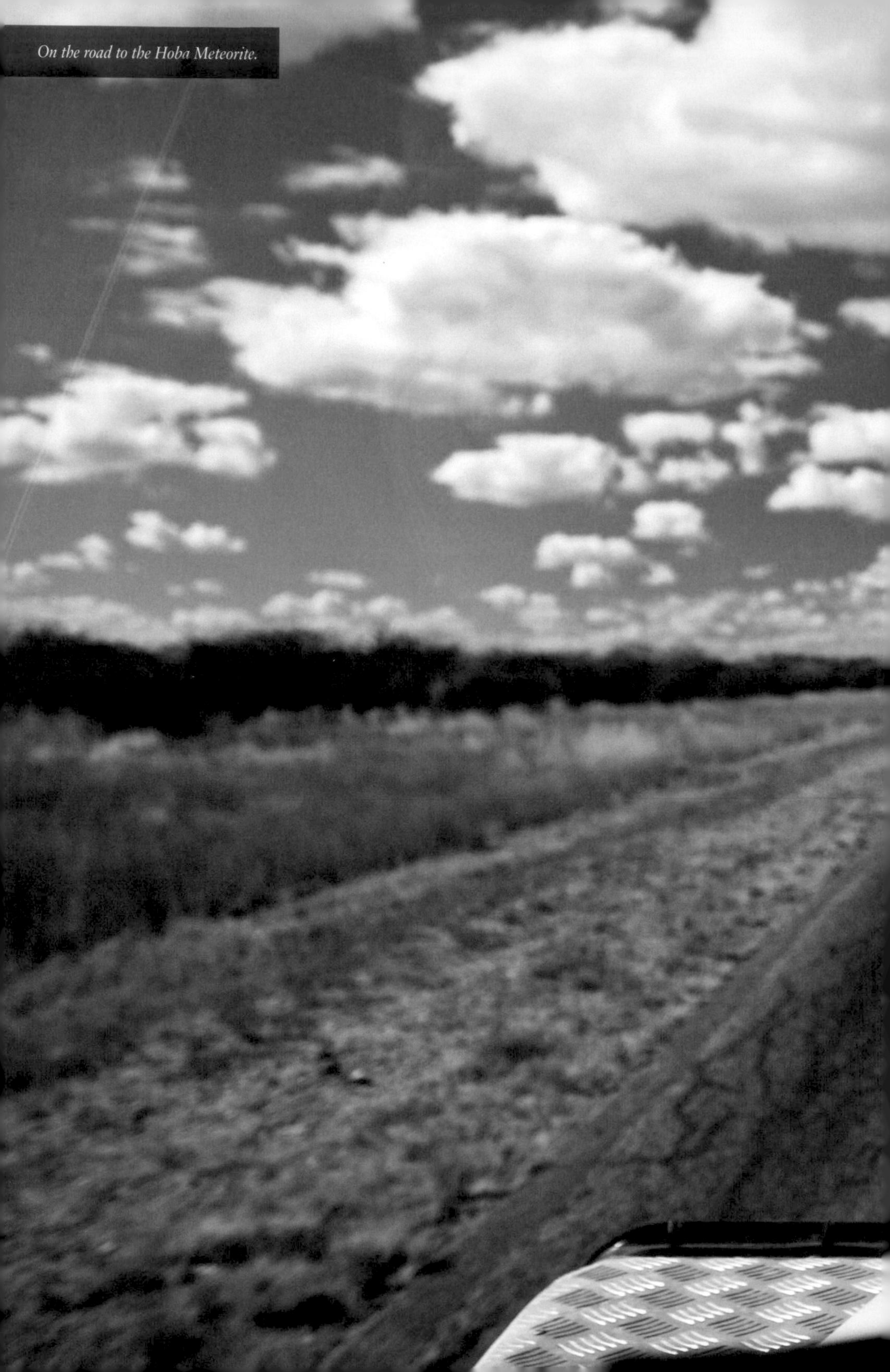

A large baobab tree near Tsumkwe.

NORTHERN NAMIBIA

The densely populated far north is Namibia's rural heartland, with traditional villages and kraals surrounded by thick bush offering a fine contrast to the arid wilds of Bushmanland.

Namibia's four northernmost regions – Oshikoto, Ohangwena, Oshana and Omusati – constitute its cultural heartland. The traditional home of the Ovambo, Namibia's largest ethnic group (in fact, before independence the area was officially known as Ovamboland), this is the most densely populated part of the country, with most people making a living as subsistence farmers growing crops of maize and millet and raising cattle and goats.

Beyond the isolated towns stretches a series of flat, scrubby plains, dotted here and there with feathery makalani palms, baobab trees and the odd clump of mopane forest. A string of small traditional villages, cattle *kraals*, roadside craft markets and *cuca* shops (grocers' stalls) complete the picture.

Crossing the line

The best time to visit the area is during May, just after the rainy season when the bush is looking splendidly verdant (this area receives the highest rainfall in the country). Summers (November–February), meanwhile, can be unpleasantly hot and sticky.

The main gateway to the north, reached by following the B1 northeast from Windhoek and Otjiwarongo through **Otavi**, is **Tsumeb** ❶ a charming town of leafy avenues set in an area whose mineral wealth embraces

vast copper deposits and more than 200 other minerals including silver, lead, zinc and cadmium. The excellent **Tsumeb Museum** (tel: 067 220447; 9am–noon Mon–Sat and 2–5pm Mon–Fri; charge), housed in an old German-built schoolhouse in Main Street, has displays on local geology and cultural history, together with a collection of retrieved German armaments dumped by retreating forces in Lake Otjikoto in 1915. For good-quality handicrafts, visit the **Tsumeb Arts and Crafts Centre** (contacts

Main Attractions
Lake Otjikoto
Ombalantu Baobab Tree
  Heritage Centre
Hoba Meteorite
Nyae Nyae Conservancy
Khaudom National Park

Items on display and for sale at the Cultural Village in Tsumeb.

and opening times as for museum) at 18 Main Street; it's run by an educational trust supporting Namibian craftsmen. Also worth a look, at the southern edge of town, the **Tsumeb Cultural Village** (tel: 067 220787) is an community project dedicated to providing visitors with an insight into traditional rural life.

Situated 24km (15 miles) northwest of Tsumeb along the B1 to Etosha's Namutoni Gate, **Lake Otjikoto** ("deep hole" in Herero) formed when the roof of an enormous underground cavern collapsed, leaving a steep-sided dolomite sinkhole some 90 metres (290 yards) deep. It's a compelling sight and well worth the detour. Otjikoto and nearby Lake Guinas are the only known habitats of the fish *Pseudocrenilabrus philander*, a species of mouth-breeding tilapia that occurs in a remarkable range of colours, from dark green to bright yellow and blue, perhaps because initially it had no natural predators in the lake and camouflage was unnecessary.

Heading north from Tsumeb, you'll have to stop at tiny **Oshivelo ❷**, some 91km (56 miles) away along the B1, in order to pass through the "Red Line", a veterinary control fence designed to block the movement of cattle (and therefore the transmission of cattle diseases such as foot and mouth) down into the ranching districts of Central Namibia.

To the west, the **Andoni Plain**, was part of Etosha National Park until the early 1960s, and home to huge herds of zebra, gnu and oryx. These days, cattle herds have displaced the wildlife, and much of the bush has been cleared to make way for flat fields sown with vegetables and grain. Part of the road north is lined by a prominent pipeline, which siphons off water from the Culevai River drainage system, a web of shallow watercourses known as *oshanas*, which fill up with water during the rainy season and then hold underground water all year round.

Just before you get to Ondangwa, you'll notice signs for the turnoff to **Olukonda** village ❸, some 10km (6 miles) southeast on the D3606. It's home to northern Namibia's oldest building, a mission house built in the

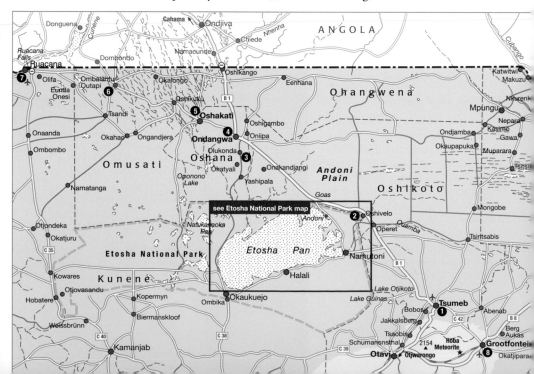

late 1870s by the Finnish missionary MarttiRauttanen. The locals called him Nakambale, or "the one with the hat", and the name stuck. Recently renovated with Finnish funding, **Nakambale House** is now a museum (tel: 065 245668; charge), that adjoins a rest camp offering accommodation in a historic mission cottage, various traditional Ovambo huts and in a campsite, too. Rauttanen is buried in the graveyard adjoining the little thatched-roof church.

If you're coming from Tsumeb, **Ondangwa ❹** is the first sizeable town you'll encounter on the B1. Before independence this was Ovamboland's main administrative centre and, while Oshakati's now taken over that role, the place still hums with life. From here, it's just 60km (37 miles) on the B1 to the Angolan border post at **Oshikango**.

Oshakati

From Ondangwa, the C46 leads northwest to Oshakati, Ovamboland's "capital". The closer you get, the more built-up the area becomes, and you'll notice a marked increase in the traffic on the road, too. Little **Ongwediva**, some 25km (15 miles) from Ondangwa, is a noted educational centre with a well-respected Teacher's Training College; of more interest to visitors, though, is the **Oshana Environment and Art Association's** shop on the main road, selling art from all over the northwest along with a good range of crafts such as jewellery, pottery and baskets.

Fast-growing **Oshakati ❺** is set near a particularly large *oshana* which habitually overflows its banks after good rains, damaging houses and other infrastructure in the process – something to bear in mind if you're travelling during the rainy season. It's a big, busy town with a lively atmosphere, but there's not really much worth stopping for here apart from the substantial covered market on the town's western boundary, which sells everything from frogs caught in local *oshanas* to woven baskets and dried mopani worms.

The road now loops northwest through the Omusati Region (*omusati* means "mopane" in Ovambo),

TIP

The former Ovamboland is in a malarial area, so consult your pharmacist and start taking prophylactics before you travel here.

Lake Otjikoto, near Tsumeb.

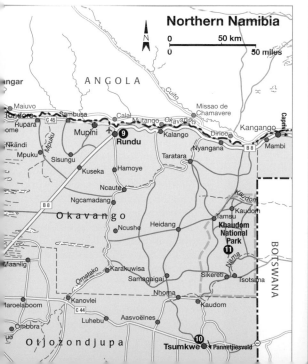

Northern Namibia

The Kavango people in Northern Namibia make baskets using all natural materials.

At Hoba Meteorite.

and you'll notice these trees becoming more prolific the further west you go. About 110km (68 miles) from Oshakati, you'll reach the dusty village of **Outapi** and the **Ombalantu Baobab Tree Heritage Community Campsite** (tel: 065 251005; www.spitzkoppereservations.com; charge). Here, an enormous 800-year old baobab tree with a trunk containing a hollowed-out "room" has been put to many different uses in the past, including stints as a church, school and even a post office! Today, it is managed as a community project with a good craft stall attached.

Ruacana Falls

Heading further northwest, you'll pass the agricultural settlement of **Mahanene** about 40km (25 miles) from Ombalantu before reaching the turn-off to sleepy **Ruacana** ⑦ some 50km (30 miles) further on. There's a petrol station and a shop here, but little activity – although you may sometimes see stately clusters of Himba clans people who have come east into town to stock up on goods before migrating back deep into the Kaokoveld.

From here, it's a scenic 25km (16-mile) drive north across the Kunene River and up into Ovamboland's only mountain range for a view into Angola and the 85-metres (280ft) high **Ruacana Falls**. Once a magnificent natural attraction, these are now dry except during the very wettest part of the rainy season (March–April), thanks to the upstream construction of a major dam in Angola. To a lesser degree, the flow is also controlled by a weir just above the falls, built to divert water into the turbines of the 320-megawatt underground hydro-electric power plant stationed on the border.

If you are planning to head into the Kaokoveld from here, Ruacana is the last place to buy fuel before **Opuwo** (see Northwest Namibia, page 204).

The Kavango region

Bordering Ovamboland to the northeast lies the lushly wooded and well-watered Kavango area. This is Namibia's second most densely populated region, with most of its inhabitants living along the banks of the Okavango River and its floodplains in scattered villages of thatched, circular huts. The traditional way of life is still strong around here and, for many Western visitors, the Kavango region and the Caprivi further east probably represent the rural African experience as they always imagined it.

The farming town of **Grootfontein** ⑧, 60km (37 miles) southeast of Tsumeb along the C42, is the main jumping off point for Kavango and the Caprivi Strip. Its only real attraction is the iron-and-nickel **Hoba Meteorite**, at 60 tonnes the largest in the world. Having blazed to earth some 30,000–80,000 years ago, it was discovered in 1920 by a local farmer and is now a national monument. It lies just 20km (12 miles) west of Grootfontein on the B8 (charge).

It's a straight 250km (155-mile) drive on a good, tarred road northeast from Grootfontein to **Rundu**, the region's main centre. About halfway

along, you'll pass through the veterinary control fence that divides the commercial cattle ranches of central Namibia from the communal land and subsistence farms of the north. Across the line, the landscape becomes markedly more Third World, with patchy fields of millet and maize linking straggling rural hamlets. Roadside stalls also start to appear, selling wooden crafts and great piles of vegetables and fruit.

In a lovely setting high above the Okavango floodplain, with good views into Angola, busy **Rundu** ❾ has a wide range of places to stay spread out along the riverfront. Most lodges offer cruises and angling trips up and down the river, too, although water levels get very low just before the rains in January. This is a good place to stock up on fuel and supplies if you're planning to drive further east to the Caprivi (see page 187) and Botswana, and don't miss the chance to visit the **Mbangura Woodcarvers' Cooperative**, either – the handicrafts sold here (chiefly made from teak) are generally to a high standard.

Bushmanland

East of Grootfontein, Central Namibia's fertile agricultural plains begin to shade into the hot and arid Kalahari sands of Otjozondjupa Region. This stretch of semi-desert – reaching all the way to the Botswana border – is still widely known by its old name Bushmanland. It is the main territory of the traditional hunter-gatherers who refer to themselves as the Ju/hoansi, but are more widely known to outsiders as San or Bushmen. Hunting is now expressly forbidden in the region, and most communities here are no longer nomadic but settled in scattered villages, where they scratch a living as subsistence farmers (see page 17).

The easiest way to get to the region's main town, **Tsumkwe** ❿, is from Grootfontein. Bear in mind, however, that Tsumkwe is little more than a dusty crossroads, offering sparse supplies and without even a petrol station

– so stock up before you go. To find it, head north on the B8 for 50km (32 miles) before turning east onto the (gravel) C44. After 32km (20 miles), you'll pass **Maroelaboom** police station; it's about another 200km (125 miles) from here.

The community-run **Omatako Valley Rest Camp** (www.omatakovalley. com) makes a good pit stop along the way – look out for signs about 88km (55 miles) after you've turned east onto the C44. It has a good craft shop selling beads, necklaces and baskets as well as cold drinks, and activities such as bush walks and village tours can be arranged.

Tsumkwe is on the borders of the 9,000-sq-km (3,475-sq-mile) **Nyae Nyae Conservancy**, which was established by a development foundation in 1997 to promote ecotourism as a way of preventing any further erosion of traditional Ju/'hoansi culture. Most hotels and lodges around Tsumkwe can arrange excursions with local guides into the conservancy, visiting villages to watch craft demonstrations and traditional dancing, or taking food-gathering trips into the bush.

FACT

Some San now sell their traditional craftwork, including necklaces and bracelets made from ostrich eggs, beads, bows and arrows, and animal hide bags.

A woman drills holes in beads at a San community near Tsumkwe.

Hollowed out ostrich eggs are used as water carriers, convenient in the dry areas of Namibia.

The general stores in Tsumkwe.

Nyae Nyae forms part of the **Pannetjiesveld**, an area speckled with small pans around which modest amounts of game collect in summer, when the ground gets very dry. Visitors can expect to spot a good range of wildlife from lion, leopard, elephant and hyena to giraffe, kudu and the roan antelope.

During the rainy season, the area's often temporarily flooded and the bigger animals move further north – although the birdlife remains abundant. After a good amount of rainfall, you can expect to see great flocks of lesser flamingos and wood sandpipers on **Nyae Nyae**, the largest pan, and perhaps even rare wader species such as the great snipe.

You can drive to Tsumkwe in an ordinary saloon car, but to explore further afield you definitely need to be part of a completely self-reliant group with at least two 4x4 vehicles between you. And, if you're planning to camp out around these parts, always sleep inside a tent due to the obvious threats from dangerous insects, reptiles and large mammals.

Khaudom National Park

Just north of Bushmanland in the region of the Botswana border, the little-known and undeveloped **Khaudom National Park** ⓫ is a wild area of dry woodland savannah on stabilised Kalahari dunes, dotted with the occasional clay pan.

Thanks to the *omurambas* (a Herero word meaning poorly-defined drainage lines) that criss-cross the area, the vegetation's pretty dense, dominated by mangetti, Rhodesian teak and false mopane on the dunes, and acacia and umbrella-thorn elsewhere.

Wildlife isn't as abundant as in the Etosha National Park, but giraffe, kudu, oryx and steenbok are present in significant numbers, alongside scarce antelope such as roan and tsessebe. A substantial lion population is boosted by leopard, cheetah, black-backed jackal and spotted hyena.

This is also Namibia's best national park for catching sight of the localised African wild dog. The main attraction, however, has got to be the very real sense that you are definitely deep in the African wild.

EXPLORING KHAUDOM

Khaudom is accessible only to well-equipped and adventurous travellers. Facilities are almost non-existent, and no official campsites or supplies are available, so visitors must bring all their own food, water and fuel. Two camps formerly maintained by Namibia Wildlife remain the best camping spots: southerly Sikereti is set in a grove of silver-leaf terminalia, while northerly Khaudom stands on a dune crest overlooking a waterhole. Access is from Tsumkwe, following the minor road that leads north out of town, and is signposted for Khaudom. Where the road splits, take the right fork for the park entrance and Sikereti camp, a total journey of about 65km (40 miles). Within the park, the roads are mainly sandy, so it's advisable to travel in a convoy of at least two 4x4s.

The Ovambo

Forming by far the largest ethnic group within Namibia's boundaries, the Ovambo comprise slightly more than half of the total population

Ovambo (or Aawambo or Ambo) is a collective name for a number of indigenous peoples living in Northern Namibia and Southern Angola who share a common origin and culture. Traditionally, the clan (*omuhoko*) was the most important political institution among the Ovambo. Four of the biggest clans live in the southern Kunene Province of Angola and eight in northern Namibia (the largest group, the Kwanyama – comprising 36 percent – is cut in two by the international boundary). Others are the Ndongo (29 percent), the Kwambi (12 percent), the Ngandjera (8 percent), and the Mbalantu (7 percent). Although each group speaks its own dialect, they are all closely related and mutually intelligible.

Many Ovambo still adhere to a traditional economy based on a combination of subsistence agriculture and animal husbandry. The main crop of the region is millet, which is used to make a stiff porridge, but other common crops include beans, squashes, and watermelons. Goats, cattle, pigs and chickens are reared in many family smallholdings. During the rainy season, when seasonal rivers fill with water from Angola, this home-grown produce is supplemented by fishing.

A tribe under pressure

The Ovambo's way of life has been under pressure since German colonial times, when an ever-increasing number of young men entered the labour market on farms, in towns and at industrial sites and mines. The introduction of the Western monetary system also brought about drastic changes to the economy, with hundreds of small Ovambo-owned shops springing up across the land. Meanwhile, most Ovambo people combine elements of a traditional belief system, which centres on a single deity called Kalunga, with a heavier dose of Christianity – Lutheranism being dominant as a result of a German and Finnish missionary influence dating to the 1870s.

After the contract labour and pass laws associated with apartheid were abolished, the southward migration of Ovambo people increased significantly.

Today, many Ovambo work in the larger towns as labourers, craftsmen and professionals.

The traditional social system reveals a close relationship with other central African Bantu cultures. A most striking feature is the predominance of matrilineal descent, a system which determines in particular the laws of inheritance and succession, as well as post-marital residency. In recent years, however, there has been a distinct shift towards a patrilineal society. External factors such as Christian doctrine, migrant labour, business enterprises undertaken by nuclear families and economic independence have all contributed to this change.

Traditionally each clan was headed by a hereditary chief or king, assisted by a council of headmen. Today, however, only three of the main clans are still ruled by chiefs-in-council; the rest have a system of senior headmen forming a council and administering their communities by joint action. Regulating the land ownership system is one of the most important roles. Personal ownership of the land is unknown, and only life-long rights of utilisation may be granted by the chief via his headmen. After the death of the tenant, the right of utilisation reverts to the next higher authority and may be assigned to somebody else. Thus land never becomes private property.

An Ovambo woman.

Animals at a watering hole.

Oryx at Etosha National Park.

ETOSHA NATIONAL PARK

Set in high savannah in the north of the country, this is one of the oldest and largest parks in Africa, and the best for big-game spotting in an arid environment.

Etosha National Park is the jewel in Namibia's wildlife crown. At first sight for the game viewer, however, it is a rather hollow jewel, for – right in the centre of that part of the park which is open to the public – sprawls an enormous saline pan. Yet it is for this pan that Etosha is famous. Measuring about 130km (80 miles) from east to west, and up to 68km (42 miles) from north to south, it covers an area of about 4,800 sq km (1,850 sq miles) and is as inhospitable as the most barren desert. Almost entirely devoid of vegetation, Etosha Pan gleams and shimmers in the noonday sun, creating the most fantastic mirages, inverting distant images and turning the black full stops of the male ostriches who stray onto its great white wastes into colons.

All this is good news for the game viewer, however, for almost all the animals are concentrated along the rim of the pan (especially along its southern side), where a string of about 50 pumped and natural waterholes create a stage attracting a constantly changing cast of players. For the enthusiastic visitor, rewarding wildlife watching is practically guaranteed.

A brief history

Etosha first gained official park status in 1907, when Governor von Lindequist of the German Colonial Government

proclaimed Game Reserves 1, 2 and 3. Game Reserve No. 2 encompassed the Etosha Pan and Kaokoland from the Kunene River in the north to the Hoarusib River in the south, a total area of 93,240 sq km (36,000 sq miles). As such, it remained intact until 1947 when the Kaokoland portion was set aside for use and occupation by the Herero. During the same year, 3,406 sq km (1,315 sq miles) were cut off from the Etosha portion and sectioned into farms, an area which became known as the Gagarus block. It then became clear,

Main Attractions
Okaukuejo Rest Camp
Fischer's Pan
Namutoni Rest Camp
Tsumcor Waterhole
Rietfontein Waterhole
Halali Rest Camp
Onkoshi Camp
Ongava Lodge and Tented Camp

Namutoni Rest Camp in Etosha.

The Etosha National Park was first established in 1907, and is now about one-quarter of its original size.

however, that the reduced park area was too small to accommodate rare species such as Hartmann's mountain zebra and black-faced impala, migratory big game such as eland and elephant, and the influx of wildlife from adjacent areas. In accordance with the Elephant Commission of 1956, the boundaries of the park were extended towards the west to include unoccupied state land between the Hoanib and the Ugab rivers.

This practically doubled the size of the park, safeguarded migration routes and created a corridor to the sea. The new park now extended from the Skeleton Coast in the west for nearly 500km (300 miles) inland to the edge of the Etosha Pan in the east, a total surface area of 99,526 sq km (38,427 sq miles).

Unfortunately, the existence of what was effectively the largest game reserve in the world was short-lived. As a result of the recommendations of the Odendaal Commission of 1963, the park area was drastically reduced, with total disregard for ecological boundaries. Solely for political reasons (that is, in order to accommodate South

Africa's policy of separate homeland development or apartheid), 71,792 sq km (27,719 sq miles) were sacrificed to the land needs of Ovamboland, Kaokoland and Damaraland. By 1970 the park had been whittled down to its present size of 22,270 sq km (8,600 sq miles), a reduction of 77 percent – just a shadow of its former grandeur. This makes it larger than the Serengeti and comparable in size to the Kruger National Park, a vast conservation area by any standards, but many wildlife experts feel that the ecological integrity of Etosha would be greatly boosted were the link with Skeleton Coast National Park to be re-established.

The pan and beyond

The park takes its name from the **Etosha Pan ❶**, the "great white place of dry water" which is the ultimate destination of channels draining from the catchment area in southern Angola. The Etosha Pan started life many thousands of years ago as a shallow perennial lake fed by the Kunene River, which subsequently changed its course, leaving behind a mineral-rich sump

Etosha
National Park

with an estimated capacity of 150–200 million cubic metres (195–260 million cubic yards), a quantity of water almost never seen in the pan today.

The pan can become partially flooded during the rainy season, but the water is too brackish for human or animal consumption; instead it supports a rich growth of blue-green algae. In a good rainy season, up to a million flamingos are lured to the pan to breed – a wonderful sight. When the water dries up, very little vegetation grows on the pan, with the exception of occasional patches of a salt-loving grass, rich in protein, which provides good grazing for blue wildebeest, springbok and zebra during the dry winter months.

To the east of the pan is the tree-less **Andoni Plain**, a typical grassland dominated by the tall perennial grass, *Sporobolus spicatus*. Along the western and northwestern shore of the pan are the **Okondeka grasslands**, and between the Haunted Wood and the Charl Marais Dam is **Grootvlakte ❷**. These two grasslands are the main summer grazing areas for plains

animals such as Burchell's zebra, blue wildebeest and springbok. The winter grazing areas, which sustain less palatable grasses, are the **Halali Plains**, extending from the waterholes known as **Charitsaub ❸** to **Nuamses** and **Gemsbokvlakte**.

The big game show

Some 114 species of mammal have been recorded in Etosha, ranging from four of the so-called Big Five – lion, leopard, elephant and black rhinoceros – to a host of smaller creatures such as rodents and bats. However, the arid nature of the terrain and lack of perennial waterways makes it ill-suited to creatures dependent on water: there are no buffalos, hippos or crocodiles in the park, and only one fish species has ever been recorded.

When the rainy season begins in November, the animals seldom need to visit the waterholes along the tourist routes, congregating instead in large herds on the grass plains west of **Okaukuejo Rest Camp ❹** and in the area around **Fischer's Pan** near **Namutoni Rest Camp ❺**. Many

TIP

When you stop to watch birds at a waterhole or along the road, keep an eye out, too, for camouflaged mammals hidden in shady places.

A game-viewing location at Okaukuejo, rated by many as one of Africa's most exciting game-viewing water-holes.

NOMADS & HOMEBODIES

Much of Etosha's wildlife, including the likes of lion, leopard, spotted hyena and steenbok, is strongly territorial, which means that a particular individual or group will almost always be found within its specific home range, which it will defend vigorously against any intruder of the same species. By contrast, some other creatures, such as elephant, eland and red hartebeest, are highly nomadic, wandering widely around the entire ecosystem, and sometimes beyond it, in search of the best grazing or browsing. Many of these nomadic creatures, including springbok, plains zebra, blue wildebeest and elephant, follow reasonably predictable migrational patterns based on the seasonal availability of grazing and rainwater, which most animals prefer to fountain or borehole water.

Dangerous animals

Namibia hosts an impressive menagerie of wildlife, and while these creatures seldom initiate attacks on humans, they are best treated with caution and respect.

Contrary to myth, most wild animals fear humans far more than we fear them, and their instinctive response to any accidental encounter is to flee in the opposite direction. At the same time, accidents can and do happen – indeed, almost any wild animal large enough to confront a human might do so when injured, cornered or provoked – so it pays to use a little common sense in the presence of potentially dangerous wildlife.

On a motorised safari, the one animal that poses a serious risk to passengers is the elephant, which is large enough to overturn a car and crush its occupant. For this reason, it's a good idea to leave the engine running when you first encounter an elephant, at least until you are pretty sure it is chilled about your presence. An elephant will almost invariably

Do not feed – monkeys and baboons become very aggressive when they learn to link people with food.

precede a proper charge with loud trumpeting and/ or a mock charge; when this happens, the best strategy is simply to back off and give it some space. It is also inadvisable to carry fruit in your car in elephant country – they have a good sense of smell and tusks make fantastic tin openers!

On foot, buffalo and black rhino probably present more of a risk than elephant. All three of these sizeable ungulates are best given a wide berth, especially if you see them before they see you, and risk surprising them at close quarters. In the unlikely event you are actually charged – and it really is unlikely – the safest course of action is usually to head for the nearest tree and climb it.

Though neither is present in Etosha, hippos and crocs are responsible for more human fatalities than any other large African animal, and both are common in the Caprivi. Hippos are not actively aggressive, but they panic easily and will mow down any person that comes between them and the perceived safety of the water, so avoid vegetated riverbanks and lakeshores in overcast weather or low light. Crocodiles seldom attack outside of their aquatic hunting environment, so you are only at appreciable risk if you bathe in crocodile-infested waters – the simple rule here is to ask local advice before you swim.

Take precautions

Never feed the wildlife, especially monkeys or baboons, which become very aggressive (and may need to be put down) when they learn to associate people with food. At campsites, be careful about where you stash fresh foodstuffs: fruit might attract elephants or monkeys to a tent, and raw meat could pique the interest of a passing predator.

Speaking of which, large predators such as lion, spotted hyena and leopard seldom attack people without provocation. Should you confront one on foot, the key thing is not to run away, which might potentially trigger its instinct to chase. Rather stand still or back off very slowly, preferably without making eye contact. Sleeping in a sealed tent practically guarantees your safety from predators after dark – but don't sleep with your head out of a flap, or you risk being decapitated through plain curiosity.

Venomous snakes and scorpions are unobtrusive, and lethal bites are rare – in neighbouring South Africa, for instance, lightning is a bigger killer than snakebite. Still, it pays to be wary when picking up firewood, and to wear solid walking boots and reasonably thick trousers as protection on game walks.

young animals are born at this time of the year, but this is also when most of Etosha's 1,500 elephants leave the tourist section and move to the northern and southern areas. Some even leave the park altogether, depending on the availability of water.

Black rhino (for which the park is famed) occur mostly in the western and southwestern areas of the park and are generally seen in the vicinity of Okaukuejo either at night at the waterhole, or in the evenings and early mornings, as they browse in the cool of the day. Giraffe are widely distributed throughout Etosha but, being browsers, they avoid the plains unless it is to drink at a waterhole, when they make a particularly dramatic sight. Lion are distributed throughout the park with concentrations where prey is plentiful, along with both cheetah and the elusive leopard. Other large mammals to look out for in Etosha are Burchell's (or plains) zebra, blue wildebeest, gemsbok, kudu, eland, red hartebeest, roan antelope and springbok. Etosha is a stronghold for the black-faced impala, which is endemic

to the Namibia/Angola border area. About 300 individuals were translocated here in the 1970s and their descendents now form half of the global population of 1,000.

Smaller species

Less-frequently seen species include secretive nocturnal predators such as the caracal, with its trademark lynx-like tufted ears, the African wild cat, the aardwolf – a smaller distant relative of the hyena – and the spotted hyena, which can sometimes be heard howling or "laughing" at night. Also encountered are black-backed jackals, warthogs, honey badgers, and smaller antelope such as steenbok and grey duiker, along with the diminutive Damara dik-dik which can be seen especially in the Klein Namutoni area. The endearing striped ground squirrel is often seen scurrying or standing along the roadside.

Of the 340 bird species which have been identified in the park, about one-third are migratory, such as the European bee-eater, European roller, barn swallow and a profusion of

The jackal usually lives and hunts in monogamous pairs.

A lion and lioness explore their territory.

The African ground squirrel lives in open, grassy areas, similar to North American prairie dogs.

Capturing a giraffe on film.

waders. During good rainy seasons large numbers of waterbirds and waders, including greater and lesser flamingo, congregate on Fischer's Pan. Namibia's national bird, the dramatic crimson-breasted shrike, is fairly common in Etosha, drawing attention to itself with its harsh loud duets. It is also possible to spot, and ponder over the identification of, no less than 12 species of lark.

Of the 35 raptor species found in the park, 10 are migratory and come to Etosha only for the summer. These include the yellow-billed kite, steppe eagle, western red-footed kestrel and the booted eagle. The smallest bird of prey in the park is the pygmy falcon. The most common species of vulture are lappet-faced and white-backed vultures but examples of Cape, Egyptian, and hooded vultures can also be spotted by the observant birdwatcher. Other rare bird species found here include the black-tailed godwit, the goliath and purple heron, the dwarf bittern and the grey crowned crane. Conspicuous ground birds include Kori bustard, red-crested korhaan, northern black korhaan, helmeted guineafowl and red-billed francolin.

Fruitful sites

The best game viewing in Etosha is generally achieved by sitting quietly at a waterhole and waiting to see what animals will turn up. This is especially true during the winter months (May–August) and before the rainy season (September–November), when the lack of standing rainwater forces thirsty animals to congregate around the watering points. If you arrive at a waterhole and it seems to be deserted, don't just drive away – stop and have a good look around. It may just be that there is a predator lurking nearby, preventing the game from coming near the water. Look carefully in all the shady places where cats might lie up out of the sun, and scan the bigger trees for leopards.

As a general rule, most visitors arriving at waterholes park where they do not obstruct the views of others. It is also good game-viewing protocol to turn off the engine, especially if you have air conditioning, as this makes things considerably quieter and allows

everybody to enjoy the natural sounds of the bush. Switching off the engine also enables photographers to lean on the vehicle's open windows without the vibration from the engine blurring their pictures. Everybody has a much more enjoyable safari if each has his or her own pair of binoculars so that no-one becomes bored while the rest of the party discusses the finer points of a twitching lion's tail, or the tusks of a distant elephant only visible through a magnifying lens!

The **Klein** and **Groot Okevi** water-holes just north of Namutoni are both frequented by black-faced impala, kudu, gemsbok, zebra, elephant and a great variety of birds, as well as predators such as leopard and cheetah. Further north is **Tsumcor ⑥**, a favourite place for pho-tographing elephants. Still further, on the Andoni Plain, is the **Andoni** water-hole **⑦**, where there are often many bird species. A new entrance gate to the park was opened here in 2003. East of Namutoni on the edge of Fischer's Pan are **Aroe**, frequented by elephant, springbok, blue wildebeest, kudu, zebra and giraffe, and **Twee Palms**, with its two landmark makalani palms, a favour-ite with photographers.

South of Namutoni lie **Chudob** and **Klein Namutoni**, both fed by artesian springs. Giraffe, black-faced impala and warthog can be observed at both of these waterholes. In the same vicin-ity is Bloubokdraai, where the Damara dik-dik can sometimes be seen at rela-tively close quarters. West of Namutoni is Kalkheuwel, where it is possible to get close to the game. During the dry season large numbers of animals come here to drink, including lion, gemsbok, giraffe and elephant.

Other waterholes

Other sites in this area include **Oker-fontein**, on the edge of the pan, where cheetah and lion are seen; **Ngobib**, which attracts kudu, zebra and elephant; **Batia**, with its large herds of springbok, blue wildebeest and elephant; and **Goas ⑧**, where you could see vast numbers of

black-faced impala, blue wildebeest, red hartebeest, elephant and zebra, as well as lion and birds of prey.

Travelling west towards Okaukuejo is **Rietfontein ⑨**, one of the best-known waterholes in the park. Many species, including leopard, are found here, as well as a wide variety of birds. **Charit-saub**, **Salvadora** and **Sueda** waterholes are situated close together further west and are a good bet for lion. Hundreds of springbok, zebra and gemsbok are often seen here too, but elephant only very rarely. Still further west is **Homob**, close to the pan and often frequented by both lion and elephant. There is also good game viewing at **Aus**, **Oli-fantsbad** and **Gemsbokvlakte**.

Furthest northwest of all is **Ozon-juitji m'Bari**, frequented by a vari-ety of animals, but is rather far from camp. Here, the road travels through the well-known **Sprokieswoud** ("Haunted Wood"), the only place in the park where the weirdly shaped African moringo is found growing in a flat area and as a dense forest. Moringos – endemic to Namibia and christened the "upside-down tree" by

An impala.

The lilac-breasted roller is commonly found through sub-saharan Africa.

Springbok gather at the Etosha Pan.

the Bushmen – normally grow on the slopes of hills and mountains. **Ombika** ❿ lies south of Okaukuejo and close to the Andersson Gate; it's visited by a variety of game, especially lion.

Etosha's rest camps

Okaukuejo, the park's oldest and most popular rest camp and its administrative HQ, lies 17km (10 miles) from the southern entrance gate, right in the centre of the park (most tourist maps show only the eastern sector, but in fact it stretches as far westwards as the C35 road at Otjovasandu). The accommodation here has recently been modernised and now offers a broad range of bungalows and rooms as well as a camping site, restaurant, shop, filling station internet café, and swimming pool. It has a wonderful floodlit waterhole, which is almost always active and can be exceptional at night, when black rhino can come almost within touching distance. Guided morning, afternoon and night drives are also offered here.

Namutoni Camp, on the eastern side of the park, has a recorded history going back to 1851, when the explorers

Sir Francis Galton and Charles Andersson camped near Namutoni Spring, a bowl-shaped limestone fountain in a marshy environment of tall reeds, once a drinking place for cattle. The first Fort Namutoni, built of unfired clay bricks, was completed in 1903 only to be razed to the ground the next year during the Herero uprising (the garrison of four soldiers and three ex-servicemen all escaped). In 1950 the rebuilt but dilapidated fort was declared a national monument; a few years later it was renovated according to the original design. First opened to tourists in 1958, the camp was greatly extended in 1983, when a shop, restaurant complex and 24 accommodation units were added. It also has a floodlit waterhole and offers guided day and night game drives.

Opened in 1967, **Halali Rest Camp** ⓫ is situated among shady mopane trees at the base of a dolomite hill about halfway between Okaukuejo and Namutoni. Here, attractions include the so-called **Tsumasa Trail** and the floodlit waterhole laid out on the hill close to the rest camp. The grounds of the camp can be a very good place to see small animals and birds, which – because they are so used to seeing people – have become very tame and can easily be approached for pictures. Once again, facilities include a shop, restaurant and bar, as well as a swimming pool.

The newest addition to the portfolio of camps within the park, **Onkoshi Camp** ⓬ opened in 2008 on a secluded peninsula nestled on the rim of Etosha Pan near Namutoni, from where guests are transported in camp vehicles. It's a low-impact eco-friendly establishment aimed at the more exclusive end of the market, comprising just 15 ethnically decorated rooms on stilted platforms that offer wonderful vistas over the pan, especially at sunset.

Although it may sound crazy, do take your binoculars to the waterholes at night. They really do enhance your night vision and help you to sort out what is a rock or a bush and what is a hyena. If you have a tripod,

it is possible to achieve interesting effects by photographing animals in the floodlights on a timed exposure – some stay still, while those that move leave ghostly images on your film.

Recent years have also seen the opening of several private lodges and conservancies bordering Etosha, some of which function as wildlife destinations in their own right, while others are essentially springboards for exploring the national park.

Foremost among those in the former category is the luxurious **Ongava Lodge and Tented Camp**, which lies on a privately managed 300 sq km (166 sq km) tract of acacia woodland abutting the southern park boundary near Okaukuejo Rest Camp. Managed by the highly regarded Wilderness Safaris, Ongava is open to lodge residents only, and guided game drives come with a high chance of sighting lion, giraffe, black-faced impala and both black and white rhino. Guided game drives out of Ongava also explore the road network within the national park, whose Andersson Gate lies about 15 minutes' drive away. Another good

base for exploring the western part of the park, Andersson's Camp , now also managed by Wilderness Safaris, is a mid-range tented camp that opened in 2008 about 5km (3 miles) from the entrance gate of the same name.

Similar upmarket bases for exploring the eastern part of the national park include the seriously luxurious **Mushara Lodge**, a family-run property situated 8km from the Von Lindequist Gate. Nearby, the more mainstream **Kempinski Mokuti Lodge**, part of an upmarket international chain usually specialising in city hotels, is set on a pedestrian-friendly private conservancy that harbours a good selection of antelope and other herbivores (including a misplaced herd of bontebok, a South African endemic), but no dangerous game. Another possible base for exploring the park is the 200 sq km (77 sq miles) **Onguma Game Reserve**, which opened in 2005 adjacent to the easterly Fischer's Pan, and offers an attractive combination of rustically comfortable accommodation and varied wildlife, including black rhino, lion and more than 300 bird species.

The mopani worm, or caterpillar, is an important source of protein in the diet of millions of indigenous Africans. The worms are eaten raw, dried, fried, and pickled.

Helmeted guineafowl in Etosha.

NAMIBIA'S CHARISMATIC BIRDS

Namibia's diverse landscapes support a wide range of unusual bird life, from the biggest bird in the world to the tiny indigenous Damara tern.

Namibia's varied habitats range from the hyper-arid sand-sea desert of the southern Namib through arid savannah and deciduous woodlands, to tropical forests and wetlands near the Kavango and Zambezi Rivers. In addition, coastal currents produce a rich marine environment, in the open ocean, along sandy and rocky shores, and in protected lagoons. This diversity results in a bird checklist that includes at least 706 of the 950-plus bird species listed for southern Africa, some 500 of which breed locally, .

Breeds Apart

A striking sight of the coastal region is the great flocks of greater and lesser flamingo, whose honking can be heard all night when the tides suit nocturnal foraging. Equally memorable are the three sandgrouse, seen in large numbers in the desert. This bird has evolved a fascinating adaptation to its arid environment: the adult's breast feathers are specially modified to absorb and hold water. When it visits a waterhole to drink, it immerses its breast so that when it returns to the nest, the young chicks can release the stored moisture by nibbling the adult's feathers. The riverine forests of the inland wetland regions, meanwhile, support rare raptors such as western banded snake-eagle and Pel's fishing owl. Namibia's largest number of endemic species is associated with the ante-Namib – the transition zone between desert and arid savannah – among them the stately Rüppell's korhaan and elusive Herero chat.

Migrating flamingos signal the start of the rainy season. Large numbers live at Walvis Bay's lagoon, while the Etosha Pan occasionally fills with enough water to be used as a breeding site.

As well as solitary hunting, Pale Chanting Goshawks also hunt prey in social groups to maximise their chances of success.

The southern yellow-billed hornbill.

A pair of ostriches in Etosha National Park.

THE BIGGEST BIRD ON EARTH

The Namib Desert doesn't support much birdlife, but what is there is memorable. The most striking desert-dweller, often spotted running elegantly across the gravel plains, is the ostrich, the world's biggest bird. Standing up to 2.5 metres (8ft) tall and weighing 135kg (300lb), this flightless bird has evolved long, powerful legs as its main form of defence. One kick from an ostrich's two-toed, sharp-nailed foot is enough to kill a man. It can sprint at 70kph (45mph) and maintain a speed of 50kph (30mph) for 30 minutes. In the wild, it occurs in flocks of up to 40 birds, which often travel alongside herds of antelope. The long neck allows an ostrich to spot enemies from a great distance, so it provides an early warning system to these other animals. True to myth, an ostrich may flatten its head to the ground if approached. Females of the same flock lay their eggs in a communal nest-scrape on the ground until a clutch of 15 to 20 has accumulated. An ostrich egg is 15cm (6ins) long and weighs as much as 36 hen's eggs.

The southern subspecies of the Kori bustard. These birds favour open grasslands and arid savannah.

A secretary bird in Etosha. Although known for killing snakes, it relies far more on rodents and insects for food.

The gregarious masked weaver, whose name derives from its method of nest-building, belongs to one of the largest bird families in Africa.

A lilac-breasted roller in
Bwabwata National Park.

THE CAPRIVI

Thanks to a generous annual rainfall, this lush northeastern region supports a wide range of wildlife in some excellent, and little-known, national parks.

Windhoek

ook at a map of Namibia and you are immediately struck by the strange panhandle of territory, the Caprivi Strip, sticking out to the northeast. Indeed, in order to keep themselves tidy, some maps detach the panhandle and print it elsewhere on the page so that its geographical eccentricity is not readily apparent. Like the straight lines that separate many African countries, the Caprivi Strip was the result of negotiations more than a century ago between colonial powers intent on getting the best deals for their various empires.

At the time, Germany had recently annexed Namibia (then South West Africa), and was seeking a trade route to the Zambezi in order – some say – to make an eventual link to Tanzania (then Tanganyika, and also in German hands). Britain was suspicious of her intentions and tried to block them by proclaiming the Protectorate of Bechuanaland (later to become Botswana), which included the Caprivi area. Eventually, both parties met at the Berlin Conference in 1890.

Land transactions

In a transaction more reminiscent of a Monopoly game than real life, Britain ceded control of both the Caprivi Strip and Heligoland (one of the North Frisian islands in the North Sea) in return for Zanzibar. The German Chancellor

at the time, Baron von Caprivi, gave his name to the country's new acquisition, and this should have been the end of the story – except that Britain took it back, along with the rest of Namibia, during World War I and governed it as part of Bechuanaland. Later, the Strip was administered by South Africa as part of South West Africa, and finally it became part of the Namibia that achieved independence in 1992.

Most people access the Caprivi area by driving up the B8 from **Grootfontein** to **Rundu** and then turning

Main Attractions
Popa Falls
Mahango Game Reserve
Lizauli Traditional Village
Mamili National Park
Katima Mulilo

Transportation in Mahango Village.

The Caprivi Strip stretches 450km (280 miles) from the northeast corner of the main part of the country eastward to the Zambezi River. Its width varies from about 32 to 105km (20 to 65 miles). The region is a flat plain, about 950m (3,100ft) in elevation.

The hippopotamus usually remains under water during the day, but will emerge at night to graze.

eastwards. About half-way up this road you leave behind the mainly white farming area with its large ranches, cross the veterinary fence erected to control cattle movements (and thus diseases) among livestock, and enter the sort of rural Africa more commonly seen in Botswana, Zimbabwe, Zambia or Angola. After driving hundreds of miles during which you will have barely seen a soul, suddenly there are villages of thatched rondavels by the roadside busy with people and animals. To reach the Caprivi proper, simply continue on the B8 from Rundu, which is tarred all the way to the border with Botswana at **Ngoma**.

Lush lands

The Caprivi is unlike anywhere else in Namibia. As distinct from the hot, dry desert areas, it is more tropical with warmer winters and the highest rainfall in the country. Some 450km (270 miles) long and 100km (60 miles) wide at its broadest, and less than 32km (20 miles) at its narrowest, it is divided into three regions: the West

Caprivi or Mukwe Area, the Caprivi Strip proper and Eastern Caprivi.

Much of the land in the neighbouring countries – Angola, Botswana, Zambia and Zimbabwe – immediately bordering the Caprivi is under some protection through conservation legislation. This, combined with the fact that there is an immensely rich variety of habitats – river systems, floodplains, riverine woodlands, and mopane and Kalahari woodlands – means that the wildlife in the Caprivi is equally rich. In a country where otherwise the only permanently flowing rivers are on its northern and southern frontiers, the presence of a constant supply of water is luxury indeed.

So flat and devoid of physical features is the region that 30 percent of the Eastern Caprivi can be flooded during the rains. One consequence of this is that you will find game in this region not found elsewhere in Namibia. Obvious water animals are hippo and crocodile but there are also antelope which are equally tied to water and more often thought of as being found in the neighbouring

Okavango Delta such as red lechwe, sitatunga and reedbuck. Other game is also here in large numbers: no less than 60 percent of Namibia's elephants and buffalo use the area and there are calculated to be close to 6,000 elephant here; no respecters of international frontiers, they regularly move between the Caprivi and the four neighbouring countries. They are considered to be part of the much larger population of approximately 125,000 elephants that live in the region.

A late start

Despite all this, it was only in the late 1990s that the Caprivi started developing as a tourist destination. Wilderness that had been a virtual war zone prior to independence – when the former South African Defence Force was engaged in a war with independence-seeking guerillas based in Angola – and wildlife that had been persecuted by both the military and the guerrillas now began to rehabilitate rapidly.

For the tourism industry this was a heaven-sent opportunity, and it wasn't long before the first luxury lodges

appeared in the far eastern end of the panhandle, where Zambia, Zimbabwe, Botswana and Namibia share a border. Western Caprivi has been slower to develop mainly as it abuts Angola, where a civil war has been raging for 25 years. Tourist accommodation around here is still rather more rustic and "no-frills" than the upmarket establishments at the other end of the strip.

Bwabwata National Park

A little over 200km (120 miles) from Rundu, you will reach **Divundu** ❶ where you leave the B8 and take the Botswana road towards **Mohembo** to reach the Okavango River at **Popa Falls** ❷. The river here forms the western boundary of the 6,275 sq km (2,422 sq mile) **Bwabwata National Park** ❸, which was formally proclaimed in 2007 and combines the former Caprivi Game Reserve (created in 1968 but largely ignored as a conservation entity since the South African Defence Force took over shortly afterwards) and the smaller but better-preserved Popa Falls and Mahango Game Reserves. The park is bisected

A mokoro moored in the Okavango delta.

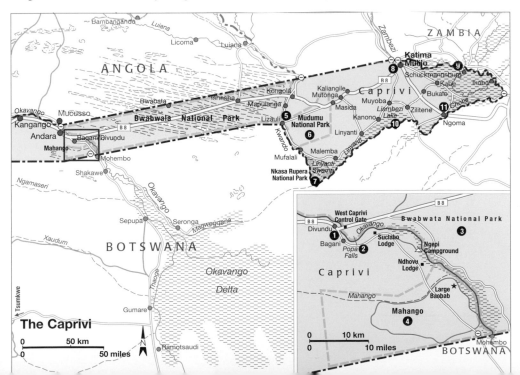

The African Elephant is extremely intelligent. Herds are usually comprised of females and their young, and are led by the matriarch.

Mahango Game Reserve.

by the main surfaced road through the Caprivi Strip for 180km (112 miles) before it reaches the Kwando River on its eastern boundary. Bwabwata is the Namibian component in the Kavango–Zambezi Transfrontier Conservation Area, which extends across 278,000 sq km (108,600 sq miles) – an area comparable to Italy – from the Caprivi into Botswana, Angola, Zambia and Zimbabwe).

A lovely spot for an overnight stay, Popa Falls is not so much a waterfall as a long set of rapids, where – thanks to a geological fault manifested here as a broad quartzite ledge – the Okavango River drops some 2.5 metres (8ft) through a maze of islands. Small it may be, but the influence of the falls on the surrounding land is immense; this is the start of the basin in which the Okavango River gradually spreads across the Kalahari to create the famous inland Okavango Delta.

The banks of the river are dominated by knob thorn acacia and other mature species, while the small islands, connected by bridges, are home to a wide variety of interesting birds including: both pied and malachite kingfishers, swamp boubou, black crake and rock pratincole.

If you continue along the Botswana road for 40km (24 miles) south of Popa Falls, you reach the former **Mahango Game Reserve ❹**, which now forms part of Bwabwata National Park. Although small, Mahango is the best part of Bwabwata for general game viewing, and many regard it as ranking among the top wildlife destinations anywhere in the country. Its tall riverine forest includes large baobabs, while the floodplains that flank the river are a good place to spot red lechwe and reedbuck. Sable and roan also do well here, and there are large numbers of elephant, buffalo, hippo and crocodile. Nevertheless, the sheer density of the vegetation, which is what the mammals find so attractive, can make game viewing a frustrating business.

Mudumu National Park

Head east along the B8, you'll exit Bwabwata National Park at the Kwando River, shortly after which a right turn onto the D3511 will lead

AN AVIAN PARADISE

Mahango Game Reserve is one of the richest ornithological sites in Namibia, with more than 400 bird species recorded. As you might expect, in the river and wetland areas there are many water-associated species, including fish eagles and various plovers, kingfishers, egrets, cranes and storks. African skimmers, a vagrant to South Africa and considered to be threatened in Namibia, nest on sandbanks in the river. These black and white birds fly along with the lower mandible of their bill, which extends beyond the upper mandible, just under the surface ready to snap up any small fish that should come their way. There are also numerous woodland species, too, including several raptors, and both Meyer's and Cape parrots.

you past signs for the **Lizauli Traditional Village ❺**, a living open-air museum. Here, you can shop for locally made handicrafts and learn about traditional Caprivian fishing and farming methods, music, basket-making and traditional medicine on an informal tour. From here it's just a short drive to the northern boundary of one of Namibia's newest national parks, Mudumu. Both this and its equally new neighbour, Mamili National Park, require a 4x4 vehicle to explore them, and both are still in the development stages as far as facilities for visitors are concerned.

Mudumu National Park ❻ is mainly a woodland park with some wetland where it flanks the Kwando River. Since being gazetted, the amount of game in the park has increased and now there are substantial numbers of impala, zebra and kudu as well as slowly growing populations of sable, roan and tsessebe. Predators tend to be rare here, although wild dog are seen from time to time. The woodland is mixed – some areas are mopane while others close to the river, consist of various figs, acacias and sausage trees. Walking tours are available, too.

Nkasa Rupara National Park

Renamed **Nkasa Rupara National Park ❼** in 2012, the former Mamili National Park, set in the very south of eastern Caprivi, where the Kwando River becomes the Linyanti, was even less developed than Mudumu prior to the opening of the exclusive Nkasa Rupara Lodge in 2011. Adjoining the Okavango Delta and based around two large wooded islands, Rupara (or Lupala) and Nkasa, the area is actually very similar to the Delta in its maze of channels, islands, lagoons and peninsulas. When flooded, about 80 percent of the park is covered by water but in the dry season there are oxbow lakes, great floodplains and large reed beds.

This is the largest protected wetland in Namibia, so game is not as abundant here as it is in some of the country's other parks (but then nor are other tourists). This is, however, an excellent area for mammals, with large herds of elephants, sitatunga, lechwe and reed buck. Both lions and hyenas are

Mahango basketry.

Two children ride on a makeshift sledge pulled by oxen.

regularly seen, too, and it's home to one of the largest concentrations of buffalo in Namibia – over a thousand animals.

Nkasa Rupara is wonderful for birds, too. At least 450 species – some 70 percent of Namibia's total – might be spotted here, including rare wattled cranes which nest in the park, three species of coucal – Senegal, coppery-tailed and black – chirping cisticola and slaty egret. Geese and ducks abound when the park is flooded, while summer migrants include squacco herons, yellow-billed kites and several roller species. The loop road through the area will return you to the B8 at **Mutonga**, about 110km (65 miles) east from where you left it.

Another 110km (65 miles) east along the B8 brings you to **Katima Mulilo** ⑧, the Caprivi's regional capital. Set on the bank of the Zambezi, Katima was established by the British in 1935 to replace the original German headquarters in the area at **Schuckmannsburg** ⑨, further east along the river. It's a thriving place with a distinct frontier feel, bolstered by the fact that you can cross the border into Zambia from here, over a newly opened bridge. Local landmarks include a giant baobab painstakingly hollowed out and fitted with a toilet by a former regional commissioner; it stands behind the Caprivi Regional Council building.

Katima is the supply hub for a growing number of tourist lodges in the area, and the urban refuge to which various safari operators are drawn when they leave the bush. It's a good place to pick up supplies (especially as it has a colourful market), get car repairs carried out and change money, but bear in mind it is also reputed to be the only town in the world where elephants have priority!

Lake Liambezi

South of Katima is **Lake Liambezi** ⑩, which now rarely holds water due to a drop in the Zambezi's flow. This peaked between 1946 and the late 1970s, when Victoria Falls carried around 1,400 cubic metres (4,592 cubic feet) of water, double the figure for the early 20th century, but it fell dramatically again in the early 1980s. As a result, Lake Liambezi filled with water in the 1950s, for the first time since the hunter Frederick Courtenay Selous recorded seeing it full in 1879, and it became an important feature of the eastern Caprivi, supporting a huge fishing industry.

The lake dried up again after 1982, giving way to cultivation and grassland for cattle, and if it is ever to flood again, it will most likely be through the Chobe River, which reverses its flow when the Zambezi is high.

To the border

From Katima, the tar road continues for a further 70km (40 miles) to the border post at **Ngoma** ⑪. Once over the border in Botswana, you can take a gravel road through Chobe National Park to Kasane. From here you can travel south into the rest of Botswana, or cross into Zimbabwe and follow the mighty Zambezi to see it plummet over the magnificent Victoria Falls.

Kavango women go about traditional tasks, such as childcare.

The Kavango

The lush floodplains of the Okavango support Namibia's second-largest ethnic group, who share their name with the river on which their livelihood depends.

The Kavango people inhabit the wide floodplains that flank the Okavango River as it runs for more than 400km (240 miles) along the border with Angola. Many of those living on the Namibian side of the river were originally based in Angola, but fled south in the 1970s to escape that country's civil war. As a result, the Kavango population of Namibia has almost doubled in size over recent years, to stand at almost 200,000 today.

Between them, the five main Kavango clans speak four different dialects. The Kwangari in the western region and their immediate neighbours, the Mbunza, speak a common language. Shishambyu and RuGciriku are also closely related, but the ThiMbukushu in the east has less affinity with other dialects.

Traditionally, the Kavango have made their living by fishing and by cultivating sorghum, millet and maize on the fertile ground. Today, however, thousands of young Kavango people work as labourers on farms, in mines and in urban centres. Another important local industry is woodcarving for tourists and the commercial market. The main technique used here is hewing with the aid of an *adze* (an instrument like an axe, with the blade at right angles to the handle); knives are only used for the fine touches. Unfortunately, most of the work is produced with the mass market in mind, but here and there a genuine work of art can be found.

As with most other groups in northern Namibia, Kavango social organisation is matrilineal. This penetrates all spheres of social life, in particular family law, the law of inheritance and succession, the marriage system, the political structure and the traditional religious system. Kavango mythology centres on a supreme being called Karunga, who is guided by celestial bodies to protect people. Stars are said to be Karunga's fireflies, which amass in the sky on moonless nights to give more light. Ancestral worship also plays a large role in traditional religion and in warding off the demonic powers of Karunga's evil servant Shadipinyi, who delights in exposing human weakness.

State of transition

As in so many parts of Africa, the Kavango are in a state of transition from the old traditional order to new forms of economic, social and political life. Christian missions have played an important part in this transition phase, a key role having been undertaken by the Catholic Congregation of the Oblates of the Virgin Mary, now deeply rooted in Kavango society. German, and later Finnish, missionaries pioneered work in the fields of education, health, agriculture and commerce here. For many years they were the dominant development agency until government bodies took over much of their work.

Numerous enterprises all over the region bear witness to the development programme carried out by the government. There are now about 100 schools. At Rundu a government hospital with three operating theatres, modern sterilisation facilities, a well-equipped X-ray section and a steam laundry were erected a few years ago. The leper and TB hospital at Mashare can accommodate over 400 patients.

In addition, where until recently vehicles had a difficult drive along deep sandy tracks – parts of which could only be negotiated by a four-wheel-drive – there are now well-constructed roads.

The Kavango people are traditionally riverine.

Children gather in a small village in northwest Namibia.

NORTHWEST NAMIBIA

Some of the country's most dramatic scenery can be found in this empty land, where ancient cultures, petrified forests and desert elephants enliven one of Africa's last true wildernesses.

nland from the desert plain of the Skeleton Coast rises an austere and rugged wilderness, one of the last real wildernesses in Africa. Although it falls within the Kunene and Erongo regions, it's still commonly referred to by its old names, **Kaokoland** (for the northern region) and **Damaraland** (for the south). Home to a unique flora and fauna as well as some hauntingly beautiful scenery, this wilderness is the least-populated part of Namibia. Damaraland's the ancestral home of the Damara people, while in the far north live the Himba, semi-nomadic pasturalists whose lives centre around their cattleherds.

A desert rich in wildlife

As the rock paintings in Damaraland's Twyfelfontein valley illustrate, wildlife has survived in this parched land for thousands of years. Today, rare desert elephants and black rhino forage alongside scattered sand-rivers such as the Hoanib and the Hoarusib, while nomadic herds of game including kudu, oryx and Hartmann's mountain zebra roam the north and the east, where the vegetation's more dense. A rich and varied birdlife – from near-endemic species such as the Herero Chat and Rüppell's korhaan to the ostrich – and a host of curious plants such as the commiphora and the *Welwitschia mirabilis* (a sort of underground tree) also

eke out an existence in these seemingly barren wastes.

Although most of the main sights in southern Damaraland are accessible in an ordinary car, a 4x4 is essential in Kaokoland or if you plan to explore away from the main highway in northern Damaraland. In Kaokoland you should always travel in convoy with a minimum of two 4x4 vehicles, carrying extra fuel and water, comprehensive maps and a gps navigation aid (though roads may be marked on the map, in practice some simply don't exist).

Main Attractions

Brandberg Mountain
Spitzkoppe
Twyfelfontein Unesco World
   Heritage Site
Damaraland
Western Kaokoland

Heading into Namibia's northwestern wilderness.

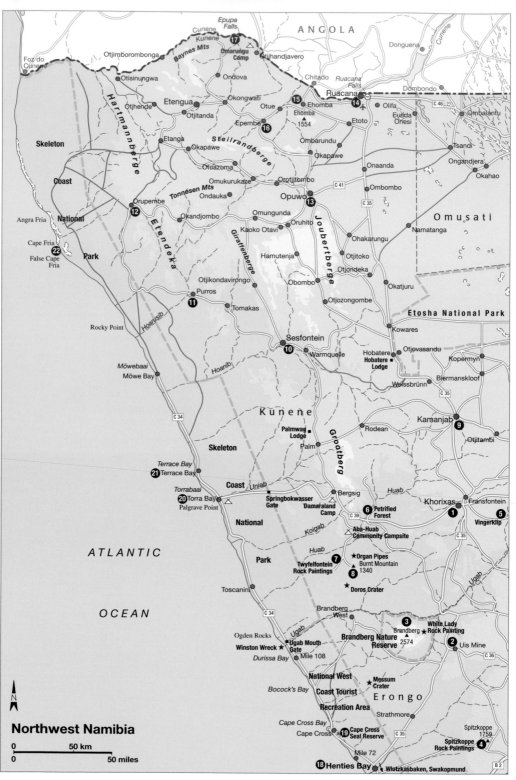

ANGOLA

Epupa
Falls
Cunene
Kunene
Otjimborombonga
Foz do
Cunene
Otisinungwa
Omarungu
Camp
Otjihandjavero
Donguena
Cunene
Baynes Mts
Chitado
Ruacana
Falls
Ondova
Dombondo
Ruacana
Olifa
Eunda
Onesi
C 46
Ombalantu
Okongwati
Ehomba
Etengua
Otjihende
Otue
Ehomba
1554
Etoto
Tsandi
Okapawe
Steilrandberge
Ombarundu
Onaanda
Ongandjera
Okahao
Etanga
Okapawe
Okapawe
Onaanda
Omukurukaze
Orotjitombo
C 41
Ombombo
Otjitanda
Epembe
Ondauka
Tonnésen Mts
Otuazuma
Opuwo
Namatanga
Omusati
Orupembe
Okandjombo
Omungunda
Oruhito
Kaoko Otavi
Ohakarungu
Angra Fria
Cape Fria
False Cape
Fria
Hamutenja
Otjitoko
Otjondeka
National
Park
Otjikondavirongo
Obombo
Okatjuru
Etosha National Park
Purros
Tomakas
Otjozongombe
Kowares
Otjovasandu
Kopermyn
Rocky Point
Sesfontein
Warmquelle
Hobatere
Hobatere
Lodge
Biermanskloof
Möwebaai
Möwe Bay
Hoanib
Weissbrünn
C 35
Kunene
Palmwag
Lodge
Rodean
Kamanjab
Otjitambi
C 34
Skeleton
Palm
Groatberg
Huab
Terrace Bay
Terrace Bay
Coast
Torrabaai
Torra Bay
Palgrave Point
Uniab
Springbokwasser
Gate
Bergsig
Damaraland
Camp
Koigab
C 39
Petrified
Forest
Khorixas
Fransfontein
Vingerklip
Abu-Huab
Community Campsite
National
Huab
Twyfelfontein
Rock Paintings
Organ Pipes
Burnt Mountain
1340
C 35
Park
Doros Crater
Toscanini
Brandberg
West
C 34
Ugab
White Lady
Rock Painting
Brandberg
2574
Uis Mine
C 36
Ogden Rocks
Winston Wreck
Ugab Mouth
Gate
Mile 108
Durissa Bay
Brandberg Nature
Reserve
Messum
Crater
National West
Coast Tourist
Recreation Area
Erongo
Bocock's Bay
Strathmore
ATLANTIC
OCEAN
Cape Cross Bay
Cape Cross
Cape Cross
Seal Reserve
C 35
Mile 72
Spitzkoppe
1759
Spitzkoppe
Rock Paintings
Hentiesbay
Wlotzkasbaken, Swakopmund
B 2

N

Northwest Namibia

0 ———— 50 km
0 ———— 50 miles

Given these conditions, by far the safest and most interesting way to experience the area is to travel with a specialist tour operator and knowledgeable guide, who can give an insight into Kaokoland's fascinating plants, wildlife and cultures.

Southern Damaraland

Nondescript **Khorixas ❶**, the former administrative capital of Damaraland, is 131km (81 miles) due west of Outjo on the C39 and well placed as a base for exploring the south and for stocking up on supplies. Otherwise, there's not much to see here, although the **Khorixas Community Craft Centre** – a project backed by the Save the Rhino Trust – at the entrance to the town is definitely worth a visit if you're interested in good-quality crafts. Note, however, that the craft centre may eventually be relocated following the town council's 2013 announcement that it may be build in new shopping mall on the site.

Follow the C35 south towards sleepy **Uis Mine ❷**, which initially evolved around a small tin mine (now closed). Just beyond the town – some 105km (65 miles) from Khorixas – turn west onto the D2359 and follow it for 28km (17 miles) to the **Brandberg ❸**, an oval-shaped massif which towers above the surrounding plains. Around 120 million years ago there was a volcano here, set in a rocky plateau. Gradual erosion of the plateau's own lava-layers has exposed this giant chunk of weather-resistant granite, whose 2,573-metre (8,440 ft) summit, known as the **Königstein** (German for King's Stone) is the highest point in Namibia.

Capturing the sunset at Brandberg.

The German name Brandberg ("Fire Mountain") refers to the burnished glow of this granite extrusion before sunset. The same phenomenon is alluded to in the Damara name Daures ("Burning Mountain"). The Herero call it Omukuruvaro, the "Mountain of Gods". Long before that, for thousands of years, nomadic hunter-gatherers sheltered in the myriad caves and overhangs of the Brandberg, as evidenced by the prolific ancient rock art that adorns the walls. The richest seam of rock art sites, comprising more than

The White Lady, amongst other figures.

THE "WHITE LADY"

The most celebrated rock painting in Namibia is the 40cm (16in) -tall humanoid first described in the 1950s by the French archaeologist Abbé Henri Breuil, who named it the "White Lady of the Brandberg". Breuil theorised that the white pigment indicated that the figure (which he thought was female) depicted a person of Mediterranean origin, an idea that was popularised by apartheid theorists as proof of an ancient European influence in the region.

The "White Lady" theory is now utterly discredited by respected rock art experts, who recognise the figure to be that of a male hunter or tribal shaman – and to be no more European in origin than are the elephants and other animals painted in white pigment on rocks elsewhere in Namibia.

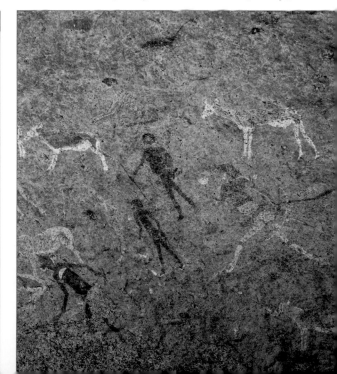

TIP

You need a permit from the NWR (Namibia Wildlife Resorts) office in Windhoek (www.nwr.com.na) if you want to visit the spectacular Doros Crater near Twyfelfontein.

40,000 individual painted figures, is to the northeast near the **Tsisab Ravine**, where you can see a painted frieze featuring the so-called "White Lady of the Brandberg" – a sweaty three-hour return walk, so avoid setting out in the heat of the day. There are at least 17 other rock-painting sites within a 1km (1-mile) radius of the White Lady, most of which depict big game such as lion, giraffe and ostrich. Guides from the local community can be hired if you want to explore the area more thoroughly.

South of Uis is the dramatic **Spitzkoppe ❹**, a pyramid-shaped mountain known as the "Matterhorn of Namibia" which offers several more rock-art sites and some good walking trails to boot. To reach it from Uis, take the C36 Omaruru road for 1km (1 mile) before turning south on the D1930 for 76km (47 miles), followed by the D3716. The site is run communally from the village of Spitzkoppe (tel: 081 211 6291 www.spitzkoppereservations.com; sunrise–sunset; charge), which can arrange knowledgeable local guides and runs a small guesthouse with camping sites and bungalows.

Around Khorixas

Just east of Khorixas is another famous local landmark, a slender 35-metre (115ft)-high monolith known as the **Vingerklip ❺** ("rock finger" in Afrikaans). Take the C39 for 46km (29 miles), followed by the D2743 for about 21km (13 miles) to reach this spectacular limestone pinnacle, poking up from the surrounding flat-topped terraces like something from a science fiction movie set. It's a favourite haunt of rock kestrels, too.

The equally odd-looking **Petrified Forest ❻** – a collection of fossilised logs that have been estimated to be between 240 and 300 million years old – lies about 42km (26 miles) west of Khorixas along the C39. Remnants of at least 50 trees can be seen, some partially buried in the surrounding sandstone. A guided tour takes about an hour (the site's open daily; small charge).

The biggest attraction around here, though, is the boulder-strewn hillside known as **Twyfelfontein ❼** (8am–5pm; charge), lying just southwest of the Petrified Forest. Inscribed as Namibia's first Unesco World Heritage

A geological feature referred to as "organ pipes" in the Brandberg Mountains.

Site in 2007, this is widely considered to be one of the richest rock-art sites in Africa, with more than 2,000 rock engravings and paintings, some dating back to before 3300 bc, depicting various animals and their spoor, as well as people. Local guides will lead visitors along the two trails that run uphill from the parking lot, past the "Doubtful Spring" after which Twyfelfontein is named, to a hillside scattered with about a dozen engraved or painted panels. Named after two of the more striking engravings on display, the Dancing Kudu and Lion Man Trails each take about one hour to walk, inclusive of stops to admire the artwork and the views, and they could be covered together in about 90 minutes. Climatically, the most comfortable time to visit is early morning, shortly after the gates open, but this is also when the site is busiest – for a more peaceful perusal, try visiting at around 4pm.

To reach Twyfelfontein, follow the C39 from Khorixas for 73km (45 miles) before turning onto the D3254 for 36km (22 miles). There's a community-run campsite at nearby **Aba-Huab**, and a couple of fine upmarket lodges too.

Other attractions worth visiting around here are the **Organ Pipes**, a mass of perpendicular dolerite slabs thought to be between 130 and 150 million years old (they're about 10km or 6 miles east of Twyfelfontein on the D3254), and nearby **Burnt Mountain** ❽. This range is pretty uninspiring when the sun is high but turns into a glowing kaleidoscope of colour – red, orange, grey and purple – when its shale slopes reflect the early morning and late afternoon light. Southeast of Twyfelfontein, meanwhile, are the equally dramatic **Doros** and **Messum Craters**, both of which can only be reached with a 4x4 vehicle.

Northern Damaraland

The further north you travel in Damaraland, the more the route begins to take on an expeditionary feel. The scenery becomes more rugged and austere,

sand dunes encroach upon the road, the sun blazes down and one can travel for miles without seeing a single soul. However, the government has set aside several large tracts of land around here for tourism (each allocated to different operators) and, although development is controlled, the region is reasonably well supplied with private lodges and camps. Prior booking is required for the community-owned (but privately managed) **Damaraland Camp** and **Desert Rhino Camp**, both of which have a collection point for those arriving by saloon car. Situated on the edge of the concessions alongside the C34, **Palmwag Lodge** is accessible in an ordinary saloon car and open to casual visitors (see Travel Tips, page 254).

The main draw around here is the wildlife, especially the desert-adapted elephants and black rhinos, although the latter are seldom seen outside the Palmwag Concession operated by Desert Rhino Camp. Most camps offer game drives and guided walks into the heart of the terracotta-coloured mountains where you could also spot gemsbok, kudu, springbok, mountain zebra

The cactus and succulent garden at the White Lady Lodge and Campsite.

People on foot in Damaraland hoping to see a rhino or elephant!

The Damara

The unsolved mystery of how a distinct ethnic group first came to Namibia fascinates historians and scientists to this day.

The Damara comprise only about 7.5 percent of Namibia's population, but they are probably one of its oldest ethnic groups. The existence of a very dark-skinned group of Negroid hunter-gatherers in this region, speaking a dialect of the click-based Khoekhoegowab language of the Central Khoisan, has for a long time aroused special interest both among scientists and the general public. The people themselves have no clear oral tradition relating to their origin and ancient history prior to arriving in their present-day homeland, and while a number of hypotheses have been postulated – most credibly that they migrated here from West Africa several thousands of years ago – the mystery is unsolved.

Traditionally, the Damara consist of 23 clans (*haoti*), each governed by its own chief, all of whom are subservient to the paramount king. Since 1994, this has been King Justus Garoëb, who became

Local transport just outside Upowo.

acting king 12 years earlier, and has also played a prominent role in national politics, as leader of the anti-apartheid Namibia National Front in the late 1970s, founder of the United Democratic Front in 1989, and a three-time presidential candidate.

In pre-colonial times, the Damara populated an extensive area from the Khuiseb River up towards the Swakop River; in the central parts from Rehoboth and Hochanas to the Khomas Highlands, west of Windhoek; and especially in the area where they are presently concentrated – northeast of the Namib around Outjo, Kamanjab, Khorixas and Brandberg.

Damara reservations

About two centuries ago, the Damara began to be ousted from their traditional areas by advancing Nama and Herero, the latter hunting them down and either killing them or carrying them off as slaves. Finally, at the request of the Rhenish Missionary Society, the Herero chief Zeraua ceded the Okombahe area to some Damara in 1870. Later, the colonial authorities created several other reserves for the Damara people, among them Otjimbingwe and Sesfontein. During the 1960s, the apartheid government bought 223 farms from European settlers and in 1973 it proclaimed an area of 11.6 million acres (4.7 million hectares) as so-called Damaraland. Within the boundaries of this territory live only a quarter of the total Damara population. The same percentage may be found in the district of Windhoek, and the remainder is distributed throughout the north-central area.

Towards the end of the 18th century the Damara first came into contact with European travellers, who usually described them as hunter-gatherers. There is, however, ample archaeological evidence to suggest not only that some clans had been keeping small herds of stock for centuries, but many were also gardeners, growing tobacco and pumpkins.

In line with their predilection for small stock farming and cattle breeding, livestock production has become an important source of income for the Damara. Today, however, many work on farms, in the urban centres and on mines. The number of independent commercial enterprises is on the increase. Hundreds of teachers, clerics and officials form a modern intelligentsia, among them some of Namibia's most eloquent politicians. In short, the Damara have succeeded in liberating themselves from their former dependency and have acquired a respected position among the people of Namibia.

and a splendid range of birds including the black eagle. If you're determined to see a desert rhino, tracking trips into Palmwag leave daily from Desert Rhino Camp.

From Palmwag, it's 118km (73 miles) to little **Kamanjab** ❾, near the western approach to Etosha. This is a useful place to stock up on fuel and essential supplies, although there's not much else to stop for and only one place to stay. Fortunately, there are a number of lodges and guest farms in the vicinity, among them Hobatere and Huab lodges which are both on large private reserves (see Travel Tips, page 254).

From Palmwag, it's 91km (56 miles) on the D3706 to Damaraland's northern boundary and the sprawling Herero settlement of **Sesfontein** ❿. Literally translating as "Spring Six", and scattered with picturesque fan palms (Hyphaene petersiana), Sesfontein has something of the feel of a desert oasis, especially after a long, dusty drive. It was a strategic military outpost for the German colonial government in the late 19th century, and the main monument from that period, **Fort Sesfontein** (1896) has

now been renovated and turned into a hotel. Also oasis-like in feel, **Ongongo Campsite** (tel: 081 211 6291, www.spitz koppereservations.com) set around a large natural rock pool and waterfall on the upper reaches of the Hoarusib River, lies to the east of the Palmwag Road some 18km (11 miles) Sesfontein.

Kaokoland

Beyond Sesfontein lies **Kaokoland**, a vast, empty and inhospitable area stretching west to the Skeleton Coast, east to Etosha and all the way north to the Kunene river on the Angolan border – a total of about 49,000 sq km (19,000 sq miles). Travelling overland here is a slow business (there are only about five driveable roads) and should never be attempted alone or without a plentiful supply of food and water, and a satellite navigation system. If you plan to do this trip, seek advice first.

It's wiser to sign up for an organised 4x4 tour; you could find yourself heading northwest along the D3707 to the community campsite at **Purros** ⓫ (tel: 081 211 6291, www.spitzkoppereservations. com), on the tree lined banks of the

A herdsman overlooks the animals at dusk.

The Himba people wear little clothing, but the women cover themselves with otjize, a mixture of ochre and animal fat, which gives their skin a reddish tinge.

A Himba man uses a gourd as a mixing bowl.

Hoarusib River. Set up to provide employment for the local Himba people as well as camping space for visitors, the campsite can also arrange escorted visits to Himba villages, and guides for game drives in an area that still supports significant numbers of elephant, giraffe and various antelope.

Ancient culture

Unlike Namibia's other indigenous peoples, the **Himba** (a subset of the Herero nation) still live exactly as they have since they migrated down from Angola and settled in this remote area some 300 years ago. It's a timeless lifestyle that requires no Western trappings or even running water – livestock (cattle and goats) constitutes wealth for this pastoral society, so the territory of each clan has to be large enough to allow them to move their herds enormous distances, following the few straggling pastures which spring up after the rains.

As they roam this huge wilderness, the Himba construct rough "camps" to sleep in, from which they can also gather roots and hunt game. When they leave to find better grazing for

their goats and cattle, household items get left behind, which they will use on their return. In a telling example of how their culture is now, having to adapt abruptly to the outside world after centuries of isolation, there have been several unfortunate incidents in the last few years where Himba camps have been denuded by unwitting tourists, who thought them abandoned.

Sensitivity towards the Himba way of life is an essential part of a Kaokoland journey. Always gain permission before you enter any of the semi-permanent Himba settlements, for instance, and ask first before you take photographs (expect to pay, too). Gifts of tobacco and mealiemeal (cornmeal), however, are usually appreciated.

Purros is about halfway to **Orupembe** ⑫, some 208km (129 miles) from Sesfontein across the wide, flat **Giribes Plains**. You'll see scattered herds of springbok as you travel, along with the odd "fairy circle" – small round patches of earth where no vegetation grows, possibly due to toxic chemicals left in the soil by long-dead *Euphorbia* bushes.

At Orupembe, the road turns east with a slow descent through rocky terrain and the dramatic Tonnesen and Giraffen passes. From here, it's about 200km (120 miles) by road through the small settlement of **Kaoko Otavi** and a north turn onto the D3705 to **Opuwo** ⑬, the only real town in Kaokoland. (If you're coming from Kamanjab, it's some 254km or 158 miles on the C35 and C41.) A dusty, somewhat shambolic place with a real frontier atmosphere, Opuwo's a good place to stock up on food and fuel. On the perimeter is a large Himba settlement where you can mingle with these strikingly dressed people – hair coiffed with mud into intricate styles, bodies shining with red ochre – as you shop at the supermarket.

If you'd prefer a self-drive 4x4 tour, you could try the circular four-day route heading north from Opuwo to Ruacana and back via Epupa Falls in the west – although it must be stressed

that it's vital to travel with at least two vehicles, to be completely self-sufficient and to carry fuel and water.

From Opuwo, take the C41 east to the C35 (the main road north to Ruacana), a journey of 142km (88 miles). Fill up with fuel in **Ruacana ⑭**; you won't have another chance until you get back to Opuwo. Now take the C46 west for a few kilometres before continuing on the D3700 for 55km (34 miles), a picturesque drive following the Kunene river to **Swartbooisdrift**, where there's accommodation and campsites at Kunene River Lodge, renowned among birders as *the* place to see Cinderella waxbill. The road west from here is atrocious; better continue south on the D3702 for 20km (12 miles) to **Ehomba ⑮**, followed by the D3702 for 10km (6 miles) then the D3701 for 31km (19 miles) to the tiny Himba settlements of **Epembe ⑯** and **Otjiveze**. Head northwest on the D3700 for 31km (19 miles) to **Okongwati**, continuing north for 73km (45 miles) to **Epupa Falls ⑰**. The Baynes Mountains, Kaokoland's highest peaks, rise to the west.

Epupa is a stunning sight, comprising a series of rapids and waterfalls, the tallest dropping 37 metres (120ft), that thunder into a palm and baobab-fringed gorge surrounded by desert. At one point, the Namibian and Angolan governments held serious talks about implementing a giant hydroelectric dam project that would have submerged the entire Kunene Valley (including the waterfalls), much of the Himba's territory, and many sacred ancestral grave and fire sites, but fortunately this idea has been shelved.

From Epupa, retrace your steps along the same route to Otjiveze and then continue south for a further 73km (45 miles) back to Opuwo.

Another option is to explore the western Kaokoveld, travelling down to Orupembe through the two long, barren but hauntingly beautiful valleys (**Hartmann's** and the **Marienfluss**) that run north to south from the western end of the Kunene River. Trips can be organised through specialist tour operators, or by booking into the superbly isolated Serra Cafema Lodge, a fly in tented camp on the dune-fringed banks of the Kunene.

The Epupa Falls along the Kunene River. The Himba people have successfully stopped the development of a dam on the river.

A Himba hut.

The Skeleton Coast is a ships'
graveyard…

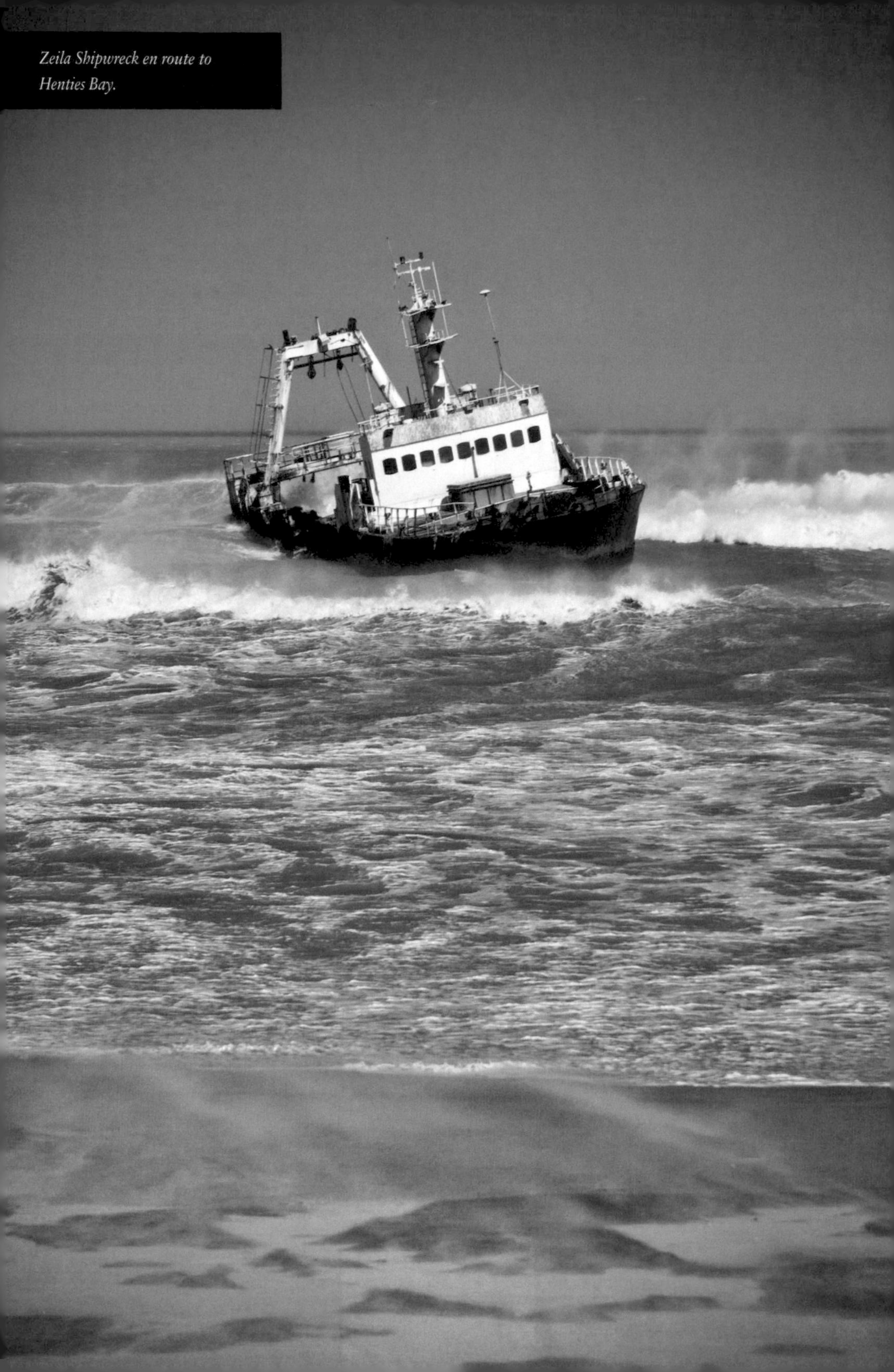

Zeila Shipwreck en route to Henties Bay.

THE SKELETON COAST

The most haunting and evocative of all Namibia's attractions, this treacherous stretch of wild Atlantic shore is backed by a bone-bleaching desert heaped high with giant dunes.

Situated in the remote north-western corner of Namibia, the Skeleton Coast, much of which is protected within an eponymous national park, is arguably one of the loneliest stretches of coastline in Africa, and certainly among the continent's most fascinating and untouched wilderness areas. Once an area for seafarers to fear and shun thanks to its treacherous shoreline flanked by bone-bleaching desert wastes – where shipwrecked sailors would almost certainly perish for lack of fresh water – it is now prized as a place of beauty and tranquillity, as well as solitude.

The southern gateway to the Skeleton Coast is the resort town of **Swakopmund** (see page 219). This port lies at the southern tip of the **National West Coast Tourist Recreation Area**, a 25km (15 mile) -wide strip that extends for 200km (120 miles) northward from the Swakop River to the Ugab River Mouth, effectively forming a southern extension to the Skeleton Coast National Park. During the hot summer months, while many Namibians escape from the heat of the interior to Swakopmund, the Skeleton Coast further north – famed for its shark and other game fish such as galjoen and kabeljou is a magnet for angling enthusiasts from all over southern Africa.

The road to nowhere.

Heading north

The coastline directly north of Swakopmund is managed as a tourist area and has extensive facilities (spaced at regular intervals) for camping and caravanning. Seen outside the holiday season, these sites seem not just empty, but bleak and inhospitable – yet once the locals pour in over the Christmas period, they take on an entirely different atmosphere. In fact, **Mile Four** is considered to be one of the biggest caravan parks in southern Africa.

Main Attractions

Henties Bay
Cape Cross Seal Reserve
Skeleton Coast National Park

FACT

Even before the name "Skeleton Coast" was coined, this treacherous region had a dread reputation among locals and outsiders alike – Portuguese navigators knew it as the "Gates of Hell" and the Nama as "The Land God Made in Anger".

Henties Bay architecture.

Thirty-two kilometres (19 miles) north of Swakopmund on the C34 is **Wlotzkasbaken**, a rather strange village of small bungalows and chalets used by the keenest fishermen. Fresh water has to be delivered and pumped to the individual water towers which stand on spidery lattice legs beside each dwelling like enormous ornate candlesticks. Some 35km (22 miles) further north on the same road you come to **Henties Bay** ⑱, the last place to obtain fuel before heading still further north.

Henties Bay is named after Major Hentie van der Merwe, a Kalkfield farmer who stumbled across a freshwater spring at the site whilst on a hunting trip in the region in 1929 – though signs of a previous camp and an old metal sign in German suggest that the *Schutztruppe* camped at the same spot in 1886, during the course of a diamond-prospecting expedition. The small town has grown from a cluster of fishing huts erected at the site by van der Merwe and his friends to become the acknowledged hub of Namibia's leisure-fishing industry,

offering some of the finest shore-based angling opportunities in southern Africa.

The best fishing spots in the vicinity of Henties Bay were once the preserve of dedicated anglers who furtively passed directions and GPS coordinates between themselves. All that changed in December 2007, however, when the local tourist association decided to erect signposts to a dozen of the region's premier fishing localities, many of them rather colourfully named: Die Walle (The Wall), Trappies (Small Steps), Popeye, Sarah se Gat (Sarah's Hole), Mile 68, Canopy, Predikantsgat (Pastor's Hole), Bakleigat (Fight Hole), Rondebos (Round Bush), Richtersfeld, Blare and Winston Wreck.

One of the most intriguing forms of plant life to occur in the deserts inland of Henties Bay and other parts of the Skeleton Coast is the lichen, a complex symbiosis of fungus and an alga. The gravel plains, rocky outcrops and mountain slopes along the Skeleton Coast are home to over a hundred species – inspect the ginger lichen fields beside the road and you

should be able to spot several different kinds. Normally hard and brittle, lichens come to life or "bloom" when water is sprinkled over them, moving visibly and becoming soft and leathery to the touch. Like other desert vegetation, lichens are dependent on fog for their survival, although they can manage without moisture for long periods of time. Visitors should take note, however, that vehicles must stay on the established roads, as their wheels destroy the lichens and leave unsightly, virtually permanent, tracks behind.

Fur seals and fishing boats

Some 53km (32 miles) north of Henties Bay, **Cape Cross Seal Reserve** ⑲ (daily 10am–5pm; charge) supports a breeding colony of around 150,000–210,000 Cape fur seals. It's a hugely impressive sight, and even more overwhelming to the other senses – the pungent smell of guano hangs over the site, and if you close your eyes, the amassed seals sound like an enormous flock of bleating ewes and lambs.

Cape Cross is also of historical interest. In 1486 the first European to set foot on the Namibian coast, the Portuguese navigator Diego Cão, erected a stone cross at the site that was later to become known as Cape Cross. Two replicas of the cross can be seen today. The first, erected by German soldiers in 1893 – after the original was taken to Germany – stands on a hillside overlooking the bay. The other is a faithful replica of the original and was unveiled in 1980 on the very spot where Diego Cão planted his cross.

Just before you reach the entrance to the national park you will see a sign pointing west to the first of the famous Skeleton Coast wrecks – that of the **Winston**, a fishing boat that ran aground here in 1970.

The Skeleton Coast National Park

The **Skeleton Coast National Park**, a narrow tract of coastline about 30–40km (20–25 miles) wide and 500km (300 miles) long between the Ugab River and the Kunene River on the frontier with Angola, was proclaimed a nature reserve in 1971. The park extends over a total area of 16,400 sq km (6,400

With a naturally deep harbour, Walvis Bay has long been a refuge for ships navigating the south tip of Africa.

The Cape fur seal colony at Cape Cross.

CAPE FUR SEAL

The Cape fur seal is a subspecies of the brown fur seal *(Arctocephalus pusillus)*, which also occurs in Australian waters, and ranks among the most common of the world's 33 species of pinniped (a family of amphibious mammals that also includes sea lions and walruses and is mostly associated with polar waters). Some two-thirds of the world's 1.5–2 million Cape fur seals are concentrated on Namibian waters, and the breeding colony at Cape Cross is the largest single aggregation anywhere, with up to 210,000 adults thought to be present in peak season, and an average of 60,000 pups born every year.

Unlike some seal species, Cape fur seals suckle their young for almost a whole year, only weaning last year's pup in order to make room for this year's.

Around mid-October the bulls, great maned beasts that grow up to 2.2 metres long (7ft) and weigh almost 360kg (800lbs), arrive to stake out their territories and defend them against intruders. By early December the young pups are born and the seals mate almost immediately afterwards although the fertilised egg remains dormant for about three months before starting to develop.

The Cape fur seal forages in the open ocean, feeding mainly on bony fish, but it will also take crustaceans and birds, and it is predated upon by the great white shark.

Famous Shipwrecks

Rocky and misty, the Skeleton Coast was most feared by the early mariners who opened up a route to the Indian Ocean.

Countless ships have come to grief along Namibia's rocky and misty coastline, but few of the wrecks have remained intact. Thanks to relentless pounding by the steel-grey Atlantic Ocean breakers and sand-blasting by the prevailing southwest wind, little more remains than twisted chunks of rusting metal, broken masts, scattered planks and a vast array of flotsam and jetsam strewn all the way up the coast.

Some of the wrecks date back to the days when Portuguese explorers and the ships of the Dutch East India Company sailed around the Cape en route to India. Their vessels not only fell victim to gales, but to the Benguela Current, too, with its sea fogs, heavy swell and deadly crosscurrents. They also had to contend with a remarkably treacherous coastline, dotted with rocky outcrops and reefs,

All washed up on the Skeleton Coast – wrecks are a common sight around here.

unexpected shoals, and sand dunes that stretch far into the sea.

Ironically, it was most likely not a shipwreck but an aircraft mishap that gave the Skeleton Coast its descriptive and appropriate name. When a Swiss pilot, Carl Nauer, disappeared along the Namibian coast in 1933, the journalist, Sam Davis, covering the accident for Reuters and the *Cape Argus*, suggested that Nauer's bones might one day be found on the "Skeleton Coast", the graveyard of ships and men. So far as can be ascertained, Nauer's body was never recovered, but the name Skeleton Coast has stuck to this day.

The shipwreck which best personifies the loneliness of Namibia's coastline, however, is that of the *Eduard Bohlen*, a steamer that ran aground in September 1909 at Conception Bay, 100km (60 miles) south of Walvis Bay. Its rusting remains can still be seen partly buried in the sand, several hundred metres inland from the present shoreline.

The Dunedin Star

The best-known wreck is that of the *Dunedin Star*, a British cargo ship which ran aground late on the night of 29 November 1942, about 40km (25 miles) south of the Kunene Mouth. The story of the rescue of the 21 passengers and crew of 85, covered at the time by maritime reporter John Marsh and subsequently published in his book entitled *Skeleton Coast*, reads as an excruciating series of disasters. One rescue boat, the *Sir Charles Elliott*, ran on the rocks, causing two members of the crew to lose their lives in their attempts to swim to safety. A Ventura bomber involved in the rescue took a nosedive into the sea, the three airmen escaping from the fuselage when it drifted ashore. In the end, the castaways only reached Windhoek on Christmas Eve, almost a month after the ship came to grief. All that can be seen today is the rusting remains of a fuel tank, part of the fated ship's cargo.

One reasonably well-preserved wreck is that of the *Montrose*, which met its fate in June 1973. It's still lying on the beach at Terrace Bay, partially buried in the sand. North of Möwe Bay, meanwhile, lie the burnt-out remains of the fishing boat *Karimona*, wrecked in September 1971.

Lastly, the rusting hull of the *Benguela Eagle*, which ran aground in June 1973, is embedded in the sand 25km (16 miles) north of the Ugab River mouth near the shattered remains of the *Girdleness*, wrecked in November 1975 on the rocks south of the Ugab.

sq miles), but the infrastructure is kept to a minimum and the number of visitors is limited, for the special qualities of the area can only be retained by minimising human impact as far as possible.

In the southern third, tourism is restricted to two angling resorts, **Torra Bay ㉚**, a caravan and camping site, and **Terrace Bay ㉑**, a small rest camp with cooking facilities or meals if you prefer. Both resorts have boundaries within which visitors must remain. Both are reached via the main coastal road from Swakopmund, passing through the **Ugab Mouth Gate**, or from the interior via the **Springbokwasser Gate** in Damaraland. Travellers must be in possession of a permit issued in Windhoek and may not leave the main roads except in the demarcated fishing areas.

If you have not booked accommodation in either of the resorts, you can obtain a permit at either one of the gates. However, you will only receive permission to use the C34 and D3245 roads in transit between the two gates, and you must enter the park before 3pm to allow time to drive through to the other gate before sunset.

Into the desert

The Skeleton Coast is part of the northern Namib Desert, which extends from the Kunene River in the north to Cape Cross in the south. A narrow band of dunes stretches along the coast, seldom reaching further than 20km (12 miles) inland, except in the far north. Saltpans occur sporadically all the way up the coast, the largest of which are the **Cape Cross saltpan** and the **Cape Fria brine-pan complex** in the far north. East of the sand desert are flat, wide gravel plains with scattered inselbergs and further east again is the escarpment, defined in the north by the Otjihipa Mountains.

The coast is pleasantly cool throughout the year, except on those days during the winter months when berg (mountain) winds blow and temperatures, higher than those in summer, are often recorded. Inland temperatures rise sharply during the day.

The landscape of the national park is probably little different from what it was 10,000, 10 million or even 100 million years ago. The richly coloured volcanic rock is interspersed

A stone and jewellery seller at Zeila Shipwreck screws up her eyes against a sandstorm.

Directions to a recreational fishing site near Henties Bay.

A black-backed jackal lounges on the beach, where the animals scavenge for Cape fur seal.

A camp on the Skeleton Coast.

with mica-schist, gneiss and granite. Towards the coast, outcrops of granitic and gneissic rocks have ghost-like, honeycomb patterns, caused by the salts contained in the coastal fog that penetrate inland during the night.

While part of the interest of the park lies in its sweeping landscapes, unchanging for many kilometres, part, too, is in the detail and for this reason you must leave your vehicle and go on foot. Long hiking trips are not practicable due to the lack of water but guided walks over a number of days are conducted by Nature Conservation officials along the Ugab River, which marks the southern border of the park. All of the river valleys running through the park repay even an hour's stroll and it is clear from the tracks that many animals use these valleys for living in and as highways.

While road access will only allow you to visit the south of the park, it is now possible to reach the interior of what is a true wilderness area by flying in to Skeleton Coast Camp, which was recently established by Wilderness Safaris built on an island in the dry Khumib riverbed, about 20km (12 miles) inland of the coast. Incredibly, this concession, which was judged the Best Overall Environmental Management System at the 2007 Imvelo Awards for Responsible Tourism, provides the only accommodation in the entire northern half of the Skeleton Coast. It caters mainly to small self-contained groups, who travel out from the camp with expert guides to see such things as the roaring dunes, Rocky Point, Agate Mountain and the remarkable white clay "temples" of the **Hoarusib Canyon**, impressive formations of yellowish-white sedimentary clay thought to be the result of the damming up of the river beyond the dunes, between 20,000 and 50,000 years ago. At **Cape Fria ㉒**, there is also a non-breeding colony of up to 40,000 seals to visit in a setting even more remote than those at Cape Cross.

Dunes on the move

Wherever you are on the Skeleton Coast, dunes are a living and integral part of the landscape. A typical dune formation is the crescent-shaped

barchan, which is formed by the prevailing southwest wind and moves in a northeasterly direction with speeds averaging between 2–3 metres (6–10ft) a year. These are best seen where they march across the D3245 road as it leaves the coast.

It is not difficult to find the tracks of black-backed jackal and brown hyena which roam the beaches along the coast, keeping them clean of dead seals, birds and fish. The most commonly seen larger mammals are springbok and gemsbok, both of which are ideally suited to an arid environment. In years when good rains occur and there is sufficient ground cover, their numbers increase and even zebra will move in from the interior, followed by beasts of prey such as spotted hyena, lion and leopard.

Droughts in the interior have, in the past, caused lions to move down the river courses to the coast where they have been observed to feed on the carcasses of Cape fur seals.

Like adjoining Damaraland, this is also one of the few places anywhere in the world where elephant, black rhino,

giraffe and lions occur in a desert environment. The "desert elephants", for example, are known to travel between feeding-grounds and waterholes as much as 70km (45 miles) apart.

Desert meets ocean

Contrasting sharply with the apparent barrenness of the desert is the immense richness of the adjacent ocean. The Benguela Current flows northwards from the Antarctic laden with oxygen and a rich variety of zoo and phytoplankton, driven to the shore by west winds. The upwelling of the current causes it to rise to the surface. Exposed to the sun, a plankton "bloom" is produced which feeds large schools of pilchards and anchovies, on which seals, cormorants, gannets and many other marine creatures feed. In rough seas the plankton washes onto the beach in large quantities of yellow froth, drying as a dull green coating on the pebbles and sand. Plenty and paucity, beauty and death, old rocks and new dunes – part of the intrigue of the Skeleton Coast is that it is full of such remarkable paradoxes.

The life span of the wild scorpion is unknown, but the oldest scorpion on record made it to the grand old age of 25.

A flock of Cape cormorants congregate on the edge of the Benguela Current.

THE LIVING DUNES OF THE NAMIB DESERT

This vast, sandy region may look remote and desolate, but in fact it's teeming with life, from plants, insects and reptiles to large mammals.

The Namib is one of the most ancient deserts in the world. Although there is some debate about exactly how old it is, it's generally accepted that this narrow coastal tract between the Atlantic and southwestern Africa's Great Western Escarpment has been at least semi-arid, and in places totally arid, for around 50 to 80 million years. The great sea of sprawling sand dunes that cascade down to the very edge of the Atlantic, however, only date back some five million years. This was when the Atlantic's icy Benguela Current – which prevents rainfall from the west and thus plays a major role in maintaining the Namib's arid conditions – became fully established, giving rise to the present southern dune field which stretches between Lüderitz and Swakopmund.

Visit some of the world's highest dunes in Sossusvlei Park at sunrise or sunset to capture their changing colours.

Something in the air

Although the Namib receives minimal amounts of rain, the coastal region has an alternative source of moisture: fog. The freezing cold waters of the Benguela Current, along with the south Atlantic's anticyclone pressure system, act together on the scorching heat of the desert to produce the swirling fogs which are so typical of the Namib coastline. Natural obstacles such as rocky outcrops cause the fog to condense and droplets to form, thus creating the possibility for plant and animal life to exist in this seemingly inhospitable terrain.

As the Welwitschia plant absorbs water through shallow-lying roots, trampling disturbs the contact between the roots and the fog-dampened ground.

A bottle tree (Pachypodium lealii) in Damaraland. The tree's swollen trunk acts as a water store while its toxic sap has been used as an arrow poison by traditional hunters.

Rock painting from the Brandberg, on the edge of the Namib.

AN AGE-OLD NAMIB RECIPE

Rock paintings are evidence that man has roamed Namibia's deserts for at least several hundred thousand years. These desert-dwellers managed to survive not just by hunting small mammals but thanks to various hardy plants that became staple foods. Take the *!nara* plant, for example, a relative of the cucumber and endemic to the Namib. Each year, the female plants (some of which live for centuries) produce dozens of melons which are avidly consumed by any creature that can break through the tough, prickly skin. Following a method devised by their forefathers, the Topnaar Nama people who live along the banks of the Kuiseb River in the central Namib scoop out the fleshy centres of the !naras before cooking them, straining off the seeds and frying them on clean sand. The flesh is also spread out to dry after which it can be rolled up and eaten – a readily portable snack. The plant itself, meanwhile, provides shelter and food for a host of other organisms such as mice, lizards and insects.

The ground-dwelling Namaqua chameleon (Chamaeleo namaquensis).

The dune grass species, here in Sossusvlei Park, sends out roots up to 20 metres (66 ft) long to take advantage of the fog water in the top surface millimetre of sand. It flowers every summer.

Lion tracks along the Skeleton Coast. Namibia's rare coastal desert lions live by scavenging carcasses thrown up by the sea and hunting fur seals.

Bojos café in Swakopmund.

SWAKOPMUND AND WALVIS BAY

Swakopmund is a pretty, historic port popular
with tourists, a centre for adventure sports and
a good place from which to explore the Skeleton
Coast and the birdlife of Walvis Bay.

Namibians calculate the vast distances between destinations in their country in hours rather than kilometres, and those in the know will tell you it is a three-and-a-half-hour drive from Windhoek to the historic port of **Swakopmund ❶**, a small slice of Bavaria sandwiched between the deserts of the Namib-Naukluft National Park to the southeast and the more northerly Skeleton Coast. Incredibly, Swakopmund is just one of three moderately substantial settlements along Namibia's 1,600km (1,000 mile) Atlantic coastline (the other two being Walvis Bay and Lüderitz, respectively 33km (20 miles) and 400km (240 miles) to the south), and the only one that could conceivably be described as a resort.

Lying directly due west of Windhoek, Swakopmund offers the closest coastal access to the capital, and as such it attracts thousands of domestic holidaymakers over the peak Christmas season. But it's not hard to see why this pretty little port is also popular with foreign visitors – the town centre has retained much of its colonial character, and it also boasts some of the best tourist facilities in the country. In addition, Swakopmund is the main springboard for exploration of the dramatic Skeleton Coast, while more immediate attractions include the bird-rich lagoon at nearby Walvis

Bay, the adventure activities operating along the dunes that separate the two ports, and Welwitschia Drive in the nearby northern Namib.

Swakopmund

The *Schutztruppe* captain Curt von François founded Swakopmund in 1892 as a competitor to nearby Walvis Bay, which remained under British control even after the rest of present-day Namibia was declared a German Protectorate in 1884. The first settlers were 120 German soldiers

Main Attractions

Swakopmund Museum
Kristall Galerie
Living Desert Snake Park
Walvis Bay Lagoon
Sandwich Harbour

Karakulia weaver in Swakopmund.

TIP

Especially if you're not exploring the more remote reaches of the Namib-Naukluft, a half-day trip from Swakopmund or Walvis Bay to Welwitschia Drive – with its fine examples of this oddball plant – is highly recommended (see page 225).

and 40 civilians who excavated caves on the beach as protection from the harsh weather prior the constructing the Alte Kaserne (Old Barracks) in late 1892. A breakwater, later known as the Mole, was built in 1898, but it silted up within a few years, and was replaced by a wooden jetty in 1904.

Swakopmund was granted municipal status in 1909. Six years later, however, during World War I, when South African forces occupied German Southwest Africa, all harbour facilities were transferred from Swakopmund to the more inherently suitable Walvis Bay, which was already controlled by South Africa. The town received an economic boost in 1976 with the controversial opening of the world's largest opencast uranium mine at Rössing, 60 km (36 miles) inland, and it has also benefited greatly from the post-apartheid tourist boom. The population today stands at around 45,000.

Swakopmund retains much of its German character and continental atmosphere. There's a good sprinkling of houses built in the Jugendstil (Art Nouveau style so popular in Germany at the turn of the last century, many of which merit a closer look, For more in-depth historical background, a visit to the **Swakopmund Museum** Ⓐ (Strand St; tel: 064 402046; www. swakopmund-museum.de; daily 10am– 5pm; charge) is a good starting point. Founded in 1951 by an itinerant German dentist, Dr Alfons Weber, it provides a comprehensive perspective of the town and its surroundings and possesses considerable historical and ethnological collections. The museum also offers half-day tours of the Rössing Uranium Mine, starting at 10am on the first Friday of every month.

Close by in Strand Street is the **Kaiserliches Bezirksgericht** Ⓑ, a stately mansion originally built as a magistrate's court but now serving as the holiday residence of Namibia's President. It is backed by municipal gardens, which are home to a 21-metre (69ft)-high stone lighthouse as well as an imposing **Marine Memorial** Ⓒ, dedicated to the German soldiers sent in to suppress the Herero uprising in 1904. Also of interest is **The Mole** Ⓓ, the original breakwater built in 1898,

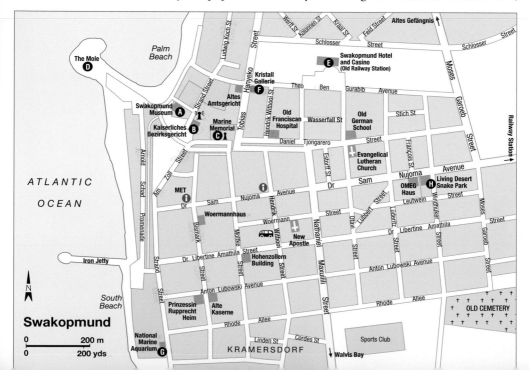

Swakopmund

and the metal **jetty**, which replaced its wood precursor in 1914, fell into disuse a year later, was boarded up as unsafe in the 1980s, but reopened in 2006 after extensive renovations.

Heading away from the beach, **Daniel Tjongarero Street** is due east across Tobias Hanyeko Street and lined with historical buildings. Then there's the **old railway station ❻** in nearby Theo-Ben Gurabib Avenue, an excellent example of Wilhelmenian-style architecture; it's now part of the Swakopmund Hotel and Casino complex.

Situated right on the corner of Theo-Ben Gurabib Avenue and Tobias Hanyeko Street, the **Kristall Galerie ❼** (Crystal Gallery; tel: 064 406080; www.namibiangemstones.com; Mon–Sat 9am–5pm; charge) houses a superb collection of semi-precious stones and other geological wonders from all around Namibia. The gallery's centrepiece is a remarkable 500-million-year-old quartzite crystal that stands twice as tall as a person – indeed, weighing in at more than 14,000kg (30,000 lb), it is credibly claimed to be the largest such formation in the world.

In terms of shopping, eating out, and entertainment, Swakopmund is – after Windhoek – the best-equipped town in Namibia, with an excellent selection of supermarkets and other shops, restaurants, delicatessens, banks, internet cafés and tour operators concentrated on and around the main drag through the town centre, Sam Nujoma Avenue. At the heart of this urban bustle, abutting the venerable Hansa Hotel on the corner of Sam Nujoma Avenue and Roon Street, an upmarket mall (simply called The Arcade) houses several good art and craft shops, the top-notch Swakopmund Buchhandlung (Bookshop), several coffee shops, and even a modern cinema complex showing recent western releases.

Sharks and sidewinders

The waterfront **National Marine Aquarium ❼** (Strand St; tel: 061 244558; Tue–Sun 10am–4pm; shark-feeding 3pm Tue, Sat, Sun; charge) on the southern outskirts of town is well worth a visit, especially on those afternoons when a diver descends into the main tank to feed the sharks. Tanks fed

You can see the strong tradition of German architecture in many of the buildings in Swakopmund.

Stones in a gem shop.

THE SWAKOP RIVER

Swakopmund – literally "Swakop Mouth" – is named after the Swakop River, a normally dry watercourse that rises in the interior near Okahandja, and whose valley supports low volumes of agriculture, including olives and tomatoes, even in years when little or no water flows. After heavy flooding, the river sometimes breaks through the sandbars on the southern outskirts of Swakopmund to flow into the Atlantic – a phenomenon that occurred most recently in 2000 (and almost happened again in the 2009 floods). The name Swakop is a bastardisation of the Nama "Tsoaxoub", literally "flowing excrement", a reference to the muddy appearance of the floodwaters when they reach the ocean laden with vast amounts of brown desert sand and other accumulated debris.

The Living Desert Snake Park in Swakopmund has both venomous and non-venomous snakes in a safe setting.

Quad-biking on the dunes near Swakopmund.

by saltwater pumped directly from the ocean house a rich variety of species associated with the chilly Atlantic, including four species of shark, great white pelican, African penguin, Cape fur seal, green and hawksbill turtle, and smaller curiosities such as anemones, sea cucumbers and sponges.

To see a very different but equally engaging animal collection, visit the **Living Desert Snake Park** ❻ (Sam Nujoma Avenue; tel: 064 405100; Mon–Fri 8.30am–5pm, Sat 8.30am–1pm, feeding time 10am Sat only; charge) immediately east of the city centre. Privately owned and managed, this herpetological zoo includes specimens of several species associated with the sandy and rocky terrain of the surrounding Namib, including the spectacular horned adder, the sidewinder-like southern dune adder, and the beady-eyed Namaqua chameleon.

Aside from being an attractive resort town, Swakopmund is now entrenched as Namibia's main centre for adventure tourism. Indeed, a good half-dozen reputable local operators scattered around town now offer visitors a wide range of day trips and activities – skydiving, quad-biking, sand boarding, dolphin cruises and deep-sea fishing, as well as township tours, nature drives into the brooding Namib dunes, or kayak excursions through choppy seas to the seal and penguin colonies around Walvis Bay – in short, enough variety to keep the most active traveller busy for days!

Walvis Bay

Driving south from Swakopmund, the road crosses the Swakop River by way of the longest bridge in Namibia (688 metres/12,250ft) to **Walvis Bay** ❷, a mere 33km (20 miles) distant. With a population of around 85,000, this is probably the second-largest town in Namibia, though it feels altogether less cosmopolitan than nearby Swakopmund, and suffers from something of a character deficit.

Despite appearances, Walvis Bay isn't lacking in historical significance. The Portuguese explorer Bartholomeu Diaz, who later pioneered a sea-route around Africa's southern tip, anchored here on 8 December 1487. If not Diaz, then it was certainly one of the many 16th century Portuguese mariners who followed in his wake that would have coined the name from which Walvis Bay derives ie Bahia das Bahleas (Bay of Whales). However, thanks to the absence of freshwater supplies, nearly three centuries were to pass before the European powers started to take an interest in this splendid natural harbour.

In 1840, Britain staked a claim on Walvis Bay and its immediate vicinity as an outpost of the Cape Colony. The port remained a British enclave in German South West Africa following the Scramble for Africa in the 1880s, but it was co-opted into the newly created Union of South Africa in 1910. Seized briefly by German troops after the outbreak of World War I, Walvis Bay was recaptured by South African troops in 1915, along with the rest of South West Africa, and it remained a South African possession until 1994,

some four years after Namibia became an independent state.

Reflecting this long association with Namibia's southern neighbour, the grid-like layout of central Walvis Bay is reminiscent of many a South African small town, as are the unmemorable architectural landmarks.

The sole attraction in the town centre is the **Walvis Bay Museum** (Nangolo Mbumba Dr; tel: 064 2013111; www.walvisbaycc.org.na; Mon–Fri 9am–12.30pm and 3–4.30pm; free) is the only real point of interest in the city centre, with displays relating to the harbour's history along with the geology and wildlife of the neighbouring Namib Desert.

Lagoons and deserts

Whatever Walvis Bay lacks for in urban charm, the immediate vicinity compensates for it terms of natural interest. Declared a Ramsar Site in 1995, Walvis Bay's **lagoon** offers some excellent opportunities for birdwatching – indeed, it's considered to be one of the most important wetlands in southern Africa, supporting, among others, almost half of the region's flamingo population. The sight of thousands of these graceful birds feeding in the shallow waters – or better still, flying overhead like thin sticks with black and pink wings – is quite breathtaking. A motorboat or canoe trip on the lagoon will not only provide good birdwatching, but may also reveal seals and dolphins too.

The lagoon can also be explored by road, heading southwest from the town centre along an extension of Nangolo Mbumba Drive. Almost immediately upon exiting the town, this road is flanked by a shallow lagoon on one side and tall dunes on the other, with a rich marine birdlife dominated by large flocks of great white pelican, the localised Damara tern, and a profusion of waders. Continue southward for another 10km (6 miles), turning right at the salt-processing plant, and you'll reach a car park (popular with local

fishermen), from where a very sandy track (suitable to experienced 4x4 drivers only) leads to Pelican Point, the site of a lighthouse and a colony of around 100 Cape fur seals.

More birdlife can be seen at **Sandwich Harbour**, which is situated almost on the **Tropic of Capricorn** about 40km (25 miles) south of Walvis. This wetland plays host to a considerable number of migratory birds en route from their nesting grounds in the northern hemisphere to the warmer climes of the Cape's west coast. In a good year, up to 50,000 wintering birds can be found here, while the occasional brown hyena, jackal or even oryx may also be seen along the shoreline.

This lagoon can only be reached by four-wheel-drive vehicle and a special permit is required, obtainable from Namibia Wildlife Resorts offices in Swakopmund and Windhoek as well as their rest camps. No vehicles are allowed beyond the northern fence of the lagoon, and visitors wishing to explore the area must do so on foot. Great care must be taken that vehicles do not get stuck.

FACT

Birders may be lucky enough to spot the rare Gray's Lark in the Kuiseb Canyon area; it's endemic to the gravel plains of Namibia and Angola.

Flamingos on the way to Sandwich Harbour.

Dead Vlei, Namib-Naukluft Park.

NAMIB-NAUKLUFT NATIONAL PARK

Thanks to the severity of its climate, the Namib
has been able to preserve itself in a near-
pristine state for 80 million years, although
it is also surprisingly accessible to visitors.

Main Attractions

The Namib Desert Park
Welwitschia Drive
Kuiseb River Canyon
Sesriem Canyon
Sossusvlei
Naukluft Mountains
NamibRand Nature Reserve

Beguiled by photographs of its
wonderful apricot dunes at
sunrise, the Namib Desert epit-
omises Namibia for many visitors.
These dunes are protected within the
49,768-sq-km (19,500-sq-mile) **Namib-
Naukluft National Park** ❸, Africa's
largest conservation area, protecting
a sweep of landscapes from the rip-
pling dunes of the Namib to the rocky
mountains of the Naukluft, as well as a
surprising amount of wildlife.

Despite its apparent remoteness,
the more developed part of **Namib-
Naukluft** – including the awesome
dunescapes around Sossusvlei – are
surprisingly accessible, whether you're
coming by light aircraft or by road.
There are two main approaches to Sossusvlei. The more direct, coming from
Windhoek, entails following the B1
south as far as Rehoboth, then turning
right onto the C24 to Solitaire and Sesriem. The more circuitous but interesting option, however, as followed in the
chapter below, involves driving east to
the ports of **Swakopmund** or **Walvis
Bay**, then following C14 through the
Kuiseb Canyon to Solitaire.

The Namib Desert Park

The park's oldest and most northerly
section, known as the **Namib Desert
Park** ❹, stretches between the Swakop
and Kuiseb Rivers. It's often simply
called the "gravel desert", and it's easy

to see why; the flat, rock-strewn landscape slopes gently away into the horizon with only the occasional isolated
inselberg (from the German for island-
mountain) breaking the monotony.

A popular half-day trip into this
section from either Swakopmund or
Walvis Bay is **Welwitschia Drive** (permit required) along the Swakop River,
where you can see some fine examples
of the *Welwitschia mirabilis* plant. First
described in 1852 by a German bota-
nist, Dr Friedrich Welwitsch, the oldest plant on the route is estimated to

En route to Welwitschia Drive.

Balloon rides over the Namib-Naukluft Park at sunrise are a popular excursion.

be close on 1,000 years old. Another botanical curiosity to look out for here is the fields of lichen, a remarkable form of plant life consisting of algae and fungi, which derive their moisture from sea fogs. You'll also drive past a curious collection of rock mounds in the bed of the Swakop River which are known as the **Mountains of the Moon**, along with a series of stark black dolerite dykes running like the plated spines of dinosaurs along the ridges of the mountains.

The Kuiseb Canyon

Another of the park's main attractions, situated about 140km (84 miles) to southeast of Walvis Bay, is the **Kuiseb River Canyon**. A geological phenomenon, it's a canyon within a canyon,

formed some 20 million years ago when the original river course gradually silted up with its own sediment, forcing the water to cut a new route.

Following the Kuiseb's course upstream brings you to a viewpoint at **Carp Cliff** offering a panorama of the escarpment and the river valley. You may spot baboon here, along with klipspringer antelope, mountain zebra and oryx. Predators include the black-backed jackal and the elusive leopard.

A second canyon, the **Gaub**, lies nearby on a tributary of the Kuiseb, and is like the latter a well-wooded and generally dry river bed, although here the underground river nourishes large trees such as the camel thorn, the false ebony tree, the shepherd's tree and the ana. Consequently, this is also

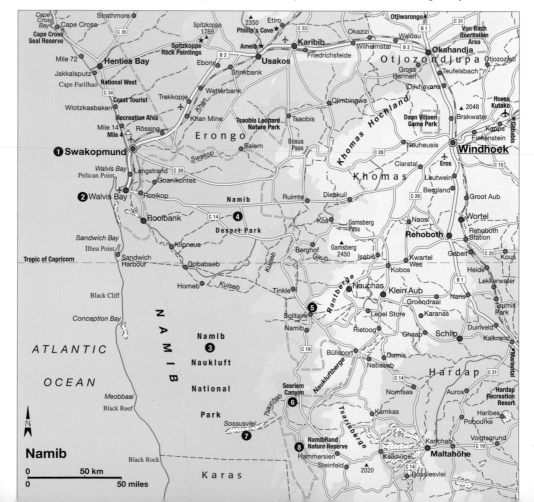

a good place to find birds and insects, and to stop for picnics.

The Solitaire area

Immediately south of the Kuiseb stretches much of the most atmospheric section of the park, the **Dune Namib**. In spite of its desolate appearance, this remains one of the most accessible of all the world's sandy deserts. The roads in the area can generally be used by two-wheel-drive saloon cars, although the going may be slow. Daytime temperatures are extremely high throughout the year and ample supplies of water should be carried as a precaution, particularly if you intend clambering to the top of a huge dune.

Over millions of years, the Orange River has carried vast quantities of sand from its origins high up in the Lesotho Highlands down to the Atlantic Ocean. The Benguela Current has then transported the sand northwards from the river's mouth and deposited it on the shore to create these coastal dunes, and from here it's been vigorously driven northeast by the wind. Currently, this "marching" of the dunes continues at a rate of 20 metres (60ft) a year.

To reach the dune fields, drive south from the Kuiseb and Gaub Canyons across the Tropic of Capricorn for about 66km (40 miles) to the tiny settlement of **Solitaire** ❺ on the C14. From here, a further 70km (44-mile) drive southwards along route 36 will bring you to the **Sesriem Canyon** ❻, where the Tsauchab River has cut a spectacular gorge some 40 metres (120ft) deep into layers of schist and gravel deposited millions of years ago. This delightful spot acquired its evocative name because early settlers required six lengths of leather thongs (*rieme* in Afrikaans) to haul water from the canyon below in order to water their teams of oxen.

A fairly steep but manageable path leads into the canyon where the conglomerate layers are clearly visible;

you can also see from the material caught high up on the walls of the gorge that it fills right up after heavy rain. There are a camp site and several lodges nearby, some of which offer the possibility of ballooning over the desert at dawn.

The heart of the Namib

An hour and a half's drive (60km/37 miles) deeper west into the desert brings you to **Sossusvlei** ❼, a huge clay-pan surrounded by massive dunes – the highest dunes of the desert in fact. Saloon cars can travel to within 4km (2.5 miles) of the *vlei* ("pan" in Afrikaans), while 4x4 drive vehicles can continue up to the parking area by the pan itself. You can walk to Sossusvlei or one of the other pans nearby such as Hidden Vlei or Dead Vlei.

This, truly, is the heart of the Namib. The yellow and grey-buff hues of the pan contrast sharply with the brick-red dunes, providing spectacular opportunities for photography, especially at dawn and dusk. The views are enhanced even further if the pan is flooded, which only happens once

The dunes at Sossusvlei Park have been formed by the wind, so the leeward side of the dune will always be much steeper than the windward side.

An abandoned car in the desert outside Swakopmund.

At Sossusvlei, the ground is baked into crazy-paving patterns.

or twice every decade, most recently in early 2011. Occasionally, the graceful shape of an oryx, standing on the crest of a dune, can be seen etched against the skyline – not as a favour to photographers, but as one of the strategies used by this desert antelope to catch the slightest breeze and reduce its body temperature.

The Naukluft Mountains

Rising to an altitude of 1,973 metres (6,430 ft) from the desert on the western edge of the main escarpment is a small range known as the Naukluft. This and a corridor of land to the west linking the mountains to the desert below used to be known as the Naukluft Park, but in 1979 were incorporated into the bigger Namib Desert Park to create the Namib-Naukluft National Park of today. The Naukluft area is best reached from the C14 between Solitaire and Maltahöhe with a turn-off on the D854. There are a few campsites, which – like the trails below – must be booked in advance in Windhoek – see www.nwr.com.na for details.

The pan at Sesriem.

Originally intended as a sanctuary for the indigenous Hartmann's mountain zebra, the area has permanent water and supports a wide range of elusive mammals and birds. The area can only be explored on foot and two circular day hikes – the 11km (7-mile) Olive Trail and 17km (11-mile) Waterkloof Trail – start at the campsite, respectively requiring about five and seven hours of fairly strenuous walking and climbing. A third, the Naukluft Trail, is a tough eight-day affair, but worth it to explore one of Namibia's most exciting landscapes. For those seeking a different type of adventure, there is also the new 73km (44 mile) Naukluft 4x4 Trail, limited to four vehicles daily, and involving an overnight stop after 28km (17 miles).

Bordering the park to the west, the 1,720-sq-km (670-sq-mile) **NamibRand Nature Reserve** ❽ (www.namibrand.com) is one of the largest private sanctuaries in southern Africa. Offering a good range of desert landscapes and game, it's home to several upmarket lodges and small camps where guests can take advantage of expert guides.

THE HIGHEST DUNES

There are a variety of sand dune shapes in the Namib, but all have gentle slopes on their exposed windward sides and are far steeper on the sheltered leeward sides.

The tallest dunes are more than 300 metres (1,000ft) high, making them the highest formations of their type anywhere in the world. Climbing to the crest of one of these mammoth sand formations is an exhilarating but exhausting experience, a steep slog through soft sand, giving fresh meaning to the expression "two steps forward, one step backward"!

Most popular with hikers, Dune 45 (which, as its name suggests, lies 45km from Sesriem along the Sossusvlei road) is best tackled in the coolness of the early morning to avoid overexposure to the blazing sun.

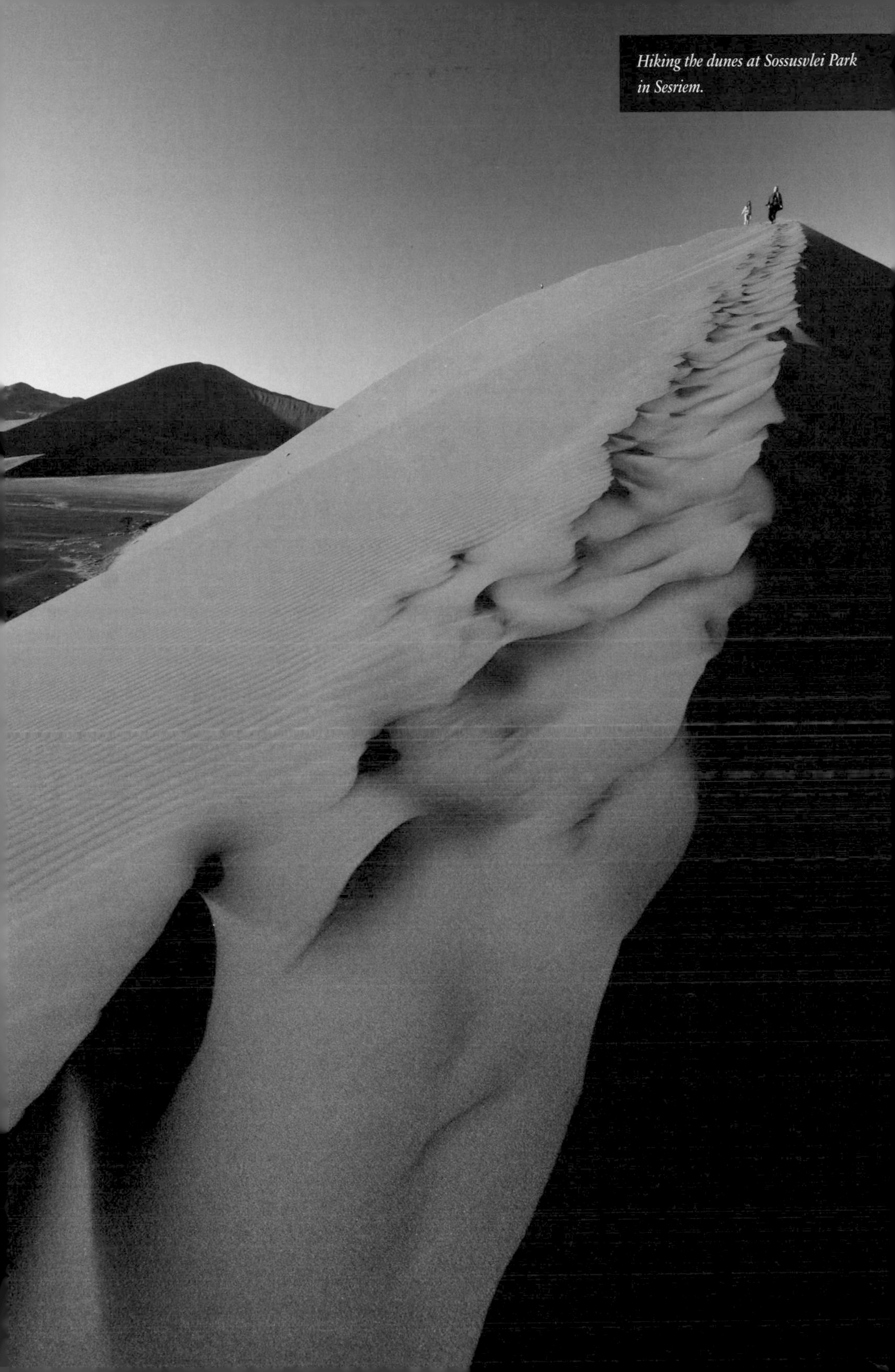

Hiking the dunes at Sossusvlei Park in Sesriem.

Fish River Canyon.

Kolmanskop, a deserted mining town near Lüderitz.

SOUTHERN NAMIBIA

The wide plains of Namibia's "Deep South" may seem arid and inhospitable, but they're home to some intriguing sights – from towns swallowed by desert dunes to the mighty Fish River Canyon.

Windhoek

tretched between the Namib Desert in the west and the dry Kalahari in the east, southern Namibia's flat, wide-open expanses are characterised by stony outcrops peppered with quiver trees and low, table-top mountains. Often neglected as a tourist destination because it lacks northern Namibia's wealth of big game, the region nevertheless contains a range of unusual sights, including one of the world's least-visited geological wonders.

Rehoboth and Lake Oanob

The quickest way to reach the south is to take the B1 from Windhoek. At first the road passes through bush interspersed with large trees, and you may even see baboons crossing the road between the capital and **Rehoboth ❶**, which straddles the Tropic of Capricorn 87km (52 miles) to the south. The main attraction in this area, 7km (4 miles) south of town, is **Lake Oanob**, which was created in 1990 when a 55-metre (180ft) dam – the highest in Namibia – was built on the eponymous river, and is now the site of the relaxed Lake Oanob Resort.

Bypassed by the main highway, Rehoboth nevertheless has an interesting history as the stronghold of the Baster community who farm the area. A mixed-race group – the progeny of

Cape Dutch settlers and the indigenous Khoikhoi – the Basters found themselves rejected by both communities. Eventually, many of them banded together and migrated northwest away from South Africa, settling around the little mission station of Rehoboth in 1870. Throughout the last century, they made many attempts to obtain home rule for their community and did, in fact, finally obtain a measure of independence when Namibia was under South African control – although, ironically, this

Main Attractions
Duwisib Castle
Mount Brukkaros
Quiver Tree Forest
Fish River Canyon Park
Kolmanskop
Lüderitz

The wild horses near Garub.

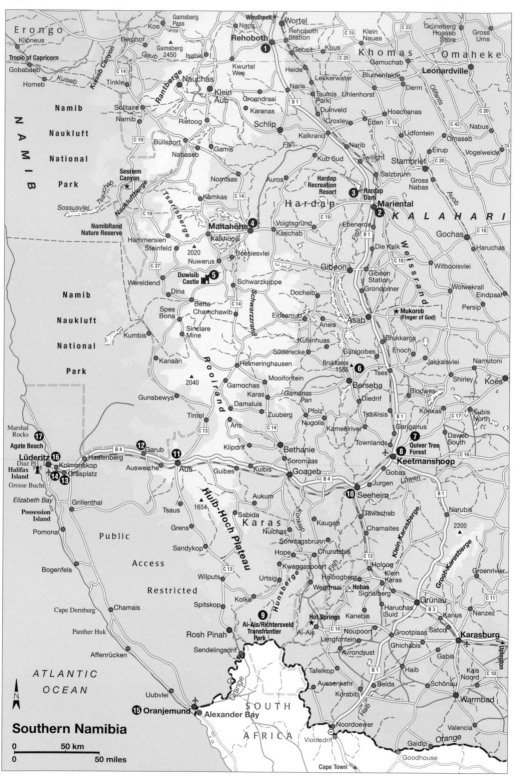

Southern Namibia

0   50 km

0   50 miles

was granted in order to strengthen the divisions within the country in the name of apartheid.

The history of the Baster people is the subject of several displays in the **Rehoboth Museum** (tel: 062 522954; www.rehobothmuseum.com; 9am–noon Mon–Sat and 2–4pm Mon–Fri; charge), which is housed in the Old Postmasters House next to the Post Office, about 300 metres from the B1. In addition to detailing the foundation of Rehoboth and the short-lived reign of the autonomous Baster government in the 1980s, the museum also hosts some interesting displays on local geology and archaeology, as well as various traditional cultures of Namibia.

Hardap Game Park

Heading south from Rehoboth, after the B1 crosses the Oanob River, the taller trees disappear, and soon after that it leaves behind the Auas Mountains – the last obvious topographical feature until it reaches **Mariental ❷**, 174km (105 miles) further south. Just before Mariental, the road drops off

the central highland plateau; a right turn along Route 93 here will take you to **Hardap Dam ❸**, the largest reservoir in Namibia with a surface area of some 25 sq km (10 sq miles). Fed by the Fish River, the lake is a haven for freshwater anglers, while the aquarium adjacent to the tourist office houses fish species from Namibia's major rivers.

An early morning or late afternoon game drive in the **Hardap Dam Game Reserve & Resort** (tel: 063-240381, www.nwr.com.na; resort gate: 6am–11pm; charge), which extends over 250 sq km (100 sq miles) on the southern and western side of the dam, can be rewarding. Along with Namibia's southernmost population of black rhino, reintroduced at the end of the last century, wildlife includes, red hartebeest, kudu, eland, oryx, springbok and Hartmann's mountain zebra. The dam is one of Namibia's only two white pelican breeding sites, but it also attracts plenty of other birds, from red-knobbed coot and squacco heron to osprey, fish eagles and cormorants.

Many plants in the region have had to adapt to the harsh environment.

The restaurant at Hardap Dam Game Reserve and Resort.

A quiver tree – a kind of aloe – grows in Giants' Playground, named for the giant rock piles scattered about, as though the playthings of giants.

Desert grasses beside the road to Lüderitz.

Mariental itself is a typically dry and dusty southern African everytown, equipped with a few small hotels, filling stations, supermarkets and restaurants. Superficially, it is an improbable setting for a flood, but that is exactly what happened here in March 2006, when the sluice gates to nearby Hardap Dam were opened too late after heavy rains, and the town was submerged waist-high in water.

To the northeast of Mariental, a clutch of newish game ranches set on the western fringe of the Kalahari makes for a convenient first stop out of Windhoek en route to the far south. The most established of these is the Intu Africa Kalahari Game Reserve, which offers accommodation in three small camps as well as guided game drives into an 180 sq km (70 sq miles) enclosure where grazers such as giraffe, dry-country antelope and Burchell's zebra cohabit with suricate, bat-eared fox and black-backed jackal. Similar but smarter, the new Bagatelle Lodge has accommodation set on the crest of a dune and a similar range of wildlife to Intu

Africa, supplemented by recently re-introduced cheetah.

Many travellers pass through **Maltahöhe** ❹, which lies 110km (65 miles) west of Mariental along the C19 at the junction of important routes north to Namib-Naukluft National Park and south to Lüderitz, but few linger very long in this nondescript town. Of greater interest, **Duwisib Castle** ❺ (tel: 066 385303; www.nwr.com.na; daily 8am–1pm and 2–5pm; charge) is an improbable neo-Baroque castle set in the heart of the desert some 72km southwest of Maltahöhe alongside the D286. Built in 1909 by Baron Captain Hans Heinrich von Wolf for his American wife, the 22-room castle was designed by the eminent architect Willi Sander, and constructed using local stone and other materials imported from Germany, and artisans from Italy, Sweden and Ireland. The Baron died in 1916 in the Battle of the Somme and his wife never returned to Namibia. Today, the castle houses a museum with an intriguing collection of 18th- and 19th-century antiques, armour and paintings, and there is a campsite in the grounds.

An unusual mountain and forest

Back on the B1, continuing southward from Mariental, you'll see the imposing sandstone mass of the Weissrand escarpment dominating the scenery to the east. Formed by the incision of the Fish River between 5 and 15 million years ago, the escarpment has been cut back at an estimated rate of 4km (2.5 miles) every million years, and has actually retreated some 40km (25 miles) from the river during this time.

Still further south, to the right of the road beyond blink-and-you'll-miss-it **Asab**, the steep outer slopes of the prominent **Mount Brukkaros** ❻, visible from 100km (60 miles) distant, lead to a 1,586-metre (5,203ft)-high rim that encloses

a 2km (1.25-mile)-wide caldera. Despite appearances, Brukkaros is not a true volcano, but was created some 80 million years ago when the combination of magma trapped underground and seeping water created a hydrostatic explosion that caused surface rocks to be blasted high into the sky, but without any issue of lava or pumice.

The spectacular and little-visited caldera can be explored on foot, and it is also possible to stay overnight at the no-frills community-run Brukkaros Campsite (tel: 063 257188/223572). To get there from the B1, turn west onto the gravel D390 at Tses, then after 30km (18 miles), about 4km (2.5 miles) before you reach the former mission station of **Berseba**, follow the signpost right to Brukkaros, which you reach after 8km (5 miles). From the end of the road, it's a 30-minute walk to the crater's floor and then about an hour's fairly steep climb up to the old observation station perched on the edge of the rim, offering superb views down to the plains below. Make sure you have sufficient water, a snack, stout walking shoes and a hat before setting off.

Back on the B1, turn left a few miles north of Keetmanshoop onto the C16 to Aroab, and then left again less than a mile further on to the C17 (signposted for Koës) to reach the **Quiver Tree Forest** ❼ (tel: 063 683421, www. quivertreeforest.com, daily; charge) some 12km (8 miles) to the east. The quiver – which grows up to 7 metres (23ft) high, and is also known as the kokerboom – is one of four Namibian aloes to be classified as a tree; around 250 such trees grow amongst the rocky outcrops here and the grove has been declared a national monument. Close by is **Giants' Playground**, a series of huge rock totems strewn across the landscape like piles of oversized tin cans. Known locally as the *Vratteveld*, these outcrops are erosional remnants of molten lava dating back some 180 million years.

The transport hub of **Keetmanshoop** ❽ is a good starting-point from which to explore Namibia's southernmost reaches. Situated some 480km (298 miles) south of Windhoek, the

A woman in Keetmanshoop, which lies on the course of The TransNamib Railway.

The Keetmanshoop Museum.

The Fish River Canyon is the largest canyon in Africa, and the second largest in the world.

The ghost town that is Kolmanskop, a former mining town.

town dates back to 1866 when a small settlement was established here by missionary Johann Schroeder and named in honour of the then president of the Rhenish Missionary Society, Johann Keetman. Of considerable architectural interest is the **Old Post Office**, which dates to 1910, but the oldest building is the imposing Rhenish Mission Church, a remarkable Gothic edifice erected in 1895 to replace an earlier structure destroyed by floods. Today, the church houses the **Keetmanshoop Museum** and is hung with memorabilia of the early days of the mission, while the gardens are dotted with wagons alongside a replica of a Nama hut (tel: 063 221256; Mon–Fri 7.30am–12.30pm and 2.30–4.30pm; free).

The town is also an important centre for Namibia's Karakul sheep-breeding industry (see page 57).

The Fish River Canyon

Vying with Ethiopia's Blue Nile Gorge for the (inherently subjective) accolade of Africa's largest canyon is the magnificent **Fish River Canyon**, the dominant topographic feature of Namibia's far south. Indeed, the canyon is one of Africa's most spectacular natural wonders, measuring about 160km (100 miles) from north to south, up to 550 metres (1,800ft) deep, and up to 26km (15 miles) wide. Formerly the centrepiece of Fish River Canyon National Park, it is now protected in the **Ai-Ais/Richtersveld Transfrontier Park** ❾. This is one of several so-called "Peace Parks" that cross Africa's international boundaries, having recently merged management with its South African component, the former Richtersveld National Park, which lies immediately south of the Orange River.

The Fish River Canyon can easily be visited as a day trip from Keetmanshoop, though it's worth staying overnight in the immediate vicinity to see it in the soft light of dusk or dawn. Either way, you need to follow the B4 southwest towards Lüderitz, then turn left at **Seeheim** ❿ onto the gravel C12, and keep heading south. Then take a right turn onto the D601 south

of **Holoog**, a left onto the D324 and a right onto the C10. If you're travelling during the rainy season, be warned the road sometimes floods, so ask about current conditions at any hotel in Keetmanshoop.

The main entrance is the **Hobas Information Centre** (www.nwr.com.na; daily 7.30am–noon and 2–5pm; charge) at the northern end of the canyon, where a lovely campsite boasts modern toilet facilities, a shop and swimming pool. From Hobas you can drive to several observation points along the eastern rim, all of which offer awe-inspiring views over the rocks and riverbed far below. Access to the bottom of the canyon is not permitted to day visitors without a permit, obtainable either at Hobas or the Ai-Ais entrance gate. If you're interested in hiking the entire canyon, bear in mind it's quite a challenge and permitted only in winter; every day between May and September intrepid walkers who have made the necessary advance booking set off from the northernmost viewpoint to hike the 85km (53 miles) from Hobas to Ai-Ais, a four- or five-day trek. A permit is required to do the hike and best bought well in advance.

From Hobas, a gravel road winds through the mountains for about 70km (43 miles) to the **/Ai-/Ais Hot Springs**. For the final 10km (6 miles,) the road twists down through a wonderful ravine between piles of loose and shattered buff and dark brown rocks; the sudden greenness around the **/Ai-/Ais** spring at the bottom comes as a real surprise. Although rather strenuous, an ascent of the hills overlooking /Ai-/Ais is rewarded with spectacular views of the rest camp down below, and the inhospitable canyon stretching away to the west.

West of the Fish River, the Hunsberg Mountains form part of the Fish River Canyon conservation area but, because of its rugged terrain, the area is not open to the public – a pity, because as well as offering beautiful scenery, it is the habitat of several rare botanical species.

Into the forbidden territory

Back on the main road (the B4) between Seeheim and Lüderitz, you will cross the Fish River just as the northernmost signs of the canyon begin to show. Continuing further west, Diamond Area I (also known as the **Sperrgebiet**, or "forbidden territory"), is entered a few miles beyond **Aus ⑪**. As the name suggests, this area is strictly controlled and it is illegal to leave the road until you get to Lüderitz. Stretching from the Orange River in the south to 26°S latitude, Diamond Area I extends about 100km (60 miles) inland from the Atlantic. Exclusive mining rights to this diamond-rich area have been granted to the Namibia Diamond Corporation (NAMDEB), which is owned in equal shares by the Namibian Government and the well-known mining multinational De Beers. As you approach **Garub ⑫**, along a stretch of road flanked by the Sperrgebiet to the south and

TIP

When you're exploring the Lüderitz peninsula, stick to hard-surface roads and avoid loose sand and the area's seemingly negotiable salt pans.

"IT COULD BE A DIAMOND..."

August Stauch was quite content with life. He had a fine position with the German railway company Lenz & Co, and his pretty wife, Ida, tended lovingly to him and their two children. If only it wasn't for the asthma… When his firm won a contract from the German Colonial Railway Building and Operating Company to build a line far away in German South West Africa, he was an obvious choice for a posting. The colony's dry, sunny climate would certainly be good for his asthma, and it was only a two-year contract. Accordingly, Stauch sadly took leave of his family and set out, landing at Windhoek in May 1907.

Stauch's main task as railway inspector was to keep part of the new track being built between Lüderitz and Aus free of sand from the shifting dunes. One day, in April 1908, an unusual stone stuck to the oiled shovel of a worker, Zacharias Lewala, who ran to his foreman: "Must give Mister little klippe (stone). Is *miskien diamant*! (is maybe diamond!)" The foreman stashed the stone away in his pocket and later told Stauch the tale, laughing. But Stauch didn't laugh; instead, he tried to cut the crystal in his pocket-watch with the stone – and succeeded. Lewala's find turned out to be a tiny part of one of the world's richest alluvial diamond fields, which today is still a mainstay of Namibia's economy.

Oysters are farmed at Shear Water Oysters in Lüderitz.

Namib-Naukluft National Park to the north, keep an eye open for the **wild horses of the Namib** which are usually seen in this vicinity; a pumping-station is maintained to provide water for them. During the German colonial period a contingent of troops was stationed at Garub and it's thought that the horses are the offspring of animals abandoned when the Germans retreated ahead of the advancing South African forces in 1915. Their numbers fluctuate from year to year, but during favourable conditions more than 100 horses roam the inhospitable desert.

A once-stately house at **Grasplatz** ⓭ serves as a reminder of the hectic period following the discovery of diamonds here in 1908 (see page 63). A few miles further west, forlorn **Kolmanskop** ⓮ rises like a ghost town out of a sea of sand. Once the centre of the flourishing diamond-mining industry, today it's a mere shadow of a more glorious era. Abandoned in 1956, nature has since reclaimed most of the town and sand has swept through broken windows and open doors, although towards the end of the 20th century some buildings such as the casino, the skittle alley and the retail shop were restored. The town can be visited only on guided tours, after a permit has been obtained from Lüderitz Safaris and Tours in Lüderitz (tel: 063 202719).

Today, the equivalent diamond-rush town is **Oranjemund** ⓯ (Orange Mouth) about 8km (5 miles) from the mouth of the Orange River near the South African border. This became the focus of Namibia's diamond industry following the discovery of diamonds here in 1928. The 100km (60-mile) stretch of coastline north of the town was once considered the world's richest alluvial diamond field, but it's now nearing the end of its lifespan and production is expected to wind down within the next 15 years. For obvious reasons, strict security measures are in force and this mining town, which appears from maps to be accessible only by air, is not open to tourists.

Lüderitz and around

From Kolmanskop, it's just 9km (5.5 miles) to the sleepy old fishing port of **Lüderitz** ⓰, whose brightly painted Art Nouveau buildings stand in pleasing contrast to the granite outcrops and tall dunes that otherwise characterise this forbidding stretch of coast. The town is named after its founder Adolf Lüderitz, a former tobacco merchant and cattle rancher who bought the peninsula known to the Portuguese as Angra Pequena (Narrow Bay) from a local Nama chief and established a trading post there. Fishing and the harvesting of guano were the main activities in Lüderitz prior to 1909, when the diamond rush began.

Today, Lüderitz vies with Swakopmund as Namibia's most engaging town. True, it has fewer facilities than Swakopmund, and attracts relatively low tourist volumes, but the compact layout and time-warped colonial architecture make it an utter delight to explore on foot. Don't miss a visit to its

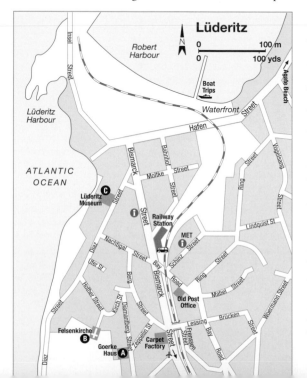

Lüderitz

most striking German colonial building, the pale blue **Goerke Haus** Ⓐ (Diamantberg Street; Mon–Fri 2–4pm and Sat–Sun 4–5pm; charge), perched on the slopes above the town centre. Designed by architect Otto Ertl, it was built in 1910 for the diamond company manager Lieutenant Hans Goerke, and while it is not typical of the local Art Nouveau architectural style, it is rich in the detail of this period.

The nearby **Felsenkirche** Ⓑ (Evangelical Lutheran Church), consecrated in 1912 and with an altar window donated by Kaiser Wilhelm II, is especially worth visiting during the late afternoon, when the setting sun illuminates the stained-glass windows beautifully. Also worth a visit, the **Lüderitz Museum** Ⓒ (Diaz Street; tel: 063-203959; Mon–Fri 10am–noon and 3.30–5pm; charge), has interesting displays about the history of the town and the local fishing and diamond industry, as well as the wildlife of the nearby desert and coast.

The Lüderitz Peninsula is characterised by numerous bays, lagoons and unspoilt stretches of beach which are accessible by car or, if one has the time and energy, on foot. At **Diaz Point**, 22km (14 miles) outside Lüderitz, a replica of the cross erected by Bartolomeu Diaz on 25 July 1488 serves as a reminder of the 15th-century Portuguese explorations. Fur seals can be seen on the rocks offshore here, while a varied marine birdlife includes the rare black oystercatcher, migrant waders such as turnstone and whimbrel, and various gulls and terns.

As an alternative (weather permitting), it's worth taking a boat trip via Diaz Point to **Halifax Island** where you can get close-up views of the African penguin colony, though sadly this was badly affected by an April 2009 oil spill in which hundreds of birds died.

The **beach** ⓲ at **Agate Bay**, 8km (5 miles) north of town, is popular with bathers, but the chances of finding any agates are slim. Another popular beach for swimming and picnicking is **Grosse Bucht** at the peninsula's southern point, while at the nearby **Sturmvogelbucht** the remains of an old Norwegian whaling station can be seen rusting away.

The lighthouse near Diaz Point.

German-style town-planning in Lüderitz.

INSIGHT GUIDES TRAVEL TIPS
NAMIBIA

TRANSPORT

GETTING THERE AND GETTING AROUND

GETTING THERE

By Air

The only direct service between Namibia and Europe is the Air Namibia flight to Frankfurt, which leaves six times per week. In addition, regional services to neighbouring countries provide convenient connections with international flights to and from other southern African capitals.

From Johannesburg, South African Airways (SAA) operates a few return flights per week to several European capitals, with easy onward connections to Windhoek, while Air Berlin and Lufthansa both fly return to Frankfurt.

From the UK, SAA and British Airways fly to South Africa, from where you can pick up a regional flight to Windhoek. It is also possible to fly directly from the US with SAA to South Africa, and then connect to Windhoek.

The cheapest flights between Johannesburg and Windhoek are operated by an excellent online booking agency: see www.kulula.com or tel: 0861 585852 from within South Africa or +27 11 921 0111 from elsewhere.
NB: the reconfirmation of return flights is essential.

For the cost of a few pounds you can make your flight carbon-neutral at either www.climatecare.org or www.carbonneutral.com.

Airports

All international flights land at Hosea Kutako International Airport (www.airports.com.na), which lies about 45km (28 miles) east of Windhoek, and is also the arrival and departure point for most scheduled regional and domestic flights to/from the capital. Eros Airport (5km/3 miles) from the city centre serves domestic and some regional charter routes.

Airline Offices

Air Namibia
Independence Avenue
Tel: 061 299 6333
www.airnamibia.aero
British Airways/Comair
Tel: 061 248528
www.britishairways.com
Air Berlin
Tel: 061 302220
www.airberlin.com
Lufthansa
Independence Avenue
Sanlam Building, Windhoek
Tel: 061 226662
www.lufthansa.com
South African Airways (SAA)
Tel: 062 540 082
www.flysaa.com
TAAG (Angolan airline)
Tel: 061 226625, www.taag.com

By Sea

Passenger liners call very infrequently at Walvis Bay en route between Southampton and Cape Town, Durban and Mauritius.

It is virtually impossible to obtain a passage on any other vessels and there is very little chance of arranging a "working" passage.

By Rail

The only cross-border rail service between Namibia and its neighbours is with South Africa. Scheduled Transnet passenger trains run from Johannesburg and Cape Town to Upington, where travellers transfer to the twice-weekly TransNamib passenger train service to Windhoek's main train station.

Passenger trains do not have dining saloons. Some trains have a catering/refreshment car for part of the journey only, so check when booking your ticket as you may need to take your own food and drink. Sleeping berths are provided for first- and second-class passengers. First- and second-class coupés accommodate two and three passengers, while first- and second-class compartments sleep four and six passengers respectively. You can provide your own bedding (sleeping bag) or buy bedding tickets when you make the reservation or on the train.

For more details contact TransNamib, tel: 061 298 1111, www.transnamib.com.na.

By Bus/Coach

The main approaches from South Africa are tarred: Johannesburg to Windhoek via Upington and Ariamsvlei (1,971km/1,225 miles), and Cape Town to Windhoek via Springbok and Noordoewer (1,493km/928 miles). It is also possible to take the asphalt Trans-Kalahari Highway from Johannesburg via Botswana to Buitepos on the border, just east of Gobabis, which is much quicker than travelling via Upington.

There is a service between Namibia, Zimbabwe and South Africa on luxury coaches with air conditioning and reclining seats. Intercape-Mainliner operates a Windhoek–Johannesburg service (19 hours) which departs three times a week via Gobabis and Botswana, and four times a week via Keetmanshoop and Upington. Coaches run between Windhoek and Cape Town (16 hours) twice weekly, and there is a once-weekly return to Victoria Falls in Zimbabwe. Intercape also runs three coaches weekly in either direction between Windhoek and Walvis Bay via Swakopmund. Tickets must be pre-paid and reservations can be made at the depot on Independence Ave (opposite Kalahari Sands), Windhoek (tel: 061 227847) or online at www.intercape.co.za. You can also book online through the South African head office (tel: 0860 287287 or 021 3804400).

GETTING AROUND

The best way to explore Namibia is in a rented car or on a small private safari. This is a country characterised by long distances and wide open spaces, and much of its scenic magic is lost if you rush around by air, though it is possible to fly to almost anywhere if you so choose, and it will save time. Public transport amounts to a few coach services and some very slow passenger trains on main routes, so it's not a realistic way of getting to see the main highlights.

Namibia's road network is well developed by African standards. All the main towns have direct links on tar roads, and the gravel roads are also in reasonably good condition (you will, however, need a 4x4 vehicle when driving in remote areas such as Kaokoland, Bushmanland and parts of the Kavango region as there are no developed gravel roads at all here).

Take great care in the rainy season, when gravel roads can be slippery. This is also when those riverbeds that are normally dry (the *omuramba*) come down in flood; they can be dangerous to cross. Also bear in mind that on gravel roads your average driving speed should not exceed 80 kph (50 mph), and estimate driving times accordingly.

All roads in Namibia are numbered and clearly signed en route. Detailed topographical maps (1: 250 000 and 1: 50 000) are very useful when travelling off the beaten track – in Kaokoland, for example. 1: 1000 000 scale maps of regions and districts are also available, as are geological maps of Namibia. Both can be bought at the Office of the Surveyor General in Windhoek, at the corner of Robert Mugabe and Lazarett Street.

By Air

Air Namibia, the country's national airline, operates regular flights from Windhoek to Walvis Bay, Lüderitz, Oranjemund, Ondangwa and Katima Mulilo. All of these flights return to Windhoek on the same day.

Other destinations in Namibia can be reached by charter flights. Here is a list of some fly-in safari operators:

Atlantic Aviation
Tel: 064 404749
www.flyinnamibia.com
Namib Wilderness Safaris
Tel: +27 11 807 1800
www.wilderness-safaris.com
Skeleton Coast Safaris
Tel: 061 224248
www.skeletoncoastsafaris.com

By Train

Although the domestic rail service operated by TransNamib (tel: 061 298 1111; www.transnamib.com) is primarily goods-oriented, passenger services are available on all routes. Passenger trains run on Tuesday, Friday and Sunday in both directions between Windhoek Station (on the corner of Bahnhof Street and Mandume Ndomufayo Avenue) and Walvis Bay. The journey takes approximately 11 hours.

Passenger trains are scheduled in both directions between Windhoek and Tsumeb on Friday and Sunday (19 hours). Services also operate between Otjiwarongo and Grootfontein; Otjiwarongo and Outjo;

Road signs warn of local hazards.

and Windhoek and Gobabis. No catering facilities are provided, but first- and second-class passengers can purchase bedding tickets either when making their reservation or on board the train. Also operated by TransNamib, the Desert Express is a very comfortable overnight tourist train that operates once weekly in either direction between Windhoek and Namibia. It departs from Windoek at around midday on Friday, and Swakopmund on Saturday afternoons, and the trip takes around 20 hours in either direction. Details are also available through the TransNamib website.

Regular fixed-departure rail safaris between Cape Town and Windhoek, typically taking 7–14 days in total, are offered by two upmarket South African companies: Shongololo Express (tel: +27 11 486 4357, www.shongololo.com) and Rovos Rail (tel: +27 12 315 8242;). An advantage of this sort of trip is that much of your travel is done by night, leaving the days free to explore places of interest, but it is obviously less flexible than a self-drive holiday.

By Bus/Coach

Intercape-Mainliner (tel: 061 227847; www.intercape.co.za) operates a luxury bus service between Windhoek and Walvis Bay three times a week. Stops along the five-hour journey include Okahandja, Karibib, Usakos and Swakopmund. Intercape-Mainliner also operates a shuttle service from

TRANSPORT
ACCOMMODATION
EATING OUT
ACTIVITIES
A – Z

Windhoek to the airport. The schedule is available at most hotels.

The Intercape-Mainliner service between Windhoek and Johannesburg operates four times weekly via Keetmanshoop and Upington, and three times per week via Gobabis and Botswana. It also operates a new service from Windhoek to Victoria Falls via Katima Mulilo in the Caprivi Strip.

Ekonolux (tel: 061 258961; www. facebook.com/EkonoluxCc) operates a thrice-weekly luxury bus service between Windhoek and Katima Mulilo. It stops at most towns en route but check the timetable, because some stops are made in the small hours of the morning.

Taxis

Taxis cruising the streets of Windhoek and other larger towns are a familiar sight, but operate mainly between the town centre and suburbs.
Dial-A-Cab, tel: 061 223531; www. dialacab-namibia.com
Dial a Driver, tel: 061 259677
Express Radio Taxis, tel: 061 239739
Some of these taxis also do airport transfers. Beware of taxis operating illegally, because they have no passenger liability insurance.

Driving

Foreign drivers' licences are accepted for stays of up to 90 days, provided that the pertinent information is written in the English language. Visitors from countries whose licences aren't in English are advised to obtain an International Driving Permit before their departure.

Driving is on the left-hand side of the road and the wearing of seat belts by the driver and front-seat passenger is compulsory. The maximum permissible alcohol level for drivers is 0.16 percent. On major

roads the maximum speed limit is 120kph (75mph) and in urban areas 60kph (37mph), unless a lower speed is indicated. The recommended speed limit on gravel roads is between 80 and 100kph (50–62mph), depending on the condition of the road.

Tourist attractions are generally well signposted and most are accessible by sedan car. A word of warning though: although roads in Kaokoland have been classified as district roads, most are impassable to cars and not signposted. The "salt" roads in Swakopmund and northwards along the coast are also particularly treacherous when wet and special caution is advisable.

Travelling at night in the rural areas can be hazardous – keep a sharp eye out for kudu and warthog, which frequently graze in the road between dusk and dawn. Guinea fowl, too, are in the habit of leaping out in front of vehicles. Stray livestock is a menace in the northern parts of the country, while gravel roads passing through farmland are often unfenced, so keep your eyes peeled for roving stock. Watch out also for the wild horses of the Namib west of Aus, especially at night when they seek the warmth of the tarred road.

Petrol and diesel are available along all major tourist routes, as well as in some state-owned rest camps. In Damaraland fuel is only available at Khorixas, Uis, Sesfontein and Palmwag, and in Kaokoland only at Opuwa. Between Rundu and Katima Mulilo the availability of fuel is reliable. There are no filling stations along the three passes linking Windhoek and Swakopmund/Walvis Bay.

Insurance

Whenever hiring a motor vehicle, insurance and collision damage waiver (CDW) is an absolute necessity. In most cases the CDW covers only 80

Restrictions on Travel

Entry into Diamond Areas 1 and 2 is strictly prohibited and visitors travelling between Aus and Lüderitz are not permitted to leave the road.

Day permits to travel through the Skeleton Coast Park can be obtained from the reservation office in Windhoek and the tourist offices at Swakopmund and Okaukuejo only and are not issued at the gates. Day visitors are not permitted to call at Torra Bay and Terrace Bay and must reach the park gates before 3pm.

Although the Caprivi Game Reserve is a declared conservation area, travellers may not leave the main road. Control points are manned by officials of the Directorate of Veterinary Services at Bagani in the west and at Kongola in the east.

percent and the rest must be paid by the driver in the case of an accident. Most accidents happen because people drive too fast or recklessly on Namibia's slippy gravel roads.

Car Hire (Windhoek)

Advanced 4x4 Car Hire
Tel: 061 246832
www.advancedcarhire.com
African Car Hire
Tel: 061 223246
www.africancarhire.de
Avis Car Hire
Aviation Road,
Tel: 061 233166
www.avis.com.na
Budget Car Hire
Windhoek Airport
Tel: 061 540160
www.budget.co.za
Odyssey Car Hire
Tel: 061 223269
www.odysseycarhire.com
Pegasus Car & Camper Hire
Tel: 061 251451
www.pegasuscar-namibia.com

Camping and 4x4 Car Rental (Windhoek)

Asco Car Hire
Tel: 061 377200
www.ascocarhire.com
Car, 4x4,and camping rental.
Britz 4x4 Rentals
Tel: 062 540 660
www.britz.co.za
South African based 4x4-rental specialist offering cross-border packages and with an office in Windhoek.

Sometimes creative thought is needed when confronted with a flat tyre.

ACCOMMODATION

HOTELS, YOUTH HOSTELS, BED & BREAKFAST

WHERE TO STAY

Visitors to Namibia are increasingly well catered for when it comes to accommodation. Indeed, there is no better indicator of how greatly the country's tourist industry has expanded since independence than the immense increase in the number, variety and overall quality of lodgings. There are smart business-style hotels in the cities and swish yet organic bush lodges in the game reserves, down-to-earth small-town guesthouses and rural guest farms, and even well equipped state-run campsites and self-catering resorts in the national parks. Standards are generally high, and rates are very reasonable by international standards, this despite a significant post-independence swing away from the budget-oriented South African self-drive market to a truly cosmopolitan clientele.

It is advisable to book hotel and lodge accommodation in advance, ideally through a reputable tour operator, particularly if you are travelling during the peak international tourist season, which runs from July to February but experiences something of a lull in October and November. If you prefer a more spontaneous approach, you're unlikely to ever experience a problem finding a room in Windhoek, and should also be able to improvise in larger towns, especially out of season, but do bear in mind that the distances between rural lodges are often daunting – you wouldn't want to pitch up in the Sesriem-Sossusvlei region, for instance, and end up having to drive from door-to-door looking for a vacant room, so do at least make a phone booking a day or two ahead.

For campsites and self-catering accommodation, advance reservations are essential during Namibian and South African summer holidays (early December to mid-January), and on most weekends and public holidays, especially around Easter. At other times of year, campsites and self-catering resorts are seldom fully booked. During the peak summer season, accommodation is restricted to three nights at each of the camps in the Etosha National Park and to 10 nights at each of the following rest camps: Ai-Ais, Gross Barmen and Daan Viljoen. Visitors should note that no refund will be made if a reservation is cancelled or altered less than 10 days prior to the first date indicated on the reservation advice.

Note that all accommodation and campsites in the national parks and other state-owned reserves and resorts (several of which are listed in the pages that follow) are managed by **Namibia Wildlife Resorts**. The main booking office in Windhoek can be contacted during the opening hours of 8am–5pm Mon–Fri (tel: 061 285 7200; email: reservations@nwr.com.na) or you can book online at www.nwr.com.na. There

Around the campfire.

are also branches in Swakopmund (tel: 064 402172; email: sw.bookings@nwr.com.na) and in Cape Town, South Africa (tel: +27 (0)21 4223761; email: ct.bookings@nwr.com.na).

For travellers who want a true taste of the Namibian rural way of life, the **Namibian Community Tourism Enterprises** (formerly Namibian Community Based Tourism Association) is a non-profit organisation, founded in 1995, to manage a selection of community-run tourism projects and campsites supporting the development of rural communities. It includes 34 sites in all, several with basic accommodation as well camping sites. Some of the more interestingly located of these sites include Aba Huab at Twyfelfontein, Brandberg White Lady Lodge & Camp, Kanamub Mountain Camp, Spitzkoppe Camp, Van Zyl's Pass Campsite, Bruckaros Campsite, Hippo Pool Campsite at the Ruacana Falls, Kunene Village Campsite and Ngoabaca Campsite near Popa Falls. All these community camps and campsites are bookable online through the Spitzkoppe Reservations and Info Centre (tel: 081 211 6291; www.spitzkoppereservations.com).

WINDHOEK AND ENVIRONS

City Centre

The accommodation listed below all lies within the city centre or easy walking distance of it.

Chameleon Backpackers Lodge
5-7 Voigt St North
Tel: 061 244347
www.chameleonbackpackers.com
This perennially popular budget lodge has a friendly vibe, the choice of private rooms, camping or dorms, good facilities including a swimming pool, pool table, satellite TV and internet, and the attached tour operator sets up budget safaris all around the country. $

Hotel Heinitzburg
22 Heinitzburg Street
Tel: 061 249597
www.heinitzburg.com
Part of the prestigious Relais and Châteaux Group, this stalwart hotel fringing the city centre is dripping with character, housed as it is in a century-old castle, complete with turrets and watchtower. It's on a hill, too, so lots of scope for photographing the sunset. Excellent food and wine with friendly service. $$$$

Kalahari Sands Hotel & Casino
Gustav Voigts Centre, Independence Avenue
Tel: 061 280 0000
www.suninternational.com/kalahari-sands
This four-star 173-room high-rise, set in the city centre above an excellent shopping mall, is Windhoek's top business-type hotel, extensively refurbished in 2011. It has a swimming pool, gym and spa facilities, as well as a restaurant with an à-la-carte menu. $$$

The Olive Exclusive All-Suite Hotel
22 Promenaden Road
Tel: 061 239199
www.theolive-namibia.com
Reopened in 2012 following extensive upgrades and refurbishments, this elegantly furnished boutique hotel has a lovely hillside location only 10 minutes' walk from the city centre. The individually designed luxury suites are large and airy, and come with high definition TV, computer with wifi, iPod dock, well-stocked mini-bar, and a sylish bathroom and spacious private deck. Other facilities include a swimming pool, sauna, a highly rated restaurant and excellent breakfasts. $$$$

Protea Hotel Fürstenhof
4 Frans Indongo Street
Tel: 061 237380
www.proteahotels.com
This four-star member of the highly regarded South African Protea chain lies a few minutes' walk from Independence Ave. It's a good-value if unremarkable hotel with a swimming pool. The classy restaurant serves French and German cuisine accompanied by a good wine list. $$$

Suburban

Hotels listed below lie some distance from central Windhoek or on the city outskirts.

Arebbusch Travel Lodge
Tel: 061 252255
www.arebbusch.com
Reminiscent of a national park rest camp (albeit without the game), this pleasant and affordable lodge lies in large acacia-studded grounds abutting the Arebbusch River. Accommodation is in en-suite chalets or rooms with a small, well-equipped kitchen, TV, direct-dial telephone and air conditioning. The lodge also has a good restaurant and pool, and a popular campsite. $$

Casablanca Hotel & Pension
52 Fritsche Str
Tel: 061 249623
www.casablancahotelnamibia.com
Mediterranean architecture reminiscent of Etosha's Fort Namutoni and a fully indigenous garden are just two distinctive features of this friendly and affordable family-run boutique hotel between the city centre and the airport. Rooms come with free WiFi and satellite TV, and facilities include a swimming pool, Jacuzzi and library. $$

Hotel Safari & Safari Court
Aviation Road
Tel: 061 2968000
www.safarihotelsnamibia.com
Located near Eros Airport, these four- and three-star hotels stand on the same grounds and have a joint capacity of 415 rooms, making it probably the largest hotel complex in the country. As with the country club above, it has all the facilities you'd expect at this price range, but comes across as rather bland. The restaurant serves Namibian game. $$$

Windhoek Country Club Resort
B1 Western Bypass
Tel: 061 2055911
www.legacyhotels.co.za/en/hotels/windhoek
This large luxury hotel is ideal for golfers or gamblers, with an 18-hole course and casino attached, and must rank among the top two or three addresses in town when it comes to service, facilities and outdoor setting, but it's also rather characterless and isolated for those who want to explore the city. $$$$

Windhoek Environs

The hotels listed below all have rural settings outside Windhoek and would form a convenient alternative to staying in the city itself.

Airport Lodge
PO Box 5913, Windhoek
Tel: 061 231491
www.airportlodgenamibia.com
Award-winning small hilltop lodge set 25km from the city centre towards Hosea Kutako Airport offering accommodation in comfortable thatched bungalows with attractive décor, scenic surroundings and a pool. $$

Auas Game Lodge
PO Box 80887, Windhoek
Tel: 061 406236
www.auas-lodge.com
Relatively near to the international airport, this 16-room lodge is a good place to stay over before leaving on a tour or leaving the country after a visit, with plenty of game around as well as good walking opportunities. Family-friendly. $$$

Daan Viljoen Sun Karros Lifestyle Resort
Tel: 061 232 393
www.sunkarros.com
Overlooking the Daan Viljoen Dam in the eponymous game reserve west of Windhoek, this plush new resort offers air-conditioned accommodation in 19 contemporary-styled African chalets, as well as camping, a restaurant, and hiking and mountain biking trails in a lovely mountainous area rich with indigenous wildlife. $$$$ (chalets), $ (camping).

Eningu Clayhouse Lodge
PO Box 21783, Windhoek
Tel: 064 581880
www.eningulodge.com
Situated on Pepperkorrell Farm on the edge of the Kalahari near Dordabis, about 45 minutes' drive southeast of Hosea Kutako International airport, this is a super alternative to staying in the city, with spacious rooms, unusual décor, plentiful wildlife, and a good selection of facilities and activities (including a swimming pool). $$$

Heja Game Lodge
PO Box 588, Windhoek

Tel: 061 257151/2
www.hejalodge.com
This well-stocked game lodge has a pleasant setting in the hills east of Windhoek, along the road to Hosea Kutako Airport. There are comfortable solar-powered rooms and decent meals, while facilities include horse-riding, game drives,

a swimming pool and inexpensive airport transfers. **$$**
Okapuka Horse Safaris
PO Box 5955,
Windhoek
Tel: 061 257087
www.okapuka.com
Situated 30 minutes' drive north of Windhoek (a good springboard

for trips to Etosha and Caprivi) this pleasant private game ranch harbours a good selection of game, and facilities include walking trails, tennis courts and a swimming pool. The main activity here, however, is horse-riding in a 350-sq-km (135-sq-mile) area in and around the ranch. **$$$$**

CENTRAL NAMIBIA

You'll never lose your way at Ombo Rest Camp (Central Namibia).

Situated about 60km (37 miles) northwest of town, this upmarket hilltop lodge has a good view over the central bushveld and a surrounding 110-sq-km (42-sq-mile) game sanctuary inhabited by introduced rhino, giraffe and antelope. Spacious rooms, good food, large swimming pool, game drives and hunting. **$$$**
Von Bach Dam Resort
Tel: 061 400205
www.tungeni.com
Situated about 10km (6 miles) south of Okahandja, this lies in a small game reserve surrounding the dam that supplied most of Windhoek's water. Recently privatised and reopened after extensive renovations, resort, it offers 11 luxury chalets, 11 more basic chalets , camping sites, a decent restaurant, a swimming pool, boat cruises and walking trails. **$$$** (chalet), **$** (camping).

Okahandja and Environs

Gross Barmen Resort
Bookings through Namibia Wildlife Resorts (see page 266).
Set on a hot springs resort and small dam about 25km (15.5 miles) southwest of Okahandja, this government-style resort offers accommodation in bungalows, camping and caravan sites, as well as a restaurant, shop, walking trails, thermal pool and swimming pool. It is closed for renovation at the time of writing, but should reopen by 2015. **$$**
Moringa Guest Farm
PO Box 65
Tel: 062 501106
www.moringasafaris.com
Longstanding family-run guesthouse offering homely accommodation, game drives and walks on a 200-sq-km (77-sq-mile) game farm stocked with giraffe, cheetah and various naturally occurring antelope and small predators. It's named after an endemic baobab-like tree commonly found on the property. **$$**

Okahandja Country Hotel
Tel: 062 504299
www.okahandjahotel.com/
Situated alongside a camelthorn-fringed watercourse 2km (1.2 miles) north of the town centre, this good-value lodge has 24 clean, functional thatched rooms, large grounds centred on a swimming pool, and a rich indigenous birdlife. An inexpensive campsite is attached. **$$**
Ombo Rest Camp
PO Box 368, Okahandja
Tel: 062 502003
www.ombo-rest-camp.com
Situated 12km (7 miles) north of Okahandja on the Hochfeld Road, this relaxed and affordable rest camp has self-catering bungalows, backpacker rooms and camping. An ostrich and crocodile farm is attached, and plenty of small wildlife is attracted to the waterhole. The restaurant specialises in venison, ostrich meat and ostrich egg dishes. **$**
Oropoko Lodge
PO Box 726
Tel: 062 503871
www.oropoko.com.na

Karibib
Etusis Lodge (south of Karibib)
PO Box 5
Tel: 064 550826
www.etusis.de
Set in beautiful surroundings on a well-stocked 210-sq km (81-sq-mile) game farm in the shadow of the Otjipareta Mountains south of Karibib, this has comfortable rooms with en-suite toilet and shower. **$$$**

Usakos
Ameib Ranch & Campsite
PO Box 266, Usakos
Tel: 081 857 4639
www.ameib.com
Simple but comfortable accommodation on a farm that now forms part of the Erongo Mountain

PRICE CATEGORIES

Based on B&B rate for twin double room.
$$$$ = above US$180 (N$2,000)
$$$ = US$130–180 (N$1,400–2,000)
$$ = US$75–140 (N$800–1,400)
$ = under US$75 (N$800)

Rhino Sanctuary Trust, and is known for its superb rock formations, prehistoric rock art and wildlife. Camping is available. **$**

Bahnhof Hotel
72 Theo Ben Gurirab Street
Tel: 064 530444
Email: bahnhof@iway.na
Set in a historic building on the main road through town, this two-star hotel has air-conditioned rooms with satellite TV and a simple terrace restaurant. **$**

Omaruru
Epako Safari Lodge
PO Box 108, Omaruru
Tel: 064 570551
www.epako.com
Renovated in 2013, this is the country's only exclusive-use, private lodge, capable of taking groups of up to 20 people. It has a lovely setting on a dry riverbank in a well-stocked 110-sq-km (42-sq-mile) game farm 22km (13.5 miles) north of town. Game drives include visits to ancient rock paintings and engravings on the property. Rooms are air conditioned and the food has a strong French influence. **$$$$**

Erongo Wilderness Lodge
PO Box 581, Omaruru
Tel: 061 239199
www.erongowilderness.com
Set about 15km (9 miles) out of town, on a rocky hill offering panoramic views, this exclusive tented camp is a walker's paradise and the surrounding country supports plenty of indigenous small mammals and birds. **$$$$**

Omaruru Game Lodge
PO Box 208, Omaruru
Tel: 064 570044

www.omaruru-game-lodge.com
Situated about 15km (9 miles) northeast of Omaruru, this is a fine Swiss-owned lodge with thatched bungalows, good food, and a wide variety of introduced game kept in semi-captivity. **$$$**

Omaruru Rest Camp & Caravan Park
Wilhelm Zeraua Road
Tel: 064 570516
Email: omarururestcamp@iway.na
This well-run municipal camp offers inexpensive hutted accommodation and campsites on the northern outskirts of town. **$**

Kashana Country House
Dr. Ian Scheepers Drive, Omaruru
Tel: 064 571434
www.kashana-namibia.com
This award-winning restaurant, guesthouse and art gallery is housed in a former mine-workers casino built in 1907. Sensibly priced accommodation is available in the main building or in thatched bungalows scattered around the gardens.

Otjiwarongo and Environs

Okonjima Lodge
PO Box 793, Otjiwarongo
Tel: 067 687032-4
www.okonjima.com
Home to the multiple award-winning AfriCat Foundation, the world's largest leopard and cheetah rescue and release programme, Okonjima consists of several lodges and an exclusive villa, all of which offer an intimate atmosphere, rustically luxurious accommodation and superb cuisine, as well as a busy activity schedule embracing open-vehicle expeditions to habituated

leopard and rehabilitated cheetah. **$$$$**

Otjibamba Lodge
PO Box 134, Otjiwarongo
Tel: 067 30313
www.otjibambalodge.com
Situated in a private game ranch just 4km (2.5 miles) south of Otjiwarongo along the B1 towards Windhoek, this popular owner-managed lodge makes for a convenient overnight stop en route to or from Etosha, with spacious rooms and a fine restaurant overlooking a waterhole. **$$**

Out of Africa Town Lodge
Long Street
Tel: 067 302230
www.out-of-afrika.com
Functional suburban hotel offering comfortable rooms, decent food and good facilities (air conditioning, satellite TV in rooms, swimming pool, bistro) at highly competitive rates. **$**

Outjo
Etosha Garden Hotel
6 Otavi Street
Tel: 067 313130
www.etosha-garden-hotel.com
Good service in a century-old building with a green suburban setting, swimming pool and a fine restaurant attached. **$$**

Etotongwe Lodge
Luiperd Street
Tel: 067 313333
www.etotongwelodge.com
This well-equipped and affordable new camp on the outskirts of town has en-suite bungalows with air conditioning, campsites, a decent restaurant, a small wildlife camp, WiFi access and a swimming pool. **$**

Otavi
Khorab Safari Lodge & Campsite
P.O. Box 186 Otavi
Tel: 067 234352
www.khorablodge.com
Situated alongside the B1, about 3km (2 miles) south of Otavi, this rustic family-run lodge is far more attractive than any of the limited options in town, offering comfortable thatched accommodation, good service and food complemented by a lengthy wine list. Campsites are available. **$$$**

Palmenecke Guesthouse
96 Hertzog Ave, Otavi
Tel: 067 234199
www.palmenecke.co.za
The best of the somewhat limited options in town, this very affordable owner-managed guesthouse has a pleasant outdoor restaurant, and a swimming pool, bar and satellite TV. **$**

The Bush Suite at Okonjima Lodge.

Tsumeb
Makalani Hotel
Ndilimani Cultural Troupe Street
Tel: 067 221051
www.makalanihotel.com
This very acceptable upper mid-range hotel has comfortable rooms, palm-shaded grounds with swimming pool and beer garden, and an above average restaurant – overall it's the most commodious option in town. $
Travel North Namibia Guesthouse
Sam Nujoma Drive (Opposite Telecom)
Tel: 067 220728
www.travelnorthguesthouse.com
Comprising just six en-suite rooms, all with WiFi, air conditioning, fridge and satellite TV, set in a pretty suburban garden, this very reasonably priced owner-managed guesthouse is affiliated to a tour operator and car rental company of the same name. $

Grootfontein
Courtyard Guesthouse
2 Gauss Street
Tel: 067 240027
Owner-managed and boasting a peaceful setting in palm-shaded gardens centred on a swimming pool, this new guesthouse is probably the best deal in town, offering air-conditioned rooms, internet access and decent à-la-carte meals. $
Fiume Lodge
PO Box 195, Grootfontein
Tel: 067 240486
www.fiume-lodge.com
Set on a small game farm alongside the B1 about 35km (20 miles) north of town, this owner-managed lodge offers comfortable and reasonably priced accommodation in six stone

and thatch chalets. Activities include game drives and bush walks guided by bushmen. $$
Roy's Rest Camp
Tel: 067 240302
www.roysrestcamp.com
This pleasant camp, which lies 55km (34 miles) north of Grootfontein along the B8 towards Rundu (just past the Tsumkwe turn-off), has rustic bungalows and camping sites, as well as a swimming pool, restaurant and bar. There's good birding in the area, and a pleasant walking trail where you are likely to see antelope. Visits to a nearby San encampment can be arranged. $$
The Stonehouse Lodge
10 Toenessen Street
Tel: 067 242842
This pleasant and very well priced suburban guesthouse has six rooms, all with air conditioning, satellite TV, mini-bar and use of swimming pool and internet facilities. $

Waterberg Plateau Park
Waterberg Camp
Bookings through Namibia Wildlife Resorts (see page 266).
Set within the park, the former Bernabé de la Bat Rest Camp is an attractive facility offering accommodation in bungalows, camping sites, and decent facilities including a shop, a restaurant and a swimming pool. The camp lies on the wooded slopes of the escarpment, and guided game drives leave daily, while a network of self-guided walking trails offers an opportunity to soak up the scenery and superb birdlife. $$$

Waterberg Wilderness Lodge
Tel: 067 687018
www.waterberg-wilderness.com
Situated on the farm Otjosongombe, which has been in the same family for almost a century and comprises the only private land on the Waterberg Plateau, this highly regarded and very exclusive lodge offers guests the opportunity for guided walks into a stretch of untrammelled bush teeming with big game (including buffalo and rhino), colourful birds and great views. The established lodge is set in a valley, but a second lodge to similar standards recently opened on a clifftop on the plateau, and there is also now a campsite for budget self-drivers. $ (camping), $$$$ (lodge).

Gobabis
Arnhem Lodge
Tel: 061 581885
www.arnhemcave.com
Situated at the Arnhem Caves, between Windhoek and Gobabis, this pleasant and affordable camp has four thatched huts, a field kitchen, camping sites, ablution blocks and a swimming pool. Guided nature walks and game drives are also offered, and there are several self-guided walking trails. $$
Gobabis Guesthouse
0 Lazarette Street
Tel: 062 563189
Just about the only option in town, this low-key guesthouse offers comfortable B&B accommodation with air-conditioning only 5 minutes' walk from the town's main shopping centre. $

NORTHERN NAMIBIA

Ondangwa
Nakambale Campsite
PO Box 2018, Ondangwa
Tel: 065 245668
www.nacobta.com.na
Part of the eponymous museum, a community project accredited by NACOBTA, and the chance to stay in an Ovambo homestead 13km (8 miles) south of Ondangwa. Campsites are available, as are traditional meals and music performances by prior arrangement. $
Protea Hotel Ondangwa
Main Street
Tel: 065 241900
www.proteahotels.com
Following several changes of name and ownership, this four-star hotel, situated southeast of the town

centre some 6km (4 miles) from Ondangwa airport, was incorporated into the South African Protea Chain a few years back. The 90 air-conditioned rooms come with coffee- and tea-making facilities, satellite television and direct-dial telephone. Facilities include a business centre, swimming pool and à-la-carte restaurant. $$

Oshakati
Oshakati Country Lodge
Robert Mugabe Avenue, PO Box 15200
Tel: 065 222380
Email: countryhotel@mweb.com.na
Relatively new lodge with 50 rooms built around a lush courtyard with swimming pool, and thatched dining and sitting area. All rooms have

telephone, TV, air conditioning and mini-bar. $$
Oshandira Lodge
PO Box 958
Tel: 065 220443
Email: oshandira@iway.na
Situated alongside the airport, this comfortable hotel has 17 air conditioned rooms with telephone and TV. Has a green setting and a good restaurant. $$

PRICE CATEGORIES

Based on B&B rate for twin double room.
$$$$ = above US$180 (N$2,000)
$$$ = US$130–180 (N$1,400–2,000)
$$ = US$75–140 (N$800–1,400)
$ = under US$75 (N$800)

Premier waterhole chalets, Okaukuejo Camp.

Rundu and Environs

Environs
Hakusembe River Lodge
Tel: 061 230066
www.gondwana-collection.com
This riverside lodge comprises 22 chalets facing the Okavango 16km (10 miles) west of Rundu. Facilities include a swimming pool and a restaurant specialising in fish dishes. Boat trips, water sports, fishing and birding are among the activities on offer. **$$$**
Kavango River Lodge
PO Box 634 Rundu
Tel: 066 255244
www.natron.net/kavango-river-lodge
With a superb location in central Rundu overlooking the Okavango River and the Angolan floodplain on the opposite bank, this popular resort consists of 8 luxury and 10 self-catering bungalows with all facilities. There's a good on-site restaurant. **$$**
N'Kwazi Lodge
PO Box 1623, Rundu
Tel: 081 2424897
www.nkwazilodge.com
Gas-lit wooden chalets in a pleasant setting near the river some 20km (12 miles) northeast of Rundu. Activities include birdwatching, riding, fishing and traditional dancing. The affiliated Nkwazi Community Trails allows visitors to experience various traditional activities as part of a community-based project. **$$**
Shamvura Camp
PO Box 183, Rundu
Tel: 066 264007
www.shamvura.com
Situated on a high sand dune overlooking a knobthorn-lined

stretch of the Okavango River about 120km (74.5 miles) east of Rundu, this wonderfully isolated self-catering camp is popular with game fishermen and offers some excellent birding, canoeing and rambling. Camping sites are available. **$$**

Etosha and Environs

Etosha National Park
Okaukuejo, Halali & Namutoni Rest Camps
Bookings through Namibia Wildlife Resorts (see page 266).
Respectively situated in the west, centre and east of the public sector of the park, all three of these camps offer self-catering accommodation in modest bungalows and camping facilities, as well as a shop, restaurant, filling station and swimming pool. Okaukuejo also has an internet café. **$$–$$$**
Onkoshi Tented Camp
Bookings through Namibia Wildlife Resorts (see page 266)
The newest and most exclusive camp in Etosha proper consists of only 15 units in a secluded location overlooking the pan. It operates much like the private camps outside the park, and rates include all meals and activities. **$$$$**

East of Etosha

Etosha Aoba Lodge
PO Box 469, Tsumeb
Tel: 067 229100
www.etosha-aoba-lodge.com
Boasting an untrammelled bush setting only 13km from Von Lindequist Gate, this small lodge luxury offers accommodation in air-conditioned thatched

bungalows overlooking a waterhole that attracts plenty of wildlife. Facilities include a swimming pool and free WiFi. **$$$$**
Kempinski Mokuti Lodge
PO Box 403
Tel: 061 388400
www.kempinski.com
Situated at the Von Lindequist entrance gate to Etosha National Park, Mokuti Lodge retains a definite African charm whilst also conforming to the high international standards one would expect of the Kempinski Chain. With more than 100 suites and rooms, it lacks the intimacy of smaller bush lodges, all rooms have air conditioning, large en-suite bathrooms, mini-bar and satellite TV, and the décor is very stylish. There's a good restaurant and spa, and a swimming pool and business centre, too. **$$$$**
The Mushara Collection
PO Box 1814, Tsumeb
Tel: 067 240020
www.mushara-lodge.com
Situated about 8km (5 miles) from the Von Lindequist entrance gate, Mushara is a small private reserve with four different lodges and camps dotted around it. The smartest is Mushara Villas, which consists of two stylishly decorated 140-sq-metre (1,500-sq-ft) villas with all mod cons, from CD player with ceiling speakers and a small library of Africa-related books to private plunge pools and a choice of indoor or outdoor showers. Mushara Lodge comprises 10 twin en-suite bungalows, while Mushara Bush Camp and Outpost are both luxury tented camps with a real bush feel. The lodges are all well positioned for game drives in eastern

Etosha and the grounds protect an exciting selection of acacia-dwelling birds. Other attractions include a swimming pool, a large thatched dining and sitting area, and excellent food. **$$$$**

Onguma Safari Camps
PO Box 6784,
Windhoek
Tel: 061 237055
www.ongumanamibia.com
Situated on the eastern border of Etosha, only five minutes' drive from the Von Lindequist entrance gate and abutting Fischer's Pan, this private reserve protects a similar range of species to the adjacent national park and offers a wide variety of accommodation, ranging from a well-equipped campsite to mid-range bush camp and a luxury tented camp. **$** (camping), **$$$** (bush camp), **$$$$** (tented camp).

South of Etosha

Ongava Game Reserve
PO Box 6850, Windhoek
Tel: 061 274500
www.ongava.com
Situated immediately south of the Andersson entrance gate, this 30-sq-km (11.5-sq-mile) private reserve, managed by Wilderness Safaris, harbours a similar selection of game to Etosha, and is particularly noted for its excellent lion and rhino (black and white) sightings. A trio of exclusive lodges is scattered around the reserve, with a total of 24 double units, all of which blend well with the environment. The most sumptuous (and expensive) lodge is Little Ongava, which consists of just three tented units with private plunge pool built on a dolomite hill, chalets are all thatched and have en-suite bathrooms. Activities include guided game drives within the private reserve and into the adjacent national park, as well as rhino-tracking walks. **$$$$**

Caprivi

Divundu/Bagani area
Divava Okavango Lodge and Spa
PO Box 90538,
Windhoek
Tel: 066 259005
www.divava.com
This lovely 20-chalet camp lies to the south of Popa Falls about 14km (8.5 miles) from the entrance to Mahangu Game Reserve. The luxury chalets have wide wooden decks offering good views of the Okavango River, as does the in-house spa,

and activities include boat trips to nearby hippo and crocodile pools. **$$$$**

Mahangu Safari Lodge
PO Box 5200 Divundu
Tel: 066 259037
www.mahangu.com.na
Situated 22km (13 miles) south of Divundu, en route to Mahango National Park, this small bush lodge has thatched bungalows and luxury tents set in beautiful grounds overlooking the Okavango River near Mahangu National Park. Camping is permitted. **$** (camping), **$$$** (bungalows and standing tents).

Ndhovu Safari Lodge
PO Box 5035,
Divundu
Tel: 066 259901
www.ndhovu.com
Situated close to the Popa Falls, this consists of eight luxury tented units with en-suite bathrooms. Plenty of wildlife and birds in the vicinity. Activities include game drives to Mahungu National Park, fishing trips, bird walks and sunset cruises. **$** (camping), **$$$** (standing tent).

Popa Falls Camp
Bookings through Namibia Wildlife Resorts (see page 266).
This government campsite with a few river cabins has communal washing, and kitchen facilities, a shop with a few basic commodities. There's no electricity, but gas lighting is supplied. **$**

Kongola, Mudumu and Nkasa Lupala
Lianshulu Lodge
P.O. Box 5072,
Windhoek,
Tel: 061 224420
www.lianshulu.com
This luxurious lodge consists of 11 thatched bungalows accommodating up to 24 guests overlooking the Kwando River about 40km (25 miles) south of Kongola in Mudumu National Park, opposite Botswana. **$$$$**

Mazambala Island Lodge
PO Box 1935, Katima Mulilo
Tel: 066 686041
www.mazambala.com
This rustic owner-managed camp consists of 16 thatched bungalows on the Kwando River south of Kongola, and it also has a campsite, bar and restaurant. There's plenty of wildlife around, including buffalo, elephant, lion, red lechwe and an immense variety of birds, and a 12-metre (40ft)-high tower with two viewing platforms from which to observe the action. **$** (camping), **$$** (bungalow).

Namushasha River Lodge
PO Box 6597,
Windhoek
Tel: 061 230066
www.gondwana-collection.com
Very well situated overlooking a hippo pool on the Kwando River south of Kongola, this recently renovated luxury lodge arranges good guided game drives and boat trips. A 4km (2.5-mile) nature walk offers the opportunity to see many of the 400 bird species recorded in the vicinity. **$$$**

Nkasa Lupala Tented Lodge
Tel: 081 147 7798
www.nkasalupalalodge.com
The only accommodation in the remote wetlands of Nkasa Lupala National Park is this lodge on Lupala island 11km (7 miles) south of Sangwali. Accommodation is in 10 luxurious ensuite safari tents set on stilted wooden platforms overlooking an area of swamp that attracts plentiful wildlife. Game drives, guided walks and boat trips are offered to guests. **$$$$**

Katima Mulilo
Protea Hotel Zambezi River Lodge
Ngoma Road,
Katima Mulilo
Tel: 066 251500
www.proteahotels.com
This 42-room hotel, part of the ever reliable Protea chain, is comfortably the best place to stay in Katima Mulilo, with an inviting swimming pool and set in large gardens on the banks of the Zambezi River. **$$**

Zambezi-Chobe Confluence
Ichingo Chobe River Lodge
PO Box 68630, Bryanston,
South Africa, 2021
Tel: +27 (0) 79 871 7603
www.ichobezi.co.za
With a beautiful setting on Impalila Island overlooking the Chobe River, this ultra-luxurious lodge offers accommodation in plush tented units with balcony set below shady jackal-berry trees. Activities include boat trips, superb guided bird walks, and excursions further afield to the likes of Victoria Falls and Chobe National Park. **$$$$**

PRICE CATEGORIES

Based on B&B rate for twin double room.
$$$$ = above US$180 (N$2,000)
$$$ = US$130–180 (N$1,400–2,000)
$$ = US$75–140 (N$800–1,400)
$ = under US$75 (N$800)

TRANSPORT

ACCOMMODATION

EATING OUT

ACTIVITIES

A – Z

NORTHWEST NAMIBIA

Khorixas and Environs

Bambatsi Holiday Ranch
PO Box 120, Outjo
Tel: 067 313897
www.bambatsi.com
Situated on the C38 midway between Outjo and Khorixas, this eight-bungalow guest farm is well positioned for visits to Vingerklip, Twyfelfontein and the Petrified Forest, while on-site facilities include a swimming pool, horse-riding, game viewing, tennis court and mountain bikes. **$** (camping), **$$$** (bungalow).

Brandberg Rest Camp
3 Uis Street, Uis
Tel/fax: 064 504038
www.brandbergrestcamp.com
Simple, clean and good value self-catering accommodation and campsites situated in Uis, close to the base of a massif known for its superb prehistoric rock art. Facilities include a restaurant, swimming pool and tennis court. **$**

Khorixas Lodge & Rest Camp
Bookings through Namibia Wildlife Resorts (see page 266)
A large, well-run, functional self-catering resort and campsite, 4km (2.5 miles) out of town and well placed for visits to the Brandberg and other rock art sites. Has 38 clean but basic bungalows and a campsite, as well as a swimming pool, shop and restaurant. **$**

Vingerklip Lodge
PO Box 1150, Windhoek
Tel: 067 290319
www.vingerklip.com.na
This medium-sized lodge consists of 22 room comfortable bungalows attractively located next to the striking

finger-like rock formation for which it is named. The panoramic views are complemented by good food, a swimming pool and a range of low-key activities such as walking and birding. **$$$$**

White Lady B&B
3rd Avenue, Uis
Tel: 064 504102
Email: whitelady@iway.na
Situated in Uis, the closest town to the Brandberg, this pleasant no-frills B&B offers clean thatched en-suite accommodation set around a sparkling pool, as well as a campsite with plunge pool and birdwatching hide. **$–$$**

Twyfelfontein and Environs

Aba Huab Campsite
PO Box 131 Khorixas
Tel: 067 331104
This once popular but now quite rundown community-run campsite has standing A-frames and camping facilities on an acacia-fringed watercourse about 10km (6 miles) from Twyfelfontein. Other facilities include a restaurant, bar and ablution block. **$**

Mowani Mountain Camp
PO Box 40788, Windhoek
Tel: 061 232009
www.mowani.com
This stylish top-of-the-range tented camp has an ideal location for exploring the rock engravings at Twyfelfontein. The 15 rooms and suites are the epitome of safari chic, and all offer sweeping views over the surrounding rocky slopes. **$$$$**

Twyfelfontein Country Lodge
PO Box 6597, Windhoek

Tel: 061 374750
www.twyfelfonteinlodge.com
This popular, comfortable 56-room lodge has a scenic setting at the base of a golden cliff just 5km (3 miles) from the Twyfelfontein rock art site. Good buffet meals, a swimming pool set amidst the rocks, and a range of guided activities in the surrounding countryside. **$$$$**

Damaraland

Damaraland Camp
PO Box 6850, Windhoek
Tel: 061 274500
www.wilderness-safaris.com
No creature comforts are lacking in this spectacular wilderness location, which lies in the heart of the territory inhabited by the legendary desert-dwelling elephants of Damaraland. Accommodation is in 10 adobe-style thatched units with en-suite bathrooms; there's also a plunge-pool and a shop. The lodge can organise game drives, walking, birdwatching and star gazing. **$$$$**

Desert Rhino Camp
PO Box 6850, Windhoek
Tel: 061 274500
www.wilderness-safaris.com
Run in collaboration with the Save the Rhino Trust, this superlative exclusive bush camp is the only permanent encampment in the vast private Palmwag concession, and game drives offer a great opportunity to see a wide selection of typical desert wildlife. Rhino-tracking walks are led by experienced guides every morning, and come with a high chance of seeing this endangered creature. **$$$$**

Huab Lodge
PO Box 103, Kamanjab
Tel: 067 312070
www.huab.com
Award-winning lodge situated on a private reserve halfway between Khorixas and Kamanjab with superb guiding, and imaginative cuisine. Offers eight comfortable thatched bungalows with free WiFi set near a dry river bed, with a pool and a thermal spring. Activities include horse-riding, game drives, guided walks and birding. **$$$$**

Palmwag Lodge
PO Box 339, Swakopmund
Tel: 061 234342
www.palmwaglodge.com
One of Namibia's oldest lodges, and blossoming under dynamic new management, Palmwag is set in an oasis-like stand of makalani palms

The view from Mowani Mountain Camp.

fed by a subterranean river in what is otherwise a rather dry region. Regularly visited by desert elephants and other wildlife, this 42-room lodge also has a restaurant, a snack bar and two swimming pools. Activities include game drives, walking trails, rhino-tracking and birding. **$$$$**

Sesfontein
Fort Sesfontein Lodge
PO Box 3676, Swakopmund
Tel: 065 685034
www.fort-sesfontein.com
This lodge comprises a restored 19th century Beau Geste-style fort in tropical gardens. The hotel sleeps up to 46 and it also has a campsite, pool and restaurant, and offers guided day tours. **$$$**
Ohakane Guesthouse
PO Box 8, Opuwo
Tel: 065 273031
Email: okahane@iway.na
Situated behind the Shelli Filling Station in Opuwo, the 'capital' of the Himba, this low-key lodge has 15 comfortable rooms, a swimming pool and a restaurant. **$$**

Opuwo and environs
Omarunga Camp Epupa
Tel: 061 234342
Fax: 061 233872
Situated within walking distance of the Epupa Falls, 180km (112 miles) northwest of Opuwo, this consists of 10 luxury en-suite tents as well as eight campsites for equipped campers. Can arrange guided walks and visits to Himba homesteads. **$$**
Omarunga Lodge
Tel: 064 403096
www.omarungalodge.com
Situated within walking distance of the Epupa Falls, 180km (112 miles) northwest of Opuwa, this recently upgraded lodge consists of 13 luxury en-suite chalets as well as nine camping sites for equipped campers. Can arrange guided walks and visits to Himba homesteads. **$$$$** (lodge), **$** (camping).
Ruacana Eha Lodge
Springbok Avenue, Ruacana
Tel: 065 271500
www.ruacanaehalodge.com.na
Situated in Ruacana about 50km (31 miles) northeast of Opuwo, this is a comfortable modern lodge with 21 en-suite rooms, a good restaurant, a swimming pool and a gym. Activities include Himba village visits and guided walks. The adjacent campsite has cheap hutted accommodation using common ablution blocks. **$** (camping), **$$** (room).

Skeleton Coast
Hoanib Skeleton Coast Camp
PO Box 6850, Windhoek
Tel: 061 274500
www.wilderness-safaris.com
The only accommodation set within Skeleton Cast National Park, this luxurious and exclusive six-room lodge, managed by Wilderness Safaris, caters to fly-in clients only, and a stay of at least four days is recommended to see the area properly. Wildlife includes desert-adapted elephant, brown hyena, cheetah and various antelope and dry-country birds. Spectacular scenic excursions are also offered, as are visits to some of the shipwrecks that gave the Skeleton Coast its name. **$$$$**
Serra Cafema Camp
PO Box 6850, Windhoek
Tel: 061 274500
www.wilderness-safaris.com
With its remote but pretty location on a Himba concession bordering the Kunene River east of the park boundary, this eight-unit wilderness camp is often visited in conjunction with Skeleton Coast Camp. The dunes that rise from the riverbank make for a spectacular setting, and activities include quad-biking in the dunes, game and birdwatching drives in the Hartmann Valley, and visits to local Himba communities. **$$$$**
Terrace Bay Restcamp
Bookings through Namibia Wildlife Resorts (see page 266).
Formerly the quarters of a mining company, this remote resort (almost 300km/186 miles north of the nearest town, Henties Bay) has well-equipped bungalows and restaurant set along the rocky Atlantic coastline. **$$$**
Torra Bay Campsites
Bookings through Namibia Wildlife Resorts (see page 266).
Very basic camp/caravan sites 100km (62 miles) south of Terrace Bay, open from 1 December to 31 January. A shop and filling station are open during the December school holidays only, when water and firewood are on sale. **$**

Henties Bay, Cape Cross and Environs
Cape Cross Lodge
Tel: 064 461677
www.capecross.org
Luxurious and wonderfully isolated oceanfront lodge situated 4km (2.5 miles) from the Cape Coast seal colony and 50km (31 miles) north of Henties Bay. Day visitors to Cape Cross are welcome to drop in for a meal. **$$$**
Mile 72, Mile 108 and Jakkalsputz Campsites
Tel: 061 400205
www.tungeni.com
Recently privatised, and reopened in December 2013 after significant upgrades, these campsites are almost exclusively used by anglers. Toilets are provided and hot showers are available. During the December school holidays a shop/kiosk is manned at all camps. Mile 72 and Mile 108 now also offer inexpensive chalet accommodation. **$**

The Namib

Swakopmund
Hansa Hotel
3 Hendrik Witbooi Street
Tel: 064 414200
www.hansahotel.com.na
This centrally located, award-winning 50-room hotel celebrated its centenary in 2005. Its vintage is reflected by its superb period architecture and characterful, stylish décor. Efficient, friendly service. Superb kitchen. Nice, intimate bar with fireplace. **$$$**
Hotel Europa Hof
39 Bismarck Street
Tel: 064 405061
www.europahof.com
This centrally located hotel combines traditional German architecture (Fachwerk) with comfortable rooms and a highly rated seafood restaurant. **$$**
Mile 14 Caravan Park
Bookings through Namibia Wildlife Resorts (see page 266).
This basic site is popular with anglers during the December school holidays, when a shop/kiosk stocks basic supplies. Otherwise, facilities are limited to toilets and hot showers. **$**
Protea Hotel Burning Shore
152 4th Street, Long Beach
Tel: 064 213700
www.africanpridehotels.com
Now part of the South African Protea chain, this ultra-chic 12-room 4-star lodge, situated 15km (9 miles) south of town along the road to Walvis Bay, is probably the smartest option in the area – and no less popular for

PRICE CATEGORIES

Based on B&B rate for twin double room.
$$$$ = above US$180 (N$2,000)
$$$ = US$130–180 (N$1,400–2,000)
$$ = US$75–140 (N$800–1,400)
$ = under US$75 (N$800)

having hosted Brad Pitt and Angelina for several weeks a few years back. $$$$

Sam's Giardino
89 Anton Lubowski Avenue
Tel: 064 403210
www.giardinonamibia.com
A must for gourmets and wine-lovers, this comfortable and affordable 10-room guesthouse is justifiably renowned for its fine five-course dinners, which reflects the nationality of the enthusiastic Swiss owner-manager, and a cellar stocked with a handpicked selection of the finest Cape wines. $$$

Secret Garden Guesthouse
36 Bismarck Street
Tel: 064 404037
www.secretgarden.com.na
This small owner-managed guesthouse is quiet, comfortable, very central and affordable. $$

The Stiltz
Tel/fax: 064 400771
www.thestiltz.com
This attractive lodge consists of nine stilted and thatched wooden bungalows linked by a raised walkway in the coastal scrub overlooking the bird-rich Swakop Lagoon within walking distance of the town centre. No restaurant. $$$

Swakopmund Hotel and Entertainment Centre
2 Theo-Ben Gurabib Avenue
Tel: 064 4105200
www.swakopmundhotel.co.za
This four-star hotel includes the old railway station (reception and small bar). The 90 en-suite rooms are very well equipped with tea/coffee makers, TV, phone, mini-bar, air conditioning and safe. Good restaurant. There is also a casino. $$$

Swakopmund Municipal Rest Camp
Private Bag 5017, Swakopmund
Tel: 064 4104618
www.swakopmund-restcamp.com
Characterless but very affordable self-catering accommodation with more than 200 units squeezed onto a flat site close to the sea and town centre. $$

Walvis Bay
Free Air Guesthouse
Cnr Esplanade & 2nd Street
Tel: 064 202247
www.namibia-walvisbay-guesthouse.com
Offering spacious accommodation with great views over the lagoon, this friendly guesthouse has a more contemporary mood and décor than most places in sleepy Walvis Bay, and it arranges a long list of activities. $$

Hotel Langholm
18-20 Second Street West

The inviting fountain at Swakopmund Hotel.

Tel: 064 209230
www.langholmhotel.com
An award-winning pension-style hotel offering comfortable accommodation, this also offers good access to the harbour and lagoon. $$

Kleines Nest B&B
76 Esplanade
Tel: 064 203203
www.natron.net/tour/kleines-nest
Welcoming owner-managed six-room lodge overlooking the lagoon. Massage and aromatherapy. $

Lagoon Lodge
2 Kovambo Nujoma Drive
Tel: 064 200850
www.lagoonlodge.com.na
Alongside the lagoon but still within walking distance of the town centre, this welcoming owner-managed lodge is probably the most comfortable option in Walvis Bay. It consists of just six individually decorated rooms centred around a swimming pool, most of which have private balconies overlooking the lagoon. $$$

Langstrand Campsite and Caravan Park
Tel: 064 215500
Pleasant campsite at Langstrand (Long Beach), about 10km (6 miles) out of town along the road towards Swakopmund. $

Walvis Bay Protea Hotel
Corner Sam Nujoma and 10th Road
Tel: 064 213700
www.proteahotels.com
Part of a highly regarded South African mid-range hotel chain, this is a clean, functional and very central three-star hotel with good facilities and reasonable rates. $$

Namib-Naukluft and Environs
Desert Homestead
Tel: 061 246788
www.deserthomestead-namibia.com

Recently relocated and rebuilt on a private concession alongside the C19 about 30km (19 miles) from Sesriem, this smart owner-managed lodge consists of 20 thatched en-suite chalets with private verandahs facing the sunset. In addition to good food and a swimming pool, the lodge offers popular horseback excursions into the dunes, as well as sundowner drives and guided excursions to Sossusvlei. $$$

Kulala Desert Lodge
PO Box 6850, Windhoek
Tel: 061 274500
www.wilderness-safaris.com
This exclusive 12-room camp has a beautiful setting on the Tsauchab River in a 320 sq km (124 sq miles) concession abutting the national park some 50km (31 miles) from Sussusvlei. Good view of the dunes to the west. Within the same concession, and also managed by Wilderness Safaris, are the even more exclusive and pricey Kulala Wilderness Camp and Little Kulala Camp. All are noteworthy for their excellent food, balloon excursions, and guided drives to Sossusvlei and surrounds. $$$$

Kulula Wilderness Camp
PO Box 6850, Windhoek
Tel: 061 274500
Fax: 061 239455
Email: info@nts.com.na
www.wilderness-safaris.com
Built on a small hill offering superb views across the arid plains, this exclusive lodge, set in an private wilderness area 30km (19 miles) from Sesriem, consists of nine thatched chalets with en-suite bathrooms and private plunge pools. The main emphasis here is on exploring the stunning landscapes around nearby Sossusvlei. $$$$

Namib Naukluft Lodge
PO Box 22028, Windhoek
Tel: 061 372100
www.namib-naukluft-lodge.com
Set on a 250-sq-km (97-sq-mile) private reserve abutting the eponymous national park, this lodge which lies between Sesriem and Solitaire consists of 16 modern rooms with private verandas. Day trips to Sossusvlei are offered, and it's well placed for day hikes in the Naukluft Mountains. **$$$**

Sesriem Campsite
Bookings through Namibia Wildlife Resorts (see page 266)
Twenty campsites set in a grove of shady camelthorn trees at the main park entrance gate, close to the Sesriem Canyon and 63km (39 miles) from Sossusvlei. There's a reasonably well stocked shop, fuel station, and ablution block, and meals are available at the adjacent Sossusvlei Lodge. **$**

Solitaire Country Lodge
PO Box 6597, Windhoek
Tel: 061 305173
www.solitairecountrylodge.com
Situated 83km (52 miles) from Sesriem, this new hotel dominates the blink-and-you'll-miss-it pit stop of Solitaire on the long dusty road towards Lüderitz. It has 25 en-suite rooms centred on a refreshing swimming pool area, and is a good base for day trips into the Naukluft Mountains and Speetshoogte Pass. Camping sites available. **$$**

Sossusvlei Lodge
PO Box 6900, Ausspannplatz, Windhoek
Tel: 063 293636
www.sossusvleilodge.com
With a prime location at the Sesriem entrance gate, this is the closest lodge to Sossusvlei and its 45 en-suite tented rooms are spacious and stylishly decorated. Facilities include a floodlit waterhole and swimming pool, as well as balloon trips and guided drives to Sossusvlei. **$$$$**

Wolwedans Collection
Tel: 061 230616
www.wolwedans-namibia.com
This quintet of superlative small lodges is set amid the dunes of the NamibRand Nature Reserve, a large private conservancy bordering Namib-Naukluft to the south of Sesriem. Consisting of 22 units in total, the five lodges all offer an exclusive wilderness experience and a wide selection of activities in the desert. **$$$$**

Zebra River Lodge
Private Bag 30547, Windhoek
Tel: 063 693265
www.zebra-river-lodge.com
Set in the rugged Tsaris Mountains, this small owner-managed lodge is popular with hikers for the several trails that run through the vast property (home to a wide variety of game) and its proximity to the Naukluft Mountains. It's also a useful base for road (or plane) excursions to Sossusvlei. Homely atmosphere and good en-suite accommodation set around a sparkling swimming pool. **$$$**

SOUTHERN NAMIBIA

Rehoboth

Lake Oanob Resort
PO Box 3381
Tel: 062 522370
www.oanob.com.na
Set on the lakeshore 7km (4 miles) west of Rehoboth, this is a comfortable and attractively situated resort with good facilities (restaurant, game-viewing hides, internet café), a good variety of rooms and self-catering units, and camping and caravan sites too. **$$**

Mariental and Environs
Auob Lodge
PO Box 6597, Windhoek
Tel: 061 374750
To the east of Mariental near Gochas, about 150km (93 miles) from the border with the Kgalagadi Transfrontier Park, this three-star lodge consists of 26 spacious rooms with a view of the Kalahari dunes. **$$**

Bagatelle Kalahari Game Ranch
Tel: 061 224712
www.bagatelle-kalahari-gameranch.com
This private ranch, about 45 minutes' drive northeast of Mariental, stocks a wide variety of game, including cheetah, giraffe, oryx and various smaller antelope. The stilted dunetop accommodation has plenty of character, great views and good facilities. **$$$$**

Hardap Recreation Resort
Bookings through Namibia Wildlife Resorts (see page 266).
Situated 25km (15.5 miles) from town overlooking the Hardap Dam, this good-value resort has bungalows, camping sites, shop, restaurant, filling station and swimming pool. It is closed for renovations at the time of writing but should reopen in 2015. **$**

Kalahari Anib Lodge
PO Box 80205, Windhoek
Tel: 061 230066
www.gondwana-collection.com
Situated on the C20 some 30km (19 miles) northeast of Mariental, this lodge consists of 35 comfortable en-suite rooms surrounded by beautiful gardens and the red dunes protected within the private Gondwana Kalahari Park. **$$$**

Mariental Hotel
Marie Brandt Street, PO Box 619
Tel: 063 242466
www.marientalhotel.com
Having celebrated its centenary in 2012, this unexpectedly good country hotel provides comfortable accommodation with en-suite bathrooms, air conditioning, satellite TV and internet access. **$**

Suricate Tented Kalahari Lodge
Tel: 061 375300
www.intu-afrika.com
This stilted lodge, set in the 200-sq-km (77-sq-mile) Intu Africa Kalahari Game Reserve (to the northeast of Mariental), supports a fair variety of desert wildlife, and is also home to one of the few remaining Bushman communities in southern Namibia. Overlooking a waterhole, the lodge offers good en-suite accommodation, a swimming pool, and the rate includes game drives and activities. **$$$$**

Keetmanshoop
Bird's Mansions Hotel
6th Avenue
Tel: 063 221711
www.birdsaccommodation.com
Situated a block up from the Central Hotel, this is similarly good value, consisting of 16 en-suite rooms with satellite TV and air conditioning, and a central lapa with swimming pool and beer garden. **$**

Central Lodge
5th Avenue
Tel: 063 225850
www.central-lodge.com
Centrally located on the site of the former Hansa Hotel (built 1910), this

PRICE CATEGORIES

Based on B&B rate for twin double room.
$$$$ = above US$180 (N$2,000)
$$$ = US$130–180 (N$1,400–2,000)
$$ = US$75–140 (N$800–1,400)
$ = under US$75 (N$800)

is probably the most popular lodge in town, and very good value. All 19 en-suite rooms have air conditioning and satellite TV, and there is a swimming pool and good à-la-carte restaurant with a budget-friendly wine list. **$**

Quivertree Forest Rest Camp
PO Box 262, Keetmanshoop
Tel: 063 683421
www.quivertreeforest.com
Located on the farm Gariganus, 13km (8 miles) northeast of town, this rest camp lies adjacent to the famous Quiver Tree Forest and the rock formations of the Giants' Playground. Accommodation options consist of a three- and four-bedroom guesthouse, as well as en-suite igloo bungalows and a campsite. **$$**

Fish River Environs
Ai-Ais Recreation Resort
Bookings through Namibia Wildlife Resorts (see page 266).
This renovated resort at the southern end of the canyon has accommodation in luxury flats, plus huts, camping sites, shop, restaurant, filling station, mineral spa and swimming pool. **$–$$$**

Canyon Lodge
PO Box 80205, Windhoek
Tel: 061 230066
www.gondwana-collection.com
Situated in Gondwana Canyon Park, a privately managed extension of the Fish River Canyon National Park, this superb lodge straddles a range of rocky hills some 20km (12 miles) from the main viewpoint over the canyon. The 30 en-suite bungalows blend attractively into the granite environment. Facilities include horseback trips, a swimming pool and a beautifully positioned restaurant in the old German farmhouse serving home-style cooking. **$$$$**

Canyon Roadhouse & Mountain Camp
Booking details as for above.
Under the same management as the Canyon Lodge, the 24-room Canyon Roadhouse is a rather culty recreation of an American roadhouse complete with self-consciously tacky period décor, only 14km (8 miles) from the main Hobas entrance gate to the canyon. It also has a campsite, though the remote self-catering Canyon Mountain Camp, which now caters to groups only, is the better bet for those seeking rural solitude, set in the mountains 6km (3 miles) from the lodge. **$** (camping or mountain camp), **$$$** (roadhouse).

Hobas Resort
Bookings through Namibia Wildlife Resorts (see page 266).

Situated at the northern entrance gate to the park, close to the best viewpoints and starting point of the Fish River Canyon hiking trail, this campsite has a shop and swimming pool. **$**

Helmeringhausen
Dabis Guest farm
PO Box 6213, Windhoek
Tel: 081 3108902
www.farmdabis.com
Situated about 30 minutes' drive north of town, this welcoming guest farm has been in the same German family since 1926, and managed by four successive generations. It will be of great interest to anybody who wants to learn about sheep ranching techniques in this arid part of the world. Delicious barbecued lamb chops are something of a speciality. A good stopover between Lüderitz/Fish River and Sesriem. **$$**

Hotel Helmeringhausen
PO Box 21, Helmeringhausen
Tel: 063 283307
www.helmeringhausen.com
This small country hotel, built in the 1930s and strong on period character, offers 20 en-suite rooms at the heart of its tiny junction village. **$$**

Grünau
Grünau Country House
PO Box 2
Tel: 063 262001
www.grunauch.iway.na
This country hotel is the top lodge in this small junction town near the South African border. **$**

Karasburg
Kalkfontein Hotel
86 Kalkfontein Street
Tel: 081 129 9754
www.kalkfonteinhotel.co.za
Situated on the southern slopes of the Karas Mountains, the 17 en-suite rooms here are a little on the basic side, but comfortable enough. **$**

Maltahöhe
Duwisib Castle
Bookings through Namibia Wildlife Resorts (see page 266).
There's a very pleasant campsite with limited facilities adjacent to Namibia's most intriguingly misplaced colonial relic. **$**

Farm Duwisib
PO Box 21, Maltahöhe
Tel: 063 293344
www.farmduwisib.com
Less than 5 minutes' walk from Duwisib Castle, this homely farm has 10 rooms available, some on a self-catering basis, others dinner, B&B. **$$**

Hammerstein Rest Camp
PO Box 250, Maltahöhe
Tel: 063 693111
www.hammerstein.com.na
Situated on the C19 between Maltahöhe and Sesriem, this mid-range camp with a swimming pool lies in a boulder-strewn farm that hosts some good rock art and a variety of desert wildlife. Situated within day-tripping distance of Sossusvlei. **$**

Aus
Klein-Aus Vista
PO Box 25, Aus
Tel: 063 258116
www.klein-aus-vista.com
Situated 3km (2 miles) from Aus on the B4 to Lüderitz, an area regularly frequented by wild desert horses, this welcoming set-up consists of the 14-room Desert Horse Inn and the more exclusive hillside Eagle's Nest Lodge. **$$$**

Lüderitz
Kapps Hotel
Bismarck Road
Tel: 063 202345
www.kappshotel.com
This central hotel, the oldest in town having celebrated its centenary in 2007, has plenty of character. The en-suite rooms, though a little rundown, are not without appeal and seem like good value. The attached Rumours Sports Bar is also pretty likeable. **$**

The Nest Hotel
Diaz Street
Tel: 063 204000
www.nesthotel.com
This is a good four-star hotel on a private beach southwest of the town centre. All 70 rooms and three suites have a sea view. The restaurant offers good meals, with seafood being the speciality. **$$–$$$**

Protea Hotel Sea-View Zum Sperrgebiet
Woerman Street, PO Box 373
Tel: 063 203411-3
www.proteahotels.com
This comfortable and modern three-star hotel with 22 rooms and a good sea view was recently added to the Protea Chain. Facilities include an indoor pool and sauna, and a very good restaurant. **$$**

PRICE CATEGORIES

Based on B&B rate for twin double room.
$$$$ = above US$180 (N$2,000)
$$$ = US$130–180 (N$1,400–2,000)
$$ = US$75–140 (N$800–1,400)
$ = under US$75 (N$800)

EATING OUT

RECOMMENDED RESTAURANTS, CAFES & BARS

LOCAL CUISINE

Like most African capitals, Windhoek boasts a cosmopolitan variety of culinary treats, and it is undoubtedly the best place for eating out in Namibia. As many as a hundred different restaurants, coffee shops and fast food outlets are dotted around the city, including good representatives of German, French, Italian, Portuguese, Chinese, Indian and even Argentine cuisine, as well as a smattering of places specialising in local, West African and even Ethiopian food – not to mention various South African or global chains such as Debonairs Pizzeria, Kentucky Fried Chicken and Nando's. In other words, there is something to suit all tastes – at prices that seem very reasonable by international standards (main courses generally fall below US$12 in all but the most swish eateries) and generally with a good choice of local beers and South African wines as accompaniment.

A far smaller but otherwise comparable selection of restaurants is to be found in the three main port towns: Lüderitz, Walvis Bay and especially the more resort-like Swakopmund. Seafood is the speciality here, though good meat dishes are also available.

Elsewhere, urban centres tend to boast just one or two steakhouse-type establishments catering to undemanding carnivorous local palates. In reality, however, few tourists will spend much time in small-town Namibia: more likely they will spend most of their nights in isolated lodges, rest camps and guest farms, which typically offer high quality (but of necessity limited) three–four-course set menus (or buffets) for approximately US$20 per head.

Guest farms and smaller establishments – particularly those in the remoter areas – serve a rather more limited selection of meals. Here, it's a question of whether or not the chef's on form the day you arrive in camp, but in the main, the food is fresh and well prepared. Indeed, the standard of the cooking at some of the more far-flung places like Kulala Desert Lodge in the Namib is remarkably good, considering the great difficulties of supply and preparation.

On a lodge safari, the restaurant choices are few but fortunately most lodges offer ample amounts of food, even if the quality is variable. In many places you'll find your evening meal served in a traditional *boma*, an open-air enclosure lit by a roaring fire, where meals are prepared and served. Often, you'll be offered buffet lunches and dinners comprising a wide range of meats, salads, vegetables and desserts.

On a camping safari guests will usually be offered a traditional *braai* (barbecue) in the evenings, complete with lots of different kinds of salads and *potjiekos* – a meat and vegetable stew simmered for hours in a three-legged cast-iron *potjie* (little pot). The following state- and privately-owned game parks/reserves have restaurants: Ai-Ais, Daan Viljoen, Etosha: Halali, Namutoni and Okaukuejo, Gross Barmen, Waterberg, Skeleton Coast Park (Terrace Bay) and Hardap. Meal times are fairly restricted, so check them carefully.

If you want to try something authentically Namibian at breakfast time, look out for (or request) *mahangu* (millet) porridge, a staple food of many black Namibians; it's surprisingly tasty.

If your itinerary includes the northern regions, you'll be able to supplement your diet with all sorts of indigenous fruit and nuts from roadside stalls – depending on the season, of course. Look out for marula fruits, the *embe* or *omuve* (bird plum), and succulent monkey oranges – great for quenching thirst on a boiling hot day.

Wine lovers will find most restaurants serve an excellent selection of sensible priced wines from neighbouring South Africa. Common reds include Cabernet Sauvignon and Shiraz, while the most conspicuous Cape whites are Chardonnay, Sauvignon Blanc and Chenin Blanc. Be sure to try Pinotage, a uniquely South African red cultivar developed from a cross between Pinot Noir and Cinsault. The Beyerskloof and Zonnebloem estates both produce easy drinking Pinotages widely available at restaurants.

TRANSPORT

ACCOMMODATION

EATING OUT

ACTIVITIES

A – Z

WINDHOEK

Am Weinberg Restaurant
13 Jan Jonker Road
Tel: 061 236050
www.amweinberg.com
Offering beautiful views over the Klein Windhoek valley, this smart fine dining restaurant, set in a national monument dating from 1901, boasts an interesting fusion menu and enjoyable garden bar.

Craft Centre Café
Old Brewery Centre, 40 Tal Street
Tel: 061 249974
www.craftcafe-namibia.com
This popular lunchtime spot with a contemporary feel serves healthy sandwiches, salads and snacks, and it's also a great place for a relaxed breakfast. **$**

Dunes Restaurant
Kalahari Sands Hotel, Gustav Voigts Centre, Independence Avenue
Tel: 061 2800344
Filling evening buffets and Sunday carveries are offered at this plush restaurant, which has indoor and terrace seating overlooking Independence Avenue. **$$$**

Fusion Restaurant
Cnr Simpson and Beethoven Street
Tel: 081 214 8404
www.facebook.com/FusionNamibia
Ideal for those with adventurous palates, this cosmopolitan eatery serves a great selection of African dishes, with occasional theme nights dedicated to one style or country. **$$$**

Garnish Restaurant
Trift Towers, Trift Street
Tel: 061 258119
www.facebook.com/GarnishFlavoursofIndia
Opened in 2013, this popular recent addition to Windhoek's culinary scene serves an exceptionally varied menu of meat and vegetarian dishes. **$$$**

Gathemann Restaurant
175 Independence Avenue
Tel: 061 223853
www.facebook.com/RestaurantGathemann
One of the smartest and long-serving restaurants in town, set in an historic building overlooking Zoo Park, this serves up delicious German and other continental fare using the very best-quality local meat and fish. **$$$$**

Gourmet Restaurant
Kaiserkrone Centre,
off Post Street Mall
Tel: 061 232360
www.thegourmet-restaurant.com
Boasting something of a beer garden atmosphere, this longstanding

Breakfast on safari, Onkoshi Camp, Etosha.

purveyor of fine German-style 'Schmecker' cuisine, housed in the former Kaiserkrone Hotel (built 1910), is also well known for its seafood. **$$$$**

Grand Canyon Spur
251 Independence Avenue
Tel: 061 231003
www.spurcorp.nl/spur/Namibia
Part of a South African chain, this family-oriented restaurant serves affordable American-style burgers, steaks and salads. **$$**

Jenny's Place
78 Sam Nujoma Drive,
Klein Windhoek
Tel: 061 269152
www.jennysplace.iway.na
Linked to one of Namibia's top arts and crafts stores, this garden café has a relaxed setting and is open Mon to Sat for coffee and cake as well as light meals. **$**

Joe's Beerhouse
160 Nelson Mandela Drive
Tel: 061 232457
www.joesbeerhouse.com
The ever-popular Joe's is open for lunch and dinner and the rustic setting is ideal for sundowners. This lively place is famed for its venison and meat dishes, but it's best to book a table at weekends. **$$**

La Marmite
383 Independence Avenue
Tel: 061 240306
A genuine Cameroonian chef ensures this centrally located, relaxed and affordable restaurant serves the best West African cuisine in town. **$$**

Luigi & The Fish
320 Sam Nujoma Drive
Tel: 061 256399
This is another Windhoek institution, specialising in seafood and pasta. **$$–$$$**

Mugg & Bean
Town Square, Post Street Mall
Tel: 061 248898
www.themugg.com
Enjoy light snacks, hot meals, all day breakfast or fresh coffee overlooking bustling Post Street Mall. **$**

O Portuga
Nelson Mandela Drive
Tel: 061 272900
This Angolan-style Portuguese eatery serves top-notch seafood at reasonable prices. It's reasonably centrally located and has long opening hours (noon–11pm seven days a week). **$$**

Protea Hotel Fürstenhof
Frans Indongo Street
Tel: 061 237380
The formal restaurant at this smart hotel serves French, German and Namibian game dishes. **$$$**

Sardinia Pizzeria & Eiscafe
47 Independence Avenue

PRICE CATEGORIES

Price categories are for a meal for one including one glass of house wine:
$ = under US$8
$$ = US$8-15
**$$$** = US$–15-25
$$$$ = more than US$25

Tel: 061 225600
This informal spot serves good, reasonably priced Italian food. **$$**
Stellenbosch Wine Bar & Bistro
78 Sam Nujoma Drive
Tel: 061 309141
www.thestellenboschwinebar.com
Steaks sourced from free-range cattle are the speciality at this classy new bistro, which also serves a

variety of other meat and fish grills, and boasts one of the best wine lists in the country. **$$$**
The Wine Bar
3 Garten Street
Tel: 061 226514
www.thewinebarshop.com
Set on a hill offering great sunset views, this extension of Windhoek's top wine shop serves tasty

continental fare and a predictable varied selection of wines. **$$$**
Zoo Café (aka Café Balalaika)
Corner Independence & Fidel Castro
Tel: 061 223479
If free WiFi, freshly brewed coffee and affordable light meals aren't enough to tempt you, then the lovely garden setting below shady trees in Zoo Park should be.**$$**

GROOTFONTEIN, TSUMEB, OUTJO AND OMARURU

Grootfontein

Purple Fig Bistro
19 Hage Geingob Avenue
Tel: 081 124 2802
Hearty German stews and lighter snacks are the speciality at this brightly decorated bistro with indoor and outdoor seating. **$**

Try ostrich meat in Grootfontein.

Tsumeb

Makalani Hotel
Ndilimani Cultural Troupe Street
Tel: 067 221051
www.makalanihotel.com
There's a quality à-la-carte restaurant at this friendly central hotel, but most people prefer to eat out in the shady

lapa – a casual spot where you can watch the game (of the football variety) on the big-screen TV. Either way, it's strong on steaks and other grills. **$$**

Outjo

Etosha Garten Hotel
Otavi Street
Tel: 067 313130
www.etosha-garden-hotel.com
The restaurant at this riverside hotel serves good venison steaks and other homely food. **$-$$**
Outjo Bäkkerei
Tel: 067 313055
9 Hage Geingob Street
Established in 1950 and still going strong, this is a very popular lunch-stop serving tasty sandwiches and burgers, as well as a range of breads, pies and assorted confectioneries. **$**

Omaruru

Main Street Café
116 Wilhelm Zeraua St
Tel: 064 570544
Under dynamic new management since mid-2013, this good-value central deli, situated next to a photographic gallery, serves freshly brewed coffee and an imaginative selection of light meals and sandwiches. **$**

KEETMANSHOOP AND LÜDERITZ

Keetmanshoop

Central Lodge
5th Street
Tel: 063 225850
www.central-lodge.com
This pleasant lodge has a good, affordable à-la-carte restaurant with a budget-friendly wine list. **$$**
Uschi's Coffee Shop
5th Street
Tel: 062 222445
Inexpensive, friendly local institution serving good coffee, sandwiches, snack, pizzas and light meals. **$**

Lüderitz

Barrel's Bar & Restaurant
Berg Street, Lüderitz
Tel: 063 202458
Pleasant drinking hole, set in a pre-World War I building, the hearty dishes of the day come with a buffet salad and an unusually generous serving of veggies. Very reasonably priced. **$$**
Diaz Point Coffee Shop
Bismarck Drive
Lüderitz Tel: 063 203147
Good central location to stop in for a light lunch, a filling sandwich or a freshly brewed cup of coffee. Closed Mondays. **$**

Ritzi's Seafood Restaurant
Hafen Road
Tel: 063 202818
Now relocated to the new Harbour Square Mall, with a balcony overlooking the harbour, this restaurant serves good quality seafood as well as various meat and chicken dishes. Well-priced wine list. **$$$**
Shearwater Oyster Bar & Restaurant
Luderitz Boatyard, Insel St
Tel: 063 204031
Oysters served raw or grilled and other seafood dishes are the specialities at this relaxed harbourfront eatery. **$$**

SWAKOPMUND

Café Anton
Hotel Schweizerhaus,
Bismarck Street
Tel: 064 400331
www.schweizerhaus.net/cafe_anton.htm
This venerable café opens for
breakfast and lunch, and is known
for its delicious coffee and pastries.
Great sea views. **$**

Erich's Restaurant
21 Daniel Tjongarero Street
Tel: 064 405141
For more than 30 years now,
this Swakopmund institution is
renowned for its varied seafood
menu. Advance reservation
recommended. **$$**

Hansa Hotel Restaurant
3 Hendrik Witbooi Street
Tel: 064 414200
www.hansahotel.com.na
This century-old hotel boasts the town's
swankiest restaurant. It has a formal
atmosphere and serves imaginative
Germanic dishes with the emphasis on
venison and seafood. **$$$$**

Kücki's Pub
Tobias Hainyeko Street
Tel: 064 402407
www.kuckispub.com
This lively German-style bar serves
very good seafood and other grills,
and the service is friendly. Bookings
often essential. **$$$**

The Lighthouse Pub and Restaurant
Pool Terrace,
off Promenade Street
Tel: 064 400894
Good views of the ocean makes
the balcony here an ideal spot for a
sundowner. The seafood and steaks
are also very good, and reasonably
priced. Booking for indoor tables
essential at weekends. Closed
Monday. **$$**

The Tug
Strand Road
Tel: 064 402356
www.the-tug.com
Fresh seafood complements
the beautiful ocean views in
this permanently grounded tug
overlooking the main beachfront.
Booking essential. **$$–$$**

Village Café
21 Sam Nujoma Ave.
Tel: 064 404723
www.villagecafenamibia.com
This cosy and central café serves
excellent coffee, shakes, savoury
and sweet filled pancakes, salads,
soups and cakes, with the emphasis
on healthy locally grown ingredients.
$

Zur Kupferpfanne
9 Daniel Tjongarero Ave
Tel: 064 405405
This new restaurant, like many in
Swakopmund, is strong on seafood
and German cuisine, but the quality is
excellent. **$$$**

Zur Kupferfanne's menu board in Swakopmund.

WALVIS BAY

Crazy Mama's
Sam Nujoma Street, opposite Atlantic Hotel
Tel: 064 207364
Relaxed atmosphere and a central
location for this Italian where there's
a wide choice but the pizzas are
especially good. **$$**

Lothar's Steakhouse
112 Sixth Street
Tel: 064 220884
www.swakop.com/OnePageWebs/
LotharsSteakHouse.htm

Open 7 days a week for lunch and
dinner, this place isn't strictly for
the carnivores – the beef and
venison steak is as good as it gets,
but there is also a varied selection
of seafood, soups and salads to
tempt pescatorians and vegeterians.
$$–$$$

Raft Restaurant
Esplanade Lagoon
Tel: 064 204877
www.theraftrestaurant.com

Under the same management
as Swakopmund's Tug, the Raft
Restaurant is an equally stylish
seafood joint offering excellent
views of the lagoon (being perched
on stilts over the lagoon, as it
were) and glimpses of dolphins on
a good day. Advance booking is
recommended. **$$$**

PRICE CATEGORIES

Price categories are for a meal for
one including one glass of house
wine:
$ = under US$8
$$ = US$8-15
**$$$** = US$–15-25
$$$$ = more than US$25

ACTIVITIES

FESTIVALS, THE ARTS, NIGHTLIFE, SHOPPING SAFARIS AND SPORTS

FESTIVALS

One of Namibia's most colourful and spectacular annual events, the **Maharero Day** celebrations of the Red Flag Herero, takes place at Okahandja on the nearest weekend to 26 August. The day's activities begin on the outskirts of the town with drilling by various units of uniformed men organised along military lines. Poems in praise of their heroes' deeds and their forefathers are intermittently chanted by the men while the women ululate. Mid-morning sees the procession of men, mounted horsemen and women in their Victorian dresses begin to make its way to the graveyard of their great leaders to pay *ombimbi* (respect) to their ancestors.

The **Mbanderu**, or Green Flag Herero, pay homage to their ancestral leaders on the weekend before or on 11 June each year, again in Okahandja. On this occasion the women all wear green Victorian dresses.

Another traditional Herero cultural event takes place on the weekend before 10 October when followers of the Herero chief **Zeraua**, also known as the White Flag Herero, converge on Omaruru.

Although not comparable with the famous carnivals of Germany or Rio de Janeiro, the most important cultural event in the capital is undoubtedly WIKA – the **Windhoek Karneval** tel: 061 228255; www.windhoek-karneval.com. It usually takes place around the end of April or early May, beginning with the Prinzenball on the Friday evening. Particularly popular are the Büttenabende (performances of

music and sketches), one of which is held in English. Another of the week's highlights is the Maskenball which takes place on the Friday evening before the Kehraus, which marks the end of the carnival. There is also a ladies' night, a Jugend-Karneval (youth carnival) and a Kinder Karneval or kiddies' carnival.

Swakopmund has its annual carnival, kuska – **Kuste Karneval** or Coast Carnival – in August/September, while Otjiwarongo and Tsumeb also have an annual carnival. An Oktoberfest is also held in Windhoek, although on a far smaller scale than the one in Munich.

Calendar of Events

Bank Windhoek Arts Festival
www.bankwindhoekarts.com.na
A varied selection of one-off plays and other performances, sponsored by the Bank of Windhoek, and running throughout the year.
Windhoek Carnival (WIKA)
Tel: 061 237656
www.windhoek-karneval.com
This venerable knees-up, usually held in April, reflects the country's strong Teutonic links with plenty of oompah bands and flowing beer.
AE//GAMS Arts and Culture Festival
Tel: 061 2902493
Usually held in September, this showcase for traditional dance and music, live bands and choral events is held in various venues in central Windhoek and Katutura.
EUNIC Film Festival
Tel: 061 225700
www.goethe.de/windhoek
First held in August 2012, this festival funded by the European Union National Institutes for Culture is

organised by and partially hosted at the Goethe Institute.
Oktoberfest
Tel: 061 235521
www.skw.com.na
This boozy Bavarian institution is held at the Sports Klub Windhoek every October.

THE ARTS

Art Galleries

The National Art Gallery of Namibia (tel: 061 231160; www.nagn.org.na) on Robert Mugabe Street, Windhoek, houses the most important permanent collection of local artwork, ranging from colonial-era landscapes to contemporary work reflecting the modern political and social situation. Entrance is free on weekdays but a small entrance fee is payable over weekends and public holidays.

Namibian works of art can be bought at several private art galleries in Windhoek and Swakopmund – Namibia could hardly be described as a thriving artistic hub, but Windhoek in particular has a few venues catering to those seeking a cultural fix.

Galleries in the capital include: **Artelier Kendzia**, 14 Volans Street, tel: 061 225991, and the **Omba Gallery** in the Namibia Crafts Centre, Tal Street, tel/fax: 061 242799, www.omba.org.na. Swakopmund has a reputation as an artist's haunt and there are a surprising number of art galleries, including: **Die Muschel**, Hendrik Witbooi Street, tel: 064 402874, www.muschel.iway.na; **Hobby Horse**, The Arcade, Hendrik Witbooi Street, tel: 064 402875 and Fine Art Gallery (34 Sam Nujoma Ave; www.art-in-namibia.com).

Theatre

A variety of plays and other theatrical entertainment, live music and dance performance are staged throughout the year by the **National Theatre of Namibia** (www.ntn.org.na), the central non-profit venue next to the National Art Gallery. Many of these are local productions, but international companies touring South Africa sometimes include Namibia on their itinerary. The theatre, which accommodates 470 people, is situated on the corner of Robert Mugabe Avenue and John Meinert Street. The reservations office is open Mon–Fri, 9am–noon and 2–4pm, tel: 061 374400.

The **Warehouse Theatre** (48 Tal Street; tel: 061 402253; www.facebook.com/WarehouseTheatreWindhoek) in the Old Brewery complex has long been the place to catch contemporary Namibian musicians in live action.

Several drama productions are also staged by the University of Namibia's **School of the Arts**. The School sees itself as instrumental in exploring a Namibian indigenous theatre and although its emphasis is mainly on experimental theatre and workshops, classical dramas are also staged. When in Windhoek phone the Department of Visual and Performing Arts (tel: 061 206 3184) for information on programmes..

Productions by other performing arts groups are occasionally staged. Watch the press for details and also check out the below.

Film/Cinema

The cinemas in Windhoek (call 061 248980/9267 for more information) and Swakopmund (tel: 064 402743) have daily screenings, including Sundays. Windhoek also has an annual film festival, classical film festival and children's film festival, presented each year by the National Theatre of Namibia (NTN). These are well advertised in the local press.
Ster-Kinekor Cinema
Maerua Mall
Cnr Robert Mugabe & Jan Jonker Streets
Tel. 061 215912
www.sterkinekor.com
Windhoek's only cinema is this five-screen complex in the city's main shopping mall. International and South African releases are shown here, and prices are extremely reasonable in comparison with Europe and the US.

Other Entertainment

There are several choir groups in Windhoek, one of the most popular being the 30-member **Cantare Audire**. Founded in 1972, the choir won the mixed choir category at the International Eisteddfod in Wales in 1985. Cantare Audire has also toured Germany, Austria and the United States where it performed

with the Mormon Tabernacle Choir. Performances are also given from time to time by Namibia's National Youth Choir.
College of the Arts (COTA)
41 Fidel Castro Street
Tel: 061 374100/081 6194239
The former Windhoek Conservatory has an active programme of cultural events ranging from art exhibitions to African dance performances and chamber recitals performed by its talented pupils. Check the notice board outside the College and the press for details.

NIGHTLIFE

If you're looking for swinging nightlife, you are likely to be disappointed. As with the arts, nightlife in Namibia is all but restricted to the capital, and even there it tends to be rather subdued by international standards. Very few hotels have nightclubs or discos, and there is generally very little entertainment for guests. Windhoek has a few nightclubs but they are not in the centre of town. Consult the newspapers and ask your hotel staff if you're keen to find out where the action is. The following venues are worth checking out:
Berty's Landing Pub & Grill
Parsival Street
Tel: 081 2791198
This family-friendly venue is popular at weekends, with jumping castles and jungle gym to amuse the children by day, and occasional live music at night. Open Mon–Sat 9am–2am.
Club London V2.0
4 Nasmith Street
Email: londonnamibia@live.com
This is probably the liveliest nightclub in Windhoek, open into the wee hours, and playing an unusually eclectic selection of African and contemporary international dance music.
Club Thriller
Goreseb St, Katatura
Tel: 061 216669
This long-serving club in Katatura isn't the place to come wearing expensive jewellery or carrying other valuables, but it has a welcoming atmosphere and plays an enjoyable selection of international and African dance music. Open Thur–Sat 10pm–5am.
Desert Jewel Casino
B1 Western Bypass
Tel: 061 205 5911
www.legacyhotels.co.za/en/hotels/windhoek

Kicking up a storm at the National Theatre of Namibia.

The only casino in Windhoek, situated on the out-of-town Windhoek Country Club Resort, it offers the usual range of card tables and gaming machines.

El Cubano
Independence Avenue
Tel: 081 2005370
Popular with the under-30s, the Cuban-themed bar in the Hilton Hotel has a chilled atmosphere and a small dance floor. Open daily 5.30pm–late.

Joe's Beerhouse
160 Nelson Mandela Avenue
Tel: 061 232457
www.joesbeerhouse.com
A Windhoek institution since it opened in 1990, this likeable and thoroughly unpretentious German-style pub attracts a mixed crowd of revellers at all hours. Open Mon–Thur 4.30pm-late; Fri–Sun 11am–late.

Vibe Pub, Club & Lounge
8 Bell Street
https://www.facebook.com/pages/Vibe-Pub-Club-Lounge/1394521134100955
Spilling across two floors, the former G-Zone Lounge Bar is a friendly and popular cocktail bar that attracts a laidback younger crowd.

The Wine Bar
3 Garten Street
Tel: 061 226514
www.thewinebarshop.com
Sample an excellent range of Cape wines at this sophisticated venue set on a hill that offers fantastic sunset views over the city centre. Open Mon–Sat 5–10.30pm.

SHOPPING

Where to Buy

Much of the informal sector is aimed at the tourist market. In Windhoek, souvenir hunters will find rich pickings at the Post Street Mall open-air market, and at the street market on the corner of Peter Müller Street and Independence Avenue. Most curio, book and jewellery shops have the following business hours: Mon–Fri 8.30am–5pm, Sat 8am–1pm.

Supermarkets usually remain open until 6pm in the evening, while the larger ones also open for a few hours on Saturday afternoon and Sundays. Bear in mind that many shops close for lunch between 1pm and 2.30pm or 3pm, especially in the smaller towns.

A Herero doll for sale on the streets of Windhoek.

What to Buy

Arts & Crafts

You'll find a wide variety of curios ranging from genuine crafts made by the indigenous people of Namibia and other neighbouring countries to the usual mass-produced articles in curio shops.

Windhoek
Namibia Crafts Centre
Tal Street in the Old Breweries Building, tel: 061 242799, www.omba.org.na.
African Curiotique
Gustav Voigts Centre, Independence Avenue, tel: 061 236191, www.african-curiotique.com
Bushman Art & African Museum
187 Independence Avenue, tel: 061 228828/229131, www.bushmanart-gallery.com
Penduka Project Centre
Goreangabdam, 8 km outside Windhoek, tel: 061 257210, www.penduka.com

Swakopmund
African Kirikara Arts and Crafts
Am Ankerplatz, Sam Nujoma Avenue, tel: 064 463146, www.kirikara.com

Clothing

Compared to European prices leather goods are very reasonable. Namibia is world-renowned for its Karakul lamb pelts also known as Swakara (south-west African Karakul). The newborn lambs are skinned rather than shorn; the more expensive 'broadtail' Karakul is taken from foetal lambs. Swakara coats, jackets and other garments, as well as furs, are produced in Windhoek. Leather goods manufactured from buffalo hide and

ostrich skins are also available, but since Namibia's ostrich industry is still in its infancy, ostrich skin products are usually imported from South Africa.

Jewellery

Hand-crafted Namibian jewellery is in demand. Jewellery from Zambia, Zimbabwe and Lesotho with its unmistakably African character is also a good buy and easy to find.

Windhoek
Canto Goldsmith and Jewellers
Levinson Arcade, tel: 061 222894.
Horst Knop Jeweller
Kaiserkrone Centre, Post Street Mall, tel: 061 228657.
Adrian & Meyer Jewellers
Carl List Mall, Independence Avenue, tel: 061 236100; www.adrian-meyer.com

Swakopmund
African Art Jewellers
Hendrik Withooi Street, tel: 064 405566.

Gemstones

A browse around the gem shops in Namibia is worthwhile. Be warned, though: some of the gemstones which are sold locally are actually imported from South America.

Windhoek
Queen of Namibia
Wernhil Park, Upper Level, tel: 061 227735; www.facebook.com/QueenOfNamibia.
The House of Gems
131 Werner List Street, tel: 061 225202; www.namrocks.com.

Swakopmund
Stonetique
27 Dr Libertine Amuthila Street, tel: 064 405403.
If you're travelling between Swakopmund and Okahandja, the Henckert Tourist Centre in the main street of Karibib (tel: 064 550700; www.henckert.com) is also worth a visit. Henckert now has a branch in Swakopmund too (tel: 064 400140; www.swakopmund.henckert.com).

Carpets and Rugs

Namibia is renowned for its outstanding handwoven Karakul carpets.

Windhoek Environs
Ibenstein Weavers
Near Dordabis, tel: 062 573524, www.ibenstein-weavers.com.na
Dorkambo Weavers Cooperative
East of Windhoek, tel: 065 248155; www.dorkambo.com

Swakopmund
Karakulia Wavers
2 Rakotoka Street, tel: 064 461415;
www.karakulia.com.na

Books

Windhoek
New Book Cellar
Fidel Castro Street, tel: 081 251 8164.
Windhoek Book Den
Cnr Hosea Kutako & Puccini St, tel:
061 239976.
Central News Agency (CNA)
Gustav Voigts Centre, tel: 061 225625,
Maerua Mall, tel: 061 242 159, and
Wernhil Park, tel: 061 224090.

Swakopmund
Swakopmunder Buchhandlung
Sam Nujoma Drive, tel: 064 402613
CNA
Hendrik Witbooi Street, tel: 064
404488.

Safari/Camping Equipment

Windhoek
Cymot
342 Independence Ave, tel: 061
237759
Holtz Safariland
Gustav Voigts Centre, tel: 061
235941, www.safarilandholtz.com
Trappers Trading Co.
Wernhil Park, tel: 061 223136.
  Camping kit can be hired at:
Camping Hire Namibia
78 Mose Tjitendero Street, Olympia,
Windhoek, tel: 061 252995,
www.orusovo.com/camphire
(See page 246)

Swakopmund
Safariland-Holtz
Sam Nujoma Drive, tel: 064 462387,
www.safarilandholtz.com

SAFARIS

The following local companies can
arrange safaris. Others are available
through the Namibian Tourist Board.
(For Tour Operators abroad see page
274).
Namib Wilderness Safaris
Tel: +27 11 807 1800
www.wilderness-safaris.com
Namibia Tours & Safaris
Tel: 064 406038
www.namibia-tours-safaris.com
Southern Cross Safaris
Tel/fax: 061 251553
www.southern-cross-safaris.com
Pack Safaris
Tel: 061 275800
www.packsafari.com

KaokoHimba Safaris
Tel/fax: 061 695106
www.kaoko-namibia.com
Small group guided travel to the
Kaokoveld
Abenteuer Africa Safaris
Tel: 064 404030
www.abenteuerafrika.com

SPORTS

Hiking

Thanks to Namibia's aridity, the
opportunities for backpacking and
trail hiking are, understandably,
limited. Nevertheless there are some
fine self-catering routes, guided
wilderness trails and day walks.
  Situated in the desolate landscape
of southern Namibia, the **Fish River
Canyon Backpacking Trail** is rated
as one of the five top routes in
southern Africa. The 85km (53-mile)
route demands a high level of fitness
and since there are no facilities
whatever, backpackers must be
totally self-sufficient. Groups must
consist of a minimum of three people.
The extreme summer temperatures
and the danger of floods rule out
any possibility of backpacking during
the summer months and the route
is open only between 1 May and 30
September.
  The spectacular **Naukluft Hiking
Trail** on the edge of the Namib
Desert traverses undulating plains
and deep ravines, affording hikers
breathtaking vistas. Hikers have an
option of a four-day route covering
approximately 58km (36 miles) or
an eight-day circular route covering
120km (75 miles).
  The steep ascents encountered
on each day's hike and the rocky
terrain underfoot are physically
demanding and the trail is not
recommended for beginners or the
unfit. On account of the excessive
summer temperatures, hiking is
permitted between 1 March and 31
October only. Groups must consist
of a minimum of three people
and are limited to a maximum of
12. Accommodation is either in
renovated farmhouses or basic
stone huts without any facilities.
Hikers must, therefore, supply
their own equipment, including
a lightweight stove since it is not
permitted to light fires on the trail.
  In addition to the two do-it-
yourself trails managed by
the Directorate of Resource
Management, outdoor enthusiasts
also have a choice of two guided

wilderness trails. The first, the three-
day **Ugab River Wilderness Trail**
in the Skeleton Coast Park, gives
hikers the opportunity to explore the
Namib Desert on foot. Only water
and firewood are supplied and
hikers must provide their own food
and equipment, including backpacks
and sleeping bags. Nights are spent
under the clear night sky. Trails
lasting four days are conducted
every second and fourth Tuesday of
the month throughout the year.
  The other is the **Waterberg
Guided Wilderness Trail** which
concentrates on the area's geology,
wildlife and history. Game tracks are
followed in pursuit of the rare game
species inhabiting the park – white
and black rhino, sable, roan and
numerous other game species. Trails
are conducted from a base camp into
the wilderness area of the park and
are tailored to suit the fitness and
interests of the group. The trail camp
comprises rustic huts equipped
with beds and foam mattresses,
cold water washing facilities and
a central fireplace. Hikers need to
supply their own sleeping bags,
food and personal items only, since
backpacks, water bottles, all cooking
and eating utensils and a basic
first aid kit are provided. Trails run
over the second, third and fourth
weekend of every month between
April and November.
  All the above-mentioned trails
must be pre-booked in Windhoek
at **Namibia Wildlife Resorts** (see
below) (Note: Hikers on the Fish
River Canyon Backpacking Trail,
the Naukluft Hiking Trail and the
Ugab River Guided Wilderness Trail
must submit a medical certificate of
fitness before commencing the trail.)
  Those with neither the time nor
the fitness for overnight hikes have
a choice of several day walks.
Routes include the **Waterkloof** and
Olive trails in the Naukluft section
of the Namib-Naukluft Park, and an
option of two routes in the Hardap
Game Reserve. There is also a
short trail at Halali Rest Camp in
the Etosha National Park, as well as
several walks in the vicinity of the
Waterberg camp at the Waterberg
Plateau Park. Outside Windhoek,
the Daan Viljoen Game Park is
traversed by the **Wag-'n-Bietjie** and
Rooibos trails.
  For more information on any of
these trails and hikes, contact:
Namibia Wildlife Resorts
Tel: 061 285 7200
Email: reservations@nwr.com.na
www.nwr.com.na

Hornbills in Etosha National Park.

Camping

Namibia offers different types of camping opportunities, from camping in the outback (self catering!) as in Kaokoland and Bushmanland, to camping at special sites and rest camps such as those in the national parks, where ablution facilities and supplies are available)

Climbing

Namibia has many superb areas for mountaineering, including the Spitzkoppe, Brandberg and Erongo mountains. The Brandberg range is the most challenging: due to the extremely rugged terrain, scarcity of water and extremes of temperatures, inexperienced or unfit climbers should under no circumstances attempt extended excursions here. Careful planning is required and an ascent of Königstein, the highest point in Namibia (2,570 metres/8,440ft), is best accomplished with a guide who knows the area. Those who do succeed in overcoming these obstacles will be rewarded with magnificent views and beautiful rock paintings.

For more information, contact the **Mountain Club of Namibia** in Windhoek, http://nam.mcsa.org.za.

Birdwatching

The northeastern part of the country is the best area for birding. To date, some 417 species have been recorded for the eastern Kavango, along with 430 species for East Caprivi. The Popa Falls rest camp and the nearby Mahango Game Reserve (both of which are accessible by car) are especially popular birding localities, particularly during the summer months. Also worth visiting is the Kaudom Game Reserve, which is accessible by four-wheel-drive vehicle only.

Another good area for birding is the Etosha National Park which has recorded some 340 species. Following good summer rains the pan attracts large numbers of waterbirds, but during dry years you are unlikely to spot more than 100 species.

The Walvis Bay wetland, which is used by up to 43,000 Palaearctic migrants, is one of Africa's ten most important wetlands. It also supports 63, 60 and 42 percent of the southern African populations of chestnut-banded plovers and lesser and greater flamingos respectively. North of Walvis Bay, the gravel plains near the coast are the habitat of 80 percent of the world's breeding population of Damara terns, while Gray's lark inhabits the gravel flats between Lüderitz and southwestern Angola.

The **Namibia Bird Club** organises regular talks and outings. For more information, see http://namibiabird club.pbworks.com.

Fishing

The coast of Namibia has long been regarded as one of the most rewarding angling areas along the southern African coastline and from mid-January to the end of March rows of sunburnt anglers are a familiar sight along the coast. But the day's bag can often be disappointing if you're not familiar with local conditions.

The **Swakopmund Rest Camp** is a popular base with anglers, as are several overnight campsites north of Swakopmund. Some basic campsites are maintained by **Namibia Wildlife Resorts** (see above) at Mile 14 (22km north of Swakopmund), Jakkalsputz (37 miles/60km north of Swakopmund), Mile 72 (115km north of Swakopmund) and Mile 108 (175km north of Swakopmund) in the National West Coast Recreation Area.

Facilities in the **Skeleton Coast Park** are limited to basic campsites at Torra Bay, which are open during the December/January period only, and fully inclusive bungalow accommodation at Terrace Bay. The most commonly caught species of fish are kabeljou (cob), steenbras, and blacktail, but galjoen is the most sought after. Barbel is commonly caught and although often discarded is particularly tasty when smoked.

What you end up with on your hook will largely depend on the bait you use. Red bait is considered a good all-purpose bait, as are fresh pilchards (unless you're after galjoen which favours white mussels and red bait). Steenbras are particularly partial to shrimps and white mussels, while kabeljou will readily take white mussels.

A permit is required to catch some species and anglers must adhere to the minimum sizes and bait collection limits. It is also important to note that it is illegal to be in possession of more than 25 galjoen at a time. For full information contact the **Ministry of Fisheries and Marine Resources** (tel: 064 4101000, www.mfmr.gov.na).

A number of ski-boat owners offer deep-sea angling trips from Swakopmund. Information on these trips can be obtained from the **Namib I office** on Sam Nujoma Drive; (tel: 064 404287/403129; www.natron. net/tour/swakop/infoe.htm) or see www.swakop.com.

The inland dams of Namibia are well stocked with freshwater species. Hardap, the mecca of freshwater anglers, is stocked with carp, yellowfish, barbel, Orange River mudfish and moggel. The Von Bach Dam just outside Okahandja, is stocked with carp, kurper and black bass, while barbel and kurper can be caught in the Otjivero Dam near Gobabis. Of the five species of fish occurring in the Fish River, the exceptionally large barbel found in the pools below the weir at the **Ai-Ais Resort** are particularly sought after.

Small- and large-mouthed yellow fish, carp and blue kurper also abound in the Fish River. Licences for freshwater angling in Namibia are obtainable at the Ai-Ais Resort, Hardap, Von Bach Recreation Resort and at Popa Falls Rest Camp or from the tourist information office. The minimum size limits for the most commonly caught species are as follows: kurper, 8 inches (20 cm); carp and bass, 10ins (25cm); yellowfish, 12ins (30cm) and barbel, 14ins (35cm). Anglers may not catch and retain more than 10 of each of these species, but there is no limit on the number of mudfish and moggel.

"Pap" (maize meal porridge), maize pips and worms are considered the best bait for carp and kurper, while artificial bait and worms are readily taken by bass. You are likely to achieve the best results with chicken liver, worms and fish heads or intestines if you're after barbel.

The Zambezi River in northeastern Namibia offers excellent opportunities for tiger-fishing which is usually most rewarding between August and December. Other species you could catch include greenhead and three-spot bream, squeaker, barbel and nembwe. Boats and fishing tackle can be hired at Katima Mulilo or, alternatively, you can join a Kalizo fishing safari. Anglers have a choice of weekend, week-long or tailor-made fishing safaris which are conducted from Kalizo's permanent fishing camp on the banks of the Zambezi River, 23 miles (37km) from Katima Mulilo. Reservations can be made with **Kalizo**, tel: 066 686802; email: info@ kalizolodge.com; www.kalizolodge.com.

Golf

The Windhoek Country Club (www.legacyhotels.co.za/en/ hotels/windhoek) and **Rossmund Golf Club** in Swakopmund (www.rossmundgolfestate.com) have 18-hole golf courses in good condition. Walvis Bay, Henties Bay and Tsumeb also offer the opportunity to play golf.

Horse- and Camel-Riding

The Namib Desert Ride (400km/250 miles) starts in the Khomas Hochland, west of Windhoek, at Farm Hilton. It ends at Swakopmund. More information can be obtained from **Namibia Horse Safari Company** (tel: 081 470 3384; www.namibiahorsesafari.com). In Swakopmund, Okakambe Trails (tel: 064 402799; www.okakambe.iway.na) can be contacted for horse-riding at the coast.

Further information is also available from:
The Namibia Equestrian Foundation
Tel: 061 309517 www.namef.org.na

River Rafting

River rafting can only be done in the extreme south (Orange River) and north (parts of the Kunene River). **Kunene River Lodge** (tel: 061 224712; www.kuneneriverlodge.com). Offers river rafting as part of their services.
Felix Unite (tel: +27 (0)84 354 0578: www.felixunite.com). Can arrange rafting on the Orange River.

4 x 4 Adventures

Namibia offers a wide range of 4x4 trails, including **The Isabis Trail**, west of Windhoek (Tel/fax: 061 248682, www.isabis4x4.com); **The Windhoek-Okahandja Trail**, north of Windhoek (tel: 061 257157); **the Omaruru 4x4 Trail** (www.hentiesbaytourism. com); the Messem Crater 4x4 Trail (www.hentiesbaytourism.com) and the Naukluft Four Wheel Drive Trail (www.namibweb.com/n4x4trail.htm).

Duneboarding and Quad-biking

The coastal dunes and environment offers duneboarding and quad-biking for the adventurous visitor. Contact: **Abenteuer Afrika**, tel: 064 404030, www.abenteuerafrika.com; or **Desert Explorers Adventure Centre**, Swakopmund; tel/fax: 081 124 1386; www.namibiadesertexplorers.com.

Ballooning

You can't beat viewing the Namib from a hot-air balloon for sheer thrills. Flights are only undertaken if the weather is suitable and a minimum of two passengers is taken per flight. Contact **Desert Explorers Adventure Centre** (see above), or **Namib Sky Adventure Safaris** (tel: 063 683188; www.namibsky.com).

Scuba Diving

Only experienced divers should attempt to dive Namibia's extraordinary subterranean lakes such as Dragon's Breath and Otjikoto Lake.

For more information, take a look at the excellent website www.diving namibia.org, which hosts the Underwater Federation of Namibia and the Windhoek Underwater Club.

Skydiving

Windhoek and Swakopmund have ideal conditions for skydiving and paragliding. More information can be obtained at tourist offices. You can also contact the **Desert Explorers Adventure Centre** (see above).

Stargazing

Namibia is one of the best locations for stargazing in the world, thanks to its non-polluted skies. There's an observatory in the Auas Mountains, south of Windhoek (www.capella-observatory.com).

Quad-biking with Desert Explorers on the dunes near Swakopmund.

A – Z

A HANDY SUMMARY OF PRACTICAL INFORMATION

A

Admission charges

An entrance fee is charged at most museums and other places of interest. Usually this is in the region of N$10–50, but some national parks are higher. Entrance permits to the premier parks (i.e. Etosha, Naukluft, Waterberg, Skeleton Coast and Fish River Canyon), cost N$80 per person. The fee for the other reserves managed by Namibia Wildlife Resorts is N$40.

B

Budgeting for your Trip

Assuming that you have pre-booked accommodation and transport, day-to-day expenses in Namibia are low by international standards. The exchange rates are currently as follows: US$1 = N$11; GBP/£1 = N$18; and €1 = N$15.
Some typical prices follow:
Car rental: from around N$300 per day (small sedan) up to N$1,000 (4x4).
Campsite: private sites around N$100-150 for two people; national park sites cost N$150-300 for two.
Accommodation: N$500–800 (small town guesthouse); N$800–2,000 (city or town hotel, or guest farm) to upwards of N$2,000 for a very smart lodge.
Petrol: N$12 per litre.
Restaurant meal: N$50 -100(à-la-carte main course) to 200-250 (set menu at lodge) excluding drinks.
Soft drink or beer: N$10–15 (pricier at some lodges).

Wine (medium quality bottle): N$80-120 white, N$100–150 red.
Airport transfer: N$200-250.
Bread loaf: N$9-10.

C

Children

There are few specific dangers inherent to travelling in Namibia with children. The main exception is the presence of malaria in the far north. It is also advisable to be careful children don't stray too far out of sight in game reserves with potentially dangerous wildlife. Most lodges are reasonably child friendly, though some will specifically exclude children younger than a certain age.
On the whole, however, the heat, long distances and lack of diversions would make Namibia less than ideal for travel with younger children, especially those with a low boredom threshold.

Climate

With an average rainfall of 270mm (10.7in), Namibia can be classified as a largely arid country. Rainfall increases markedly from the coast, where less than 15mm (0.6in) per annum is recorded, to the interior (Windhoek has 375mm/14.8in) and from less than 50mm (10in) in the south to more than 500mm (19.7in) in the north and northeast. On average, Namibians enjoy around 300 days of sunshine a year. There are two main seasons, the reliably dry winter and more unpredictable but seldom very wet summer. There is not really an identifiable spring or autumn, but conditions tend to veer

between summery and wintery in the cusp months.

Winter (May–September)

This is the best time to visit the interior. Days are generally warm to hot, and cloudless with clear blue skies. Average daily maximum temperatures fluctuate between 22 and 27°C (71–80°F) in the south, between 20 and 26°C (68–80°F) in the central region, and 25 and 30°C (86°F) in the north. Evenings are cold, ranging between 5 and 10°C (42–49°F) in the south, 6 and 12°C (43–53°F) in the central areas and 6 and 10°C (42–50°F) in the north. Frost, quite severe at times, can be expected over large areas of the country, although by 11am the temperature has usually risen to 20°C (68°F). Due to the absence of rain during winter, the air is very dry.

Summer (October-April)

Days are very hot and nights quite cool. Average maximum temperatures in the interior generally exceed 30°C

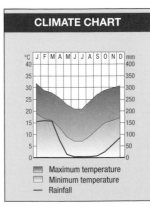

CLIMATE CHART

Maximum temperature
Minimum temperature
Rainfall

TRANSPORT
ACCOMMODATION
EATING OUT
ACTIVITIES
A – Z

(86°F), with temperatures in excess of 35°C (95°F) not uncommon (under these conditions, a mid-afternoon siesta is advisable!). Summer temperatures are usually a few degrees lower in the central highlands, and the moderating influence of the Atlantic Ocean makes the coast a popular destination at this time – despite the fog, which often lingers from late-afternoon to mid-morning.

More than 80 percent of Namibia's rain is recorded between November and March, and occurs as thunderstorms, with large masses of cloud frequently building up during the late afternoon. However, even the wet summer months are dry by most other standards, except in the far northeast. Rainfall everywhere is unpredictable, and the evaporation rate is extremely high. Fortunately, the rain cools the air sufficiently to avoid the mugginess usually associated with tropical summers.

What to Wear

Dress is generally casual in Namibia and there are few restrictions on what to wear. Men are not expected to wear a jacket, collar and tie in restaurants and cocktail bars in the evening, but on the other hand, shorts, T-shirts and jeans are not allowed in the restaurants and bars of the more upmarket hotels. For a night out at the theatre, smart-casual clothes are perfectly acceptable.

Pack for a warm climate; loose-fitting cotton clothing is the most comfortable and practical. However, thanks to the cool and often windy conditions prevailing along the coast, as well as the early morning and afternoon fog which rolls off the sea, some warm clothing (a windbreaker, for example) is essential throughout the year.

In summer, lightweight dresses or skirts, shorts and short-sleeved shirts/blouses are ideal for day-time wear, while long-sleeved shirts and trousers help keep mosquitoes at bay at night. Equip yourself with a wide-brimmed sunhat or a hat with a neck flap and make sure you have a raincoat for late afternoon thunderstorms.

In winter, light to medium-weight clothing is suitable for daytime use. The variation in day and night temperatures, however, makes warm clothing essential, especially during the early mornings and late afternoons, and in the central highlands. Trousers, long-sleeved tops and a warm fleece will come in handy. If you plan to explore some of Namibia's attractions on foot, take

a pair of well-worn, comfortable and sturdy walking shoes with leather uppers and rubber soles.

Public nudity is not acceptable at all and is a punishable offence in Namibia; bathers are expected to wear a swimming costume on the beach and at swimming pools.

If you're going on a safari, it won't be necessary to bring along everything you might need – several shops in Windhoek, in particular, specialise in safari clothing and outdoor wear.

Crime and Safety

Overall, Namibia is a fairly safe country in which to travel, but in the larger towns it is advisable to take care with valuables like wallets, jewellery, watches and photographic equipment, and to avoid overt displays of wealth.

Never leave a vehicle unattended with valuables inside. Vehicle theft is worsening in Namibia and care must be taken. Common sense and precautions should ensure that your holiday is not spoiled.

Customs Regulations

Unused personal effects, sporting and recreational equipment, laptops, cameras and accessories may be temporarily imported duty-free. It is also permitted to bring into the country 400 cigarettes, 50 cigars and 250g cigarette or pipe tobacco; 2 litres wine and 1 litre spirits; 50ml perfume and gifts with a total value not exceeding N$50,000. The import of agricultural or horticultural produce, or pets, is not permitted. A yellow fever vaccination certificate is required from travellers arriving from infected areas elsewhere in Africa or South America.

Non-residents may import or export up to N$50,000 in local currency. There is no limit for travel between Namibia and Botswana, Lesotho, South Africa and Swaziland, as they all belong to the same common monetary area. You can bring an unlimited amount of foreign currency into the country, provided that it's declared upon arrival, and can export anything up to the amount declared on arrival provided departure is within 12 months of that.

Disabled Travellers

Namibia is not yet very well geared up for people with disabilities, but is busy improving the situation. Prospective

travellers should inquire from Namibian tour operators about their special needs.

Electricity

Electricity: 220 Volts. The supply is reliable in towns but many bush lodges use solar or generator-driven power, which may only operate during specific hours.

The main type of socket in use, as in neighbouring South Africa, is earthed with three round pins.

It's a good idea to carry an adaptor though many lodges will have them in the rooms or sell them at their gift shop.

Embassies and Consulates

Foreign embassies in Namibia

British High Commission
116 Robert Mugabe Avenue, PO Box 22202, Windhoek
Tel: 061 274800
www.gov.uk/government/world/namibia

Embassy of the United States of America
14 Lossen Street, Private Bag 12029, Windhoek
Tel: 061 295 8500
http://windhoek.usembassy.gov/

The Consulate of Canada
Suite 403, First Floor, Office Tower, Maerua Mall, Jan Jonker Street, Windhoek
Tel: 061 251254
www.canadainternational.gc.ca

New Zealand Consulate
125 Middel Street, Nieuw Muckleneuk, Pretoria, South Africa
Tel: 27 12 435-9000
http://new-zealand.visahq.com/embassy/namibia/

Netherlands Embassy
18 Liliencron Street, Unit 4 Windhoek
Tel: 061 223733
http://zuidafrika.nlambassade.org

High Commission of the Republic of South Africa
c/o Jan Jonker/Nelson Mandela rsa House, Windhoek
Tel: 061 501 7111
http://www.dirco.gov.za/windhoek/

Nationals of the following countries should contact their nearest consulate in South Africa:
Ireland (Pretoria, South Africa, www.embassyireland.org.za)
Australia (Pretoria, South Africa, www.southafrica.embassy.gov.au)

Namibian embassies abroad

Belgium & EU
Avenue de Tavuren 454 B1150
Brussels
Tel: +32-2-771 1410
www.namibiaembassy.be

Germany
Wichmannstrasse 5 2nd Floor 10787
Berlin
Tel: +49-30-254-0950
www.namibia-botschaft.de

South Africa
197 Blackwood Street, Arcadia,
Pretoria
Tel: +27-12-4819100
www.namibia.org.za

United Kingdom
6 Chandos Street London W1G 9LU
Tel: +44 20 7636 6244
www.namibia.embassyhomepage.com

USA
1605 New Hampshire Ave, N.W.
Washington D.C. 20009
Tel: +1-202-986 0540
www.namibianembassyusa.org

Emergencies

The emergency number from a land
line is 081112 and from a mobile
phone just dial 112.

In the case of a medical emergency,
dial 061 **211111** to reach an operator
who will contact an ambulance.

The police countrywide emergency
number is **10111**.

Pharmacies can be found all over
the country in major towns.

Etiquette

Visitors should show respect to the
local people by exercising sensitivity,
tolerance and common sense. A few
"don'ts" might be helpful:
Don't photograph anyone without
their consent, not even in the heart of
the bush.
Don't make a show of your wealth
anywhere. The obvious temptation is to
relieve you of it in one way or another.
Don't break the law, of course. For
tourists, the main hazards are illegal
deals with foreign exchange, the
traffic regulations, and the ordinances
against prostitution, sexual offences
and drug taking.

G

Gay and Lesbian Travellers

The attitude towards homosexuality in
Namibia is somewhat ambiguous but,
as with many African countries, it is
not practised openly and gay visitors
are advised to be discreet. The law
expressly forbids discrimination on
the grounds of sexual orientation and
Namibia's high court ruled in 1999 that
gay couples have the same rights as
heterosexual couples. However, male
homosexuality is illegal, based on the
common law offence of committing "an
unnatural sex crime". The last case was
tried in the late 1980s. It is not clear
whether lesbian acts are an offence.
Up until fairly recently, President Sam
Nujoma, plus other Ministers and
Deputy Ministers openly attacked
homosexuals. The Rainbow Project has
challenged these attacks and provides
support for homosexuals in Namibia.
Sister Namibia (women's human
rights organisation; PO Box 40092,
Windhoek, tel: 061 230618;
www.sisternamibia.org.

H

Health and Medical Care

Health Hazards

The only mandatory health
requirement for Namibia is a **yellow
fever** inoculation. Prospective visitors
should, however, make inquiries when
booking their holidays as the situation
could change.

Malaria is endemic in the
northern areas of the country,
including the Etosha National Park,
so prophylactics are essential.
Take pills as prescribed two weeks
before arrival, during the stay and
for two weeks after departure. Other
preventive measures include using an
insect repellent, wearing long-sleeved
shirts and trousers in the evening and
sleeping under a mosquito net.

No preventive medication
is available against **bilharzia**
(schistosomiasis) which occurs in
the Kavango and Caprivi. Visitors are
advised to avoid drinking from and
washing or swimming in standing
or slow-flowing water with marginal
or submerged vegetation, since
the snail hosts usually prefer these
environments. If you notice blood in
your urine or stools after about six
weeks, consult a doctor immediately.

Cases of **tick-bite fever** are
occasionally reported, but you are
unlikely to suffer any adverse effects
if the tick is removed within an hour.
This is usually best accomplished by
covering it with Vaseline or whatever
greasy substance is available and
pulling the tick gently away from the
skin. The bite should be disinfected
well. If the bite becomes infected
a doctor should be consulted
immediately. The symptoms of tick-
bite fever – including aching limbs,
headache, fever and swollen glands
– usually manifest themselves within
seven to 14 days after the bite. It is
advisable to seek medical advice as the
disease is easily cured with antibiotics.

Aids (HIV) In common with much
of sub-Saharan Africa, Namibia has a
high rate of HIV infection and the risks
associated with unprotected casual
sex barely need stating. Should you
require a blood transfusion, however,
you can be reassured that all blood
is screened for the HIV virus and
hepatitis B by the Namibian Blood
Transfusion Service.

High standards of **hygiene**
are maintained at commercial
establishments throughout the
country and a meal in a restaurant
is generally quite safe. However, at
informal markets hygiene standards
leave much to be desired and meat
and fish sold there should be avoided.
Tap water in Namibia the water
is potable and safe. Sometimes the
taste is not that pleasant, but it's still
safe to drink. It is not advisable to
drink water directly from dams and
rivers. Namibia is a very arid country
and water is a very scarce resource
and should not be wasted.

Medical Insurance

Visitors are strongly advised to obtain
medical insurance in their countries
of origin prior to their departure since
there is no national health welfare
scheme in Namibia.

Emergency Services

Emergency services throughout the
country are provided by International
SOS Namibia (tel: 061 2890906;
www.internationalsos.com/en/europe-
middle-east-africa_namibia.htm) and
E-MedRescue Namibia (tel: 081
924; www.emed24.net). Ambulance
services are also provided by private
hospitals and state hospitals. In the
case of a medical emergency, dial
061 **211111** to reach an operator
who will contact an ambulance.

Medical practitioners

Medical practitioners in Windhoek are
listed under "Medical" in the Namibia
telephone directory, but elsewhere
they are listed under their surname –
usually quite easy to spot. Although
there are a number of doctors in
Windhoek, getting an appointment
can be problematic. The Kalahari
Sands and the Safari hotels in
Windhoek both have a doctor on call,
while a fully trained nurse is available
at Mokuti Lodge.

Pharmacies can be found all over the country in major towns.

Hospitals

There are well-equipped hospitals and clinics in Windhoek and every other major town. Windhoek has four hospitals. The privately owned **Mediclinic Windhoek** (tel: 061 4331000; www.mediclinic.co.za) caters for private patients and is equipped to deal with all categories of medical care, including surgery, orthopaedics, paediatrics and intensive care. Patients are usually admitted on the recommendation of their doctor, but in the event of an emergency patients will be admitted. The **Roman Catholic Hospital** (tel: 061 270 2004; www. rcchurch.na/windhoek/health/wdh-hospital.htm) in the centre of town also caters for private patients, while the **Windhoek Central Hospital** (tel: 061 309 9111) has all the necessary facilities for specialised medical care. **Rhino Park Private Hospital** (tel: 061 375000) is the latest addition to affordable medical services.

Elsewhere in the country, there are state-run hospitals in several towns, as well as good private Mediclinics (www.mediclinic.co.za) in Otjiwarongo (tel: 065 1303734) and Swakopmund (tel: 46 441 2200), and a Roman Catholic hospital at Usakos (tel: 064 530013).

I

Internet

Browsing and email facilities are available at most city hotels of any quality, but generally not in more remote game lodges and guest farms, though this improves all the time, and many lodges now have WiFi facilities. You'll find fast and affordable internet cafés scattered around the larger towns, though the connection can be slow and pricey in smaller towns. Depending on your route through Namibia, you might want to warn business associates (or anxious relatives) that it is quite possible you will spend periods of up to a week without an opportunity to check email.

M

Maps

The best available is a free map compiled by the tourist board and distributed at most local and overseas tourist information offices. It is very accurate when it comes to road conditions and distances, and is regularly updated. Good commercial maps are published by Map Studio (a subsidiary of Struik/New Holland) and by Freytag & Berndt and should be available at Stanfords in the UK. Ordinance survey maps (1: 250 000 and 1: 50 000) can be bought at the Surveyor General's Office on Robert Mugabe Avenue in Windhoek

All roads in Namibia are numbered and clearly signed en route.

Media

Radio and Television

The Namibian Broadcasting Corporation (NBC; www.nbc.na) is a statutory body governed by an independent board which is appointed by the Minister of Information and Broadcasting. The NBC has eight radio services broadcasting in several languages on the FM, SW and MW bands. The National Service broadcasts mainly in English.

NBC is currently covering the old single-channel English-medium analogue television service to a 21-channel digital service, a process that should be complete some time in 2015. Most city hotels (but generally not lodges in game reserves) subscribe to the South African satellite service DSTV, a package that includes several international news and sports channels. This may become less common once the new state digital service is fully operational.

Newspapers

Considering its small population, Namibia has a surprising number of newspapers. The emphasis is primarily on local news and, since the Constitution guarantees a free press, newspapers are often extremely critical of government policies and actions.

Three English newspapers are published in Namibia: *The Namibian* (Mon–Fri; www.namibian.com.na), the weekly *Windhoek Observer* (www.observer24.com.na), and *New Era* (www.newera.com.na), a government-owned newspaper published weekly by the Ministry of Information and Broadcasting and distributed countrywide. *The Namibia Economist* (www.economist.com.na) is a weekly business newspaper. Afrikaans and German newspapers are also published.

Since all local newspapers are printed in Windhoek, it usually takes a day or two (or even longer) before they are available elsewhere in the country.

The Namib Times (www.namibtimes. net) is published twice weekly in Walvis Bay and focuses primarily on news from Swakopmund and Walvis Bay. South African morning and Sunday newspapers, on the other hand, are usually obtainable in Windhoek later the same day. German newspapers are available a few days after publication from the Windhoeker Buchhandlung (tel: 061 225216; www.wbuch.iway.na) in Independence Avenue (opposite the municipal offices).

A wide selection of international magazines, paperbacks and coffee table books are available from bookshops in Windhoek, Walvis Bay, Swakopmund and Lüderitz, while South African magazines are available at corner shops (known locally as cafés) and supermarkets throughout the country.

Money

The Namibian dollar (N$), divided into 100 cents, was introduced in September 1993 as a replacement for the South African rand (ZAR). However, the N$ remains pegged to the ZAR, which is also an accepted currency in Namibia and directly convertible with the Namibian dollar (approximately one-for-one).

Most currencies are easily exchanged for Namibian dollars at banks (and, more expensively, in some hotels), with the US dollar, British pound sterling, and the euro being the most widely accepted. All towns of any substance will have at least one bank offering foreign exchange facilities.

Depending on your route, however, the long distances between towns means that you may go several days at a stretch without an opportunity to change money, so plan accordingly, bearing in mind that car fuel (petrol or diesel) must always be paid for with N$ or ZAR cash throughout the country.

There are a few Bureaux de Change at Windhoek's Hosea Kutako International Airport. You should change any remaining Namibian dollars before departure, as they cannot be exchanged at any European banks, and only at very few South African banks.

Travellers' cheques and credit cards bearing the Visa or MasterCard insignia are widely accepted, but most other credit cards (including American Express) are of limited use. In most towns you can draw local currency (usually to a daily maximum of N$1,000) from at least one 24-hour ATM (auto-teller), but be wary of scams involving 'helpful' locals, especially if you draw money outside of normal banking hours in Windhoek.

O

Opening hours

Government offices: Mon–Fri 8am–1pm and 2–5pm. Cashier's office: 8am–1pm.
Banking hours: Mon–Fri 9am–3.30pm (in Windhoek), 9am–1pm and 2–3.30pm (country towns); Sat 8.30–11am.
Shopping hours: Mon–Fri 8 or 8.30am–5 or 5.30pm, Sat 8 or 8.30am–1pm. Supermarkets are generally open until Mon–Fri 7pm, Sat 4–7pm, Sun 10am–1pm and 4–7pm.
Post offices: Mon–Fri 8–4.30pm (closed 1–2pm in country towns); Sat 8.30am–noon.
Namibia Wildlife Resorts Office: Mon–Fri only, 8am–1pm and 2–5pm (reservations and cashier's office: 8am–1pm and 2–3pm).

P

Photography

Because of the bright sunlight and glare, the best light for wildlife and scenic photography is in the early mornings and late afternoons. The vertical shadows and harsh light between around 9am and 4pm tend to produce ugly, bleached results. Instead of travelling mile after mile looking for animals, you are more likely to be successful if you wait for them at a waterhole. Pack a picnic basket and book for when nothing much is happening. Use a beanbag or tripod to keep the camera steady when shooting wildlife from a car.

To protect photographic equipment against sand and fine dust, keep your equipment stowed in your camera bag when not in use. A filter is useful not only to keep dust and sand off the lens, but will also help to reduce glare. Temperatures can also become unbearably hot inside vehicles and equipment should be well insulated and never left in the sun.

Namibians will usually allow you to take photos of them, but you should always ask their permission first and they will often give their consent only once you have agreed to pay them.

There are few restrictions on photography, but you are not allowed to take snaps of State House, the airport, military installations, police stations or prisons. It is also not advisable to take photographs of uniformed personnel.

Photographic shops in Windhoek and Swakopmund offer a wide variety of equipment, but you should remember to pack a spare camera battery, since these are not always available in a wide range.

Postal Services

Post is relatively reliable and very inexpensive, but delivery times are slower than most Westerners are used to. Expect mail to or from Europe to take at least 10 days to arrive, and mail to the Americas, Asia or Australia to take considerably longer – in other words, odds are that you will arrive home before any holiday postcards you might have sent!

Public Holidays

Although most businesses are closed on public holidays, many supermarkets in Windhoek and the larger towns do open for a few hours in the morning and late afternoon. Note, too, that when the normal date for a public holiday falls on a Sunday, the Monday is often taken as a holiday. Namibia has 12 public holidays:
1 January: New Year's Day
21 March: Independence Day
March/April: Good Friday and Easter Monday
1 May: Workers' Day
4 May: Cassinga Day (commemorates those killed by the South African Defence Force in an attack on a SWAPO refugee camp at Cassinga in Southern Angola in 1978)
May: Ascension Day
25 May: Africa Day (anniversary of the founding of the Organisation of

Bank sign in Lüderitz.

African Unity in 1963)
26 August: Heroes' Day (anniversary of the launch of the liberation struggle in 1966)
10 December: Namibia Women's Day
25 December: Christmas Day
26 December: Family Day

R

Religious Services

There are churches in every town – lots of them – with Lutheran and Catholic churches particularly well represented. Services are held at most churches every Sunday and on all Christian holidays. Visitors will be made welcome. Other religions are poorly represented.

T

Telephone

Namibia has developed an excellent communications system for both domestic and international services. Direct dialling is available between most centres in the country, and a full international std system has been introduced. Main international codes to other countries are 0027 to South Africa, 0044 to the UK, 001 to the USA or Canada, 0061 to Australia, 0064 to New Zealand and 00353 to Ireland.

The code for overseas calls to Namibia is 264 followed by the area code and the subscriber's number. The '0' preceding the area code in the Namibian directory is omitted. The cheapest rate is Mon 9pm–7am Sat and 1pm Sat–7am Mon (bear in mind these discounted rates are only applicable to calls made in Namibia and to South Africa).

Mobile/Cellular phones

MTC is Namibia's main service provider; most major towns are covered, as are the main camps in Etosha National Park, but most rural parts of the country have no reception. The system used in Namibia is the GSM900/1800 network and visitors from countries using this system can operate their cell phones here without problems. All mobile numbers in Namibia have an 081 prefix.

It's also possible to hire cellular phones in Namibia. If you want to stay in regular touch with home, or to have the facility to phone ahead to lodges and hotels, then it's worth thinking about buying a local SIM card (giving you a local number) to insert in your own phone for the duration of your stay. This takes a minute to set up, and once you have paid the starting fee of around US$15, you can send text messages very cheaply.

Time Zones

GMT + 1hour April through August (winter) or +2 hours September through March (summer).

Tipping

The rules that you probably use at home should also apply in Namibia. For instance, it is customary to add around 10 percent to a restaurant bill unless a service charge is included (or you feel that the service was inadequate). It is also customary to tip most service personnel including hotel porters and other attendants – though be warned that most lodgings in Namibia (even some very upmarket ones) will not offer to help guests carry their luggage to their rooms.

Tourist Information

The Namibia Tourist Board (www.namibiatourism.com.na) is well organised and produces a wide range of useful booklets. The head office in Windhoek is represented by a kiosk on Independence Avenue next to Zoo Park, or can be contacted at tel: 061 290 6000. There are also branches in most of the larger towns in Namibia, as well as information offices in Johannesburg (tel: 011 702 9602) Cape Town (tel: +27 21 422 3298; email: namibia@saol.com), Frankfurt (tel: +49 69 133 7360, www.namibia-tourism.com) and London (tel: +44 (0)87 0330 9333, email: info@namibiatourism.co.uk).

Tour Operators

Expert Africa
Tel: +44 20 8232 9777 or (US toll-free) 1-800-242-2434 www.expertafrica.com
The UK's leading Namibia specialist operator, twice voted "Top Tour Operator" by readers of the travel magazine Wanderlust.
Rainbow Tours
Tel: +44 20 7666 1250
www.rainbowtours.co.uk
Another award-winning London-based southern Africa specialist with a strong emphasis on responsible tourism.
Audley Travel
Tel: +44 1993 838000
www.audleytravel.com
Naturetrek
Tel: +44 1962 733051
www.naturetrek.co.uk

Taga Safaris
P O Box 3208 Parklands, Johannesburg, Gauteng, 2121, South Africa
Tel: +27 11 465 5678
www.tagasafarisafrica.com

V

Visas and Passports

All visitors to the country need a passport valid for at least six months after the intended date of departure. Visas are also required, unless you're a national of a country with which Namibia has a reciprocal visa waiver arrangement for stays of up to three months. These countries are: the UK, France, Ireland, Germany and other EU states, Angola, Australia, Botswana, Canada, Finland, Iceland, Japan, Kenya, Mozambique, New Zealand, Norway, Sweden, Singapore, South Africa, Switzerland, Russia, Tanzania, the US, Zambia and Zimbabwe.

Entry permission is usually granted for one month, though this can be extended to cover up to three months on request. On arrival, immigration officials may ask to see your return ticket (or proof that you have the means to buy one), and you might also need to provide proof that you can support yourself financially during your stay in Namibia. This sort of request is increasingly uncommon, however, and in both instances a credit card should suffice as proof. Entry regulations are subject to change, so it is essential to consult the nearest Namibian Embassy or High Commission, or your travel agent, for the most up-to-date information before you travel.

All visitors planning to remain in Namibia longer than 3 months should apply for an extension well in advance to the Ministry of Foreign Affairs, Private Bag 13347, Windhoek, tel: 61 2829111, www.mfa.gov.na. If you're already in the country, you can call personally at the ministry's office in the Cohen Building, on the corner of Kasino Street and Independence Avenue, open Mon–Fri 8am–1pm.

W

Weights and measures

Namibia uses the metric system and all distances are given in kilometres.

What to Bring

Besides a camera and binoculars for viewing game, other equipment

is not necessary, unless you intend to engage in some particular activity such as golf or fishing.

For the few photographers who still use film, it is expensive in Namibia and often not available in smaller towns, so the best advice is to bring your own. A day pack will be useful if you're keen on rambling, while a money belt (preferably one that can easily be concealed under your clothing) is handy to keep documents and cash safely on your person.

A sleeping bag is essential if you've booked for a guided wilderness trail and, in most instances, for safaris where tented accommodation is provided. A wide range of camping equipment ranging from teaspoons to tents can be hired on a daily basis. This service is particularly useful since state-owned rest camps and resorts, with the exception of the luxury flats at Ai-Ais, do not supply eating or cooking utensils.

Toiletries, make-up, sunblock and insect repellent are available locally but most are imported and comparatively expensive. It is best to bring your own. Also bring enough personal prescription medicines to last throughout your stay in Namibia.

Points for electric shavers are available at major tourist hotels and most state-owned rest camps and resorts. It is nevertheless advisable to bring battery-operated or disposable razors, especially if visiting the more remote areas.

Women Travellers

Women travellers, especially those on a guided tour, have very little to fear from Namibia on a gender-specific level. Indeed, a great many women travel there on their own without hassle. Culturally, the country is rather conservative, but in a way that is more likely to be reassuring to single women travellers than to make them feel threatened.

It would, however, pay to dress down more than you might at home, especially in urban areas, where revealing clothes may be perceived to make a statement that is not intended from your side.

Some single women also like to wear a wedding ring (and to invent plausible details of a temporarily absent husband) when they travel. Otherwise, apply the same common sense rules you might do at home – avoid travelling alone or walking the streets in the cities after dark, and nip any unwanted male attention in the bud as soon as possible.

FURTHER READING

BIRDWATCHING

Birds of Namibia by Jackie & Ian Sinclair. Useful but non-comprehensive beginners guide.
Roberts Birds of Southern Africa by P. Hockey. W Dean, P. Ryan et al (7th edition). Definitive ornithological overview of the region, but too bulky for use in the field.
Roberts Bird Guide by Hugh Chittenden. The daypack-friendly condensed version is now the pick of several excellent field guides that provide comprehensive coverage of the Southern African sub-region.

TREES

Trees of Southern Africa by Keith Coates Palgrave. The definitive guide to the region's trees.
Regional Flora
The four locally published guides listed below are out of print and not always easy to locate, but they remain invaluable resources for the regions they cover.
Damaraland Flora – Spitzkoppe, Brandberg, Twyfelfontein by P Craven and C. Marais.
Namib Flora – Swakopmund to the Giant Welwitschia via Goanlkontes by P. Craven & C. Marais.
Waterberg Flora – Footpaths in and around the Camp by P. Craven & C. Marais.
Damaraland Flora by P. Craven & C. Marais.

GEOLOGY

Field Guide to Rocks & Minerals of Southern Africa by Bruce Cairncross. Useful and compact overview of this geologically rich region.

PEOPLE AND CULTURE

Peoples Of Namibia by J.S. Malan. Out of print but useful cultural overview, still available through some online booksellers.

MAMMALS AND REPTILES

A Complete Guide to the Snakes of Southern Africa by Johan Marais. Useful introduction to the region's scaled creatures.

Send Us Your Thoughts

We do our best to ensure the Information in our books is as accurate and up-to-date as possible. The books are updated on a regular basis using local contacts, who painstakingly add, amend and correct as required. However, some details (such as telephone numbers and opening times) are liable to change, and we are ultimately reliant on our readers to put us in the picture.

We welcome your feedback, especially your experience of using the book "on the road". Maybe we recommended a hotel that you liked (or another that you didn't), or you came across a great bar or new attraction we missed.

We will acknowledge all contributions, and we'll offer an Insight Guide to the best letters received.

Please write to us at:
 Insight Guides
 PO Box 7910
 London SE1 1WE
Or email us at:
 insight@apaguide.co.uk

Smither's Mammals of Southern Africa edited by Peter Apps. Every mammal in the region depicted and described.
Southern African Wildlife by Mike Unwin. Supplements detailed coverage of mammals with useful starter sections on reptiles, birds and other smaller creatures.

HISTORY AND POLITICS

A History of Namibia: From the Earliest Times to 1990 by Marion Wallace. This pioneering one-volume history of pre-20th century Namibia is both readable and highly informative.
The Kaiser's Holocaust: Germany's Forgotten Genocide and the Colonial Roots of Nazism by David Olusoga & Casper Erichsen. The most detailed account to date of the genocide that took place in Namibia under German rule.
Africa: A Biography of the Continent by John Reader. Readable overview of Africa's past, placing Namibia in a continental perspective.

MISCELLANEOUS

The Sheltering Desert by Henno Martin. This is a classic account of the author's ordeal surviving in the Namibian desert from 1939 to 1942.
Skeleton Coast by A. Schoeman. Reprinted in 2011, this stunning coffee-table book covers the northern coast of Namibia.
Etosha: Rhythms of an African Wilderness by Claudia & Wynand Du Plessis. Striking coffee-table book about Namibia's greatest wildlife destination.

CREDITS

Photo Credits

123RF 57, 101, 107, 109, 110, 111, 114, 217ML
akg-images 35
Andy Selinger/fotoLibra 161
AREVA 54, 58, 61
AWL Images 66, 215B
Bigstock 102, 122
Clare Louise Thomas/Apa Publications 1, 2/3, 4M, 4MR, 4B, 5TR, 5ML, 5BL, 5BR, 6T, 6B, 7T, 8/9, 10/11, 12/13, 14, 15T, 15B, 16, 18, 19, 20, 21, 23, 24/25, 26TL, 28, 29, 30, 31, 50, 55, 56, 60, 62BR, 62BL, 63BR, 63BL, 64/65, 67, 68, 69, 70, 71, 72, 76, 78, 79, 81, 83, 84, 85, 86, 88, 89, 93, 108R, 124, 128/129, 130/131, 134, 135T, 138/139, 140, 141, 143B, 143T, 144, 145, 146, 147T, 147B, 148, 149T, 149B, 150/151, 153, 157, 158, 160, 162/163, 164, 165, 167, 168T, 168B, 169, 170T, 170B, 174, 175, 176, 177, 180B, 181, 194/195, 196, 197, 199T, 199B, 200, 201T, 201B, 202, 203, 204B, 204T, 205B, 208, 210, 211T, 211B,

213T, 213B, 216BR, 216BL, 216/217T, 217BL, 217TR, 218, 219, 221B, 221T, 222B, 222T, 223, 224, 225, 226, 227B, 227T, 228T, 229, 232, 233, 235T, 236B, 236T, 237B, 237T, 238T, 238B, 240, 241B, 241T, 242, 244, 246, 249, 256, 259, 262, 263, 265, 268, 269, 273
Corbis 27T, 27B, 40, 59, 62/63T, 63ML, 91, 206/207
Dreamstime 7B, 74, 104, 105, 115, 117L, 117R, 119, 126
Felix Unite 87
FLPA 98, 103, 120
Fotolia 82, 100, 112, 123, 186
Getty Images 17, 33, 41, 44, 45, 46, 47, 49, 51, 52, 75
iStock 5MR, 5TL, 4/5T, 53, 63TR, 99, 132/133, 172/173, 179T, 182T, 182B, 184BR, 184/185T, 184BL, 185BL, 185TR, 189, 209, 212, 214B, 214T, 215T, 230/231, 267, 275
Johannes Haape/Südwest-Archiv 38, 39

Mary Evans Picture Library 42, 43, 48
Mowani Mountain Camp 254
Namibia Tourism Board 185BR
Namibia Wildlife Resorts 92, 94, 95, 96, 97, 179B, 185ML, 190T, 235B, 247T, 252, 260, 261
National Art Gallery 77
National Theatre 80, 264
Okonjima Lodge and the AfriCat Foundation 152, 156, 159, 178, 246/247B, 250
Photoshot 73
Public domain 26MR, 34, 37
Scala Archives 32
SuperStock 217BR
TopFoto 36
Ute von Ludwiger/Namibia Tourism Board 22, 90, 106, 108L, 113, 116, 118, 121, 125, 127, 135B, 171, 180T, 183T, 183B, 187, 188, 190B, 191T, 191B, 192, 193, 205T, 228B, 245
Zenodot Verlagsgesellschaft mbH 26BR

Cover Credits

Front cover: masks *AWL Images*
Back cover: (top) Namib Naukluft Park *Clare Louise Thomas/Apa Publications*; (middle) Herero women *Clare Louise Thomas/Apa Publications*

Front flap: (from top) Luderitz *Clare Louise Thomas/Apa Publications*; Land Rover *Clare Louise Thomas/ Apa Publications*; The White Lady rock painting *Clare Louise Thomas/ Apa Publications*; zebra *Clare Louise*

Thomas/Apa Publications
Back flap: Kolmanskop *Clare Louise Thomas/Apa Publications*
Spine: oryx *iStock*

Insight Guide Credits

Distribution
UK
Dorling Kindersley Ltd
A Penguin Group company
80 Strand, London, WC2R 0RL
sales@uk.dk.com

United States
Ingram Publisher Services
1 Ingram Boulevard, PO Box 3006,
La Vergne, TN 37086-1986
ips@ingramcontent.com

Australia and New Zealand
Woodslane
10 Apollo St, Warriewood,
NSW 2102, Australia
info@woodslane.com.au

Worldwide
Apa Publications GmbH & Co. Verlag
KG (Singapore branch)
7030 Ang Mo Kio Avenue 5
08-65 Northstar @ AMK
Singapore 569880
apasin@singnet.com.sg

Printing
CTPS-China
© 2015 Apa Publications (UK) Ltd
All Rights Reserved

First Edition 1994
Fourth Edition 2015

www.insightguides.com

Project Editor
Carine Tracanelli
Author
Philip Briggs
Picture Editor/Art Editor
Tom Smyth/Shahid Mahmood
Map Production
Original cartography Polyglott
Kartographie, updated by
Apa Cartography Department
Production
Rebeka Davies

Contributors

Philip Briggs is a travel writer based in the Ukhahlamba-Drakensberg region of South Africa. The author of more than 10 travel guides to African destinations, Briggs contributes regularly to a number of leading wildlife periodicals in South Africa and in the UK.

About Insight Guides

Insight Guides have more than 40 years' experience of publishing high-quality, visual travel guides. We produce 400 full-colour titles, in both print and digital form, covering more than 200 destinations across the globe, in a variety of formats to meet your different needs.

Insight Guides are written by local authors who use their on-the-ground experience to provide the very latest information; their local expertise is evident in the extensive historical and cultural background features. All the reviews in **Insight Guides** are independent; we strive to maintain an impartial view. Our reviews are carefully selected to guide you to the best places to stay and eat, so you can be confident that when we say a restaurant or hotel is special, we really mean it.

Legend

City maps

- Freeway/Highway/Motorway
- Divided Highway
- Main Roads
- Minor Roads
- Pedestrian Roads
- Steps
- Footpath
- Railway
- Funicular Railway
- Cable Car
- Tunnel
- City Wall
- Important Building
- Built Up Area
- Other Land
- Transport Hub
- Park
- Pedestrian Area
- Bus Station
- Tourist Information
- Main Post Office
- Cathedral/Church
- Mosque
- Synagogue
- Statue/Monument
- Beach
- Airport

Regional maps

- Freeway/Highway/Motorway (with junction)
- Freeway/Highway/Motorway (under construction)
- Divided Highway
- Main Road
- Secondary Road
- Minor Road
- Track
- Footpath
- International Boundary
- State/Province Boundary
- National Park/Reserve
- Marine Park
- Ferry Route
- Marshland/Swamp
- Glacier — Salt Lake
- Airport/Airfield
- Ancient Site
- Border Control
- Cable Car
- Castle/Castle Ruins
- Cave
- Chateau/Stately Home
- Church/Church Ruins
- Crater
- Lighthouse
- Mountain Peak
- Place of Interest
- Viewpoint

INDEX

INSIGHT GUIDES

INSPIRING YOUR NEXT ADVENTURE

Insight Guides offers you a range of travel guides
to match your needs. Whether you are looking for
inspiration for planning a trip, cultural information,
walks and tours, great listings, or practical advice, we
have a product to suit you.

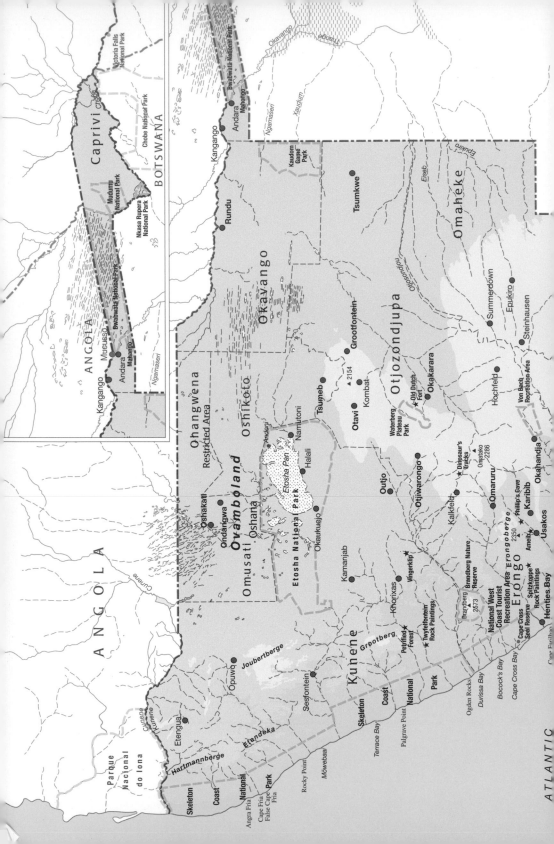